Lifelong
Learning
Programme

Schriftenreihe des Arbeitskreises
Europäische Integration e.V.

Band 88

Tim Krieger | Bernhard Neumärker |
Diana Panke [eds.]

Europe's Crisis

The Conflict-Theoretical Perspective

 Nomos

This project has been funded with support from the European Commission. This publication reflects the views only of the authors, and the Commission cannot be held responsible for any use which may be made of the information contained therein.

Die Deutsche Nationalbibliothek lists this publication in the Deutsche Nationalbibliografie; detailed bibliographic data is available in the Internet at http://dnb.d-nb.de

ISBN   978-3-8487-2149-8 (Print)
          978-3-8452-6248-2 (ePDF)

British Library Cataloguing-in-Publication Data
A catalogue record for this book is available from the British Library.

ISBN   978-3-8487-2149-8 (Print)
          978-3-8452-6248-2 (ePDF)

Library of Congress Cataloging-in-Publication Data
Krieger, Tim / Neumärker, Bernhard / Panke, Diana
Europe's Crisis
The Conflict-Theoretical Perspective
Tim Krieger / Bernhard Neumärker / Diana Panke (eds.)
225 p.
Includes bibliographic references.

ISBN   978-3-8487-2149-8 (Print)
          978-3-8452-6248-2 (ePDF)

1. Edition 2016
© Nomos Verlagsgesellschaft, Baden-Baden, Germany 2016. Printed and bound in Germany.

Contents

Contents

E. About the authors

List of abbreviations

AEI	Arbeitskreis Europäische Integration
AG	Advocate General
AfD	Alternative für Deutschland
BE	Belgium
BG	Bulgaria
BVerfG	Bundesverfassungsgericht (German Constitutional Court)
CDU	Christlich Demokratische Union
Ch.	chapter
CJEU	Court of Justice of the European Union
CSU	Christlich-Soziale Union
CY	Cyprus
DAAA	Discursive Actor Attribution Analysis
DE	Germany
DK	Denmark
ECB	European Central Bank
ECJ	European Court of Justice
EE	Estonia
EEC T	European Economic Community Treaty
EMU	Economic and Monetary Union
ES	Spain
ESS	European Social Survey
ESM	European Stability Mechanism
EU	European Union
FDP	Freie Demokratische Partei
FI	Finland
FRG	Federal Republic of Germany
GATT	General Agreement on Tariffs and Trade
GB	Great Britain
GDP	Gross Domestic Product

gov.	Government
H	Hypothesis
IE	Ireland
IMF	International Monetary Fund
KKE	Kommounistikó Kómma Elládas
KOF	Konjunkturforschungsstelle (KOF Swiss Economic Institute)
N	number of observations
ND	New Democracy
NL	Netherlands
OECD	Organization for Economic Cooperation and Development
OMT	Outright Monetary Transactions
opp.	Opposition
para	paragraph
PASOK	Panellinio Sosialistiko Kinima
PL	Poland
SE	Sweden
SGP	Stability and Growth Pact
SK	Slovakia
SI	Slovenia
SMP	Securities Markets Program
SPD	Sozialdemokratische Partei Deutschlands
SYRIZA	Synaspismos Rizospastikis Aristeras
TEEC	Treaty of Rome
TFEU	Treaty of the European Union
U.S.	United States of America
WTO	World Trade Organization

A. Introduction

Introduction

Tim Krieger, Bernhard Neumärker and Diana Panke (University of Freiburg)

When the housing market bubble burst in the US in 2007, neither scholars nor practitioners would have predicted that the crisis not only reaches Europe relatively quickly, but will still be in the limelight of the news in 2015. The EU's periphery (e.g. Greece, Ireland, Portugal and Spain) came under pressure once doubts about the structure of financing of private individual and collective endeavors, such as housing, the building sector, and banking spread (Dokko et al. 2011). The main concern was that credits were insufficiently backed up by guarantees, and once the creditors stopped prolonging credits, the debtors were unable to pay off their debts and the system was close to a collapse. Unemployment rates went up, tax revenues went down and the economy in the peripheral EU member states came almost to a halt. At the same time, the continental European states, such as Germany, Austria and the Netherlands, were not as strongly hit by the economic downturn, not the least since the investors regarded these countries as 'safe havens' into which they redirected the financial streams (Sinn 2014a,b; Landmann 2011). The immediate response to financial and economic difficulties was national rather than European in character and turned out to be inadequate. Some of the countries (e.g. Ireland) came even to the brink of bankruptcy during their quest to rescue failed banks. Quickly, the domestic crises in peripheral countries of Europe turned into a European crisis and triggered a European response. Although the Treaties related to the Economic and Monetary Union (EMU) did not foresee an institutionalized crisis management system entailing substantive funds and credits for Eurozone members under pressure, the Heads of States and Governments agreed on establishing a European Stability Mechanism (ESM). The ESM provided guarantees totaling more than €500 billion, enabling countries hit by the crisis to obtain credits on the world's financial markets. This, however, turned out to be inoperable, because the guarantees are conditional on domestic economic reforms overseen by the Troika. Thus, affected countries, above all Greece, have not managed to overcome the crisis. Even in June 2015, Greece is still struggling with domestic problems, such as high unemployment rates, lack of structural reforms in the economic sector, insufficient systems concerning tax collection and public administration and ongoing outflows of capital.

Since 2008, the European economic, employment and financial crisis has been repeatedly in the limelight of German and European media and the topic has not lost any of its importance. This is not the least due to the fact that the crisis has led to several conflicts in the political, economic and societal sphere. In the scholarly community, the European crisis has predominantly been analyzed from a macroeconomic perspective and the solutions reflect this focus. Thus, there is plenty of work on how monetary policy should be adapted or changed (Joyce et al. 2012; Dokko et al. 2012), a rich body of research on fiscal solutions either proposing to engage in deficit spending or campaigning for austerity measures (De Grauwe and Ji 2014; De Grauwe 2013; Sinn 2014a,b; Siems and Schnyder 2014). What is lacking in the scholarly debate is to approach the topic from a different angle: the conflict theoretical perspective (Garfinkel and Skaperdas 2007; Schelling 1980; Hirshleifer 1978, 2001). This approach places emphasis on the origins of the conflict, the nature of the related distributional problems, the underlying conflict dynamics and the strategies to cope with conflicts. Thus, this perspective offers a different take on the European crisis and provides, for example, insights into how the costs of the crisis should be distributed between the 'crisis-ridden' periphery and seemingly stable core (Skaperdas 2011).

This volume offers an interdisciplinary approach on the conflicts related to the European crisis. It is based on a workshop taking place at Albert-Ludwigs University Freiburg in the fall of 2014 and we would like to thank all participants for the lively and insightful discussions. Also, we are grateful for the financial support of the workshop and the book project through the Arbeitskreis Europäische Integration (AEI) and Prof. Dr. h.c. Horst Weitzmann.

The economic, social scientist, and legal contributions provide a novel analysis on the emergence of the crisis and its dynamics on member state and European level. In addition, the contributions provide insights into the various implications of the crisis for the future of European integration and shed light on potential remedies. The book draws on a broad variety of economic, social scientist and legal methods. Thus it allows for a comprehensive analysis and provides novel insights for scientists, practitioners and the interested public. The remainder of the introduction offers a short synapsis of the book.

The economic contributions

Usually, economists focus on economic causes and consequences of behavior, decisions and external parametric changes. They investigate the behavioral causes and social cost of the European crisis, the origins and effects of the crisis on unemployment, growth rates, capital allocation, public debt sustainability, contagion effects of running excessive domestic deficits, and so on and so forth. Normative implications are, then, formulated under consideration of the consequentialist efficiency or welfare criterion. Interestingly enough, the contributions of the economic part in this book focus more on the analysis and derivation of rules, procedures and institutions for the conflict management of the European crisis. As it is self-evident for economists, these investigations are based on predictive models of strategic behaviour.

In his contribution, "Any Solution in Sight to Europe's Crisis? Some General Thoughts from a Conflict Theoretical Perspective", Tim Krieger argues in favor of using economic conflict theory as the main tool for interpreting the European crisis. He shows that in the existing institutional framework with the Council of the European Union in charge, conflict resolution is power-based, making it extremely difficult to end the crisis both quickly and consensual. Therefore, the author advocates a rule-based mechanism for resolving conflicts resulting from unilateral deviations from Union-wide agreements. Specifically, he proposes to put a price tag on excessive public debt by allowing each member state to decide whether to withdraw their pro rata shares in, for instance, agricultural subsidies for the country that breached the Maastricht criteria, making sanctions a national rather than supranational decision. Only this way, the specific interests of the member states resulting from different exposure to the crisis are accommodated appropriately.

While Tim Krieger's proposal is based on a GATT-like mechanism, in "Could Exit Rules be Self-Enforcing in the EU? The Cases of France and Germany" Robert Kappius and Bernhard Neumärker introduce the self-enforcement constraint well known from the WTO's set of rules on trade liberalization to the European conflict on voluntary or involuntary member state exit. First, the authors argue that self-enforcement is a neglected but an essential requirement for durable agreements between the EMU member states. Only if the full set of fiscal rules is self-enforcing, conflicts between member states, e.g. on debt restructuring and welfare state reforms, vanish due to truly voluntary exits which are preferred by all countries. Then, Kappius and Neumärker show that to be sustainable the fiscal constitution of the EMU needs specific exit rules which differ for the potential cases of "downward exits" (like France or Greece), and "upward exits" (like Germany). In the seemingly more relevant downward case the other member states have to pay out the leaving country, i.e., an EMU agreement needs rules for exit transfers. Without such self-enforcing exit clauses the EMU can only be saved by a European central or hegemonic authority so that problematic states can be excluded from the monetary union. Despite current evolutionary tendencies towards the ECB as such a relevant central and independent authority and Germany as the hegemonic state, the authors prefer the self-enforcing mechanism of voluntary exiting which is clearly in the spirit of founding the European Union without powerful central actors and with sovereign member states. In the case of Greece, one could thus define only the exit of Greece under the self-enforcing exit agreement the institutional case of "Grexit", whereas the other uncooperative solution should be labeled "Graccident".

Maximilian Stephan, in his contribution "Debt Restructuring in Times of Crisis: A European Perspective", discusses the dimensions of conflict that may arise between different actors in debt restructuring, thereby particularly focusing on the European debt crisis. Conflicts on debt restructuring may arise between debtors and creditors, among creditors, and between domestic groups in a debtor country. The difficulties that give rise to these conflicts may result from asymmetric information, uncertainty during the restructuring, a low willingness-to-pay, run-for-the-exit problems and holdout behavior of some investors. The author also takes a close look at the Greek debt overload, arguing that the struggle between the Greek government, representing the debtor, and the Troika, representing the creditors, was so strong that Syriza was able to win the Greek election in 2015. He argues that this situation has to be interpreted as an indication of Greek moral hazard. This is because the role of the Troika is to gather information about the financial situation of the debtor allowing the creditors to judge whether and to which extent a haircut is necessary. Greece, however, seems not to be willing to support the Troika on this task, as it hopes for a too generous haircut. Stephan suggests punishing this uncooperative behavior, thereby also reducing potential conflicts between creditors among the European member states due to different evaluations of the Greek financial status.

The chapter "Two Level Reform Game Problems of Greece", written by Martha Kontodaimon and Bernhard Neumärker, focuses on the problem that Greek politics have to perform on two levels, the international one with EMU countries and the IMF as the contracting partners and the national level. Political decisions of economic reform on the national level are described by a conflictual "war of attrition" game between the interest groups of Greece showing delay as a rule in debt reducing reforms. This is caused by the nature of stabilization and public debt reforms as public goods under asymmetrically distributed information which produces in the end allover absolute winners but some relative losers (Alesina and Drazen 1991). Whenever due to a partial shift of the Greek debt burden to the international level, the burden relief on the domestic level can be freely distributed between the interest groups generating relative losers and winners, reform delay may increase. If the share of the other member states is assigned only to the relative losers of the Greek war-of-attrition reform after a reform took place, the international burden sharing will lead to a relative acceleration of stabilization, privatization and debt restructuring reforms. The latter timing of the international aid and the negotiation processes concerning this matter appears to be the best international support to reform activities in Greece.

The social scientific contributions

The current financial and economic crisis in the European Union is not only in the limelight of economic research, but also prevalent in social science scholarship. The political scientists and sociologists in this edited volume examine how political and societal actors respond to Europe's Crisis. The contributions all share the assumption that conflict and sometimes also crisis are imminent features of politics, to which state and society have to respond. The chapters show that there is considerable variation in how political actors as well as societies react to and cope with challenging situations and argue that differences in responses to conflict are not only indicative for deeply rooted differences in societal or political underpinnings, but also offer windows of opportunities to tackle the crisis by adjusting political institutions and norms.

In "The Eurozone Crisis and Party Conflicts in Greece and Germany – Discursive Struggles about Responsibility" Moritz Sommer, Jochen Roose, Franziska Scholl, and Dimitris Papanikolopoulos examine how political parties react to the Eurozone crisis. To this end, the authors focus on one country deeply affected by the crisis as debtor (Greece) and one country as a major creditor (Germany) and examine the political media discourse in order to uncover how responsibility is attributed in these two contexts. They examine how the Eurozone crisis shapes the party conflict in Greece and Germany in shedding light on who is attributing responsibility in what way to whom. In both countries, political parties play major roles in the public media discourse. Comparing Greece and Germany, the most striking differences are in the extent of party political conflict as well as in the usage of dominant attribution types. While in Germany the conflict between political parties is limited, it is intense in Greece. In the latter the most common attribution of responsibility is domestic in character (between and within opposition and government) while European actors feature only occasionally as addressees in the 'party blame game'. In Germany, the dominant attribution is not so much about who to blame, but rather focuses on questions of crisis management. The chapter explains these observed differences with reference to political culture and path dependency theories as well as variation in issue saliency and electoral competition.

The chapter "Euro Crisis, German Hegemony and the New Geography of the European Union" by Rafal Ulatowski argues that the current Eurozone crisis could be a turning point in the history of European integration. Based on hegemonic stability theory, the chapter examines whether the crisis has triggered a shift in the distribution of power between the EU member states and sheds light on whether and how Germany as an increasingly hegemonic actor facilitates stability and deeper cooperation in the EU. The chapter observes that the Franco–German tandem is no longer the driving force behind deepened European integration, not the least due to the diverging economic developments of both countries during the recent financial and economic crisis. While Germany's economy is doing well, France is stagnating. This, together with the fact that the EU is no longer divided along an old-new member axis, but far more diverse opens a window of opportunity for hegemonic leadership. However, Germany does not act in accordance with this role. Rather than engaging in unilateral attempts to further develop the EU in response to the crisis, Germany is engaging in coalition-building and pushes for adjusting the European integration project together with the other (smaller), economically successful countries as the new European "core". Thus, the institutional architecture of the EU arising from the response to the financial and economic crisis does not bear the hallmark of strengthened supranationalism per se, but is intergovernmental and focused on stronger integration within the Eurozone.

In "Increasing Winners-Losers Gap? Increasing Euroscepticism? The Crisis and Citizens' Attitudes toward the Economy and the EU", Karsten Mause and Bernd Schlipphak examine the effects of the financial and economic crisis in the Eurozone on citizens' perceptions about whether they are on the winning or losing side and, related to this, their attitudes towards the EU. Mause and Schlipphak use data from the European Social Survey and from Eurostat (2006 and 2012) and argue that the EU's crisis increased the number of citizens perceiving being on the losing side. Yet, this effect is mediated by country specific factors. Most notably, the severity of the crisis increases the likelihood that the respective citizens perceive themselves as economic losers. Also, there is evidence that the EU's crisis has led to an increasing gap between those who regard themselves as winners and those who think they have lost out. Again, country-level effects matter. The higher the unemployment has become in the wake of the EU's crisis in a country, the more pronounced the gap between winners and losers. This is also linked to the attitudes of the respective citizens towards the EU as a whole. The stronger the negative economic effect of the crisis in a country, the more inclined its citizens are to exhibit EU-skeptical attitudes. The chapter concludes with reflections on how citizens' attitudes could constrain political leaders in their responses to the EU's crisis. A permissive consensus to react to financial and economic crisis with 'austerity' measures in crisis-ridden countries and to increase public debt in economically better off states to financially support poorer and strongly hit member states might be lacking, as is also indicated by the rise of anti-EU and populist political parties.

The legal contributions

In the early days, the process of European integration was fostered by politicians and lawyers who believed strongly in „integration through law". By continuously expanding and unifying the European legal framework they sought to conclude not only the common market, but ultimately also a political union of EU member states. In today's crisis, with political scientists and economists in the lead in political and academic debates, this appears like a vision from a distant past. Nowadays, conflicts in Europe seem to be resolved mainly politically with the economically strongest member states in the best position, while little regard is still given to the existing legal rules. This, however, ignores the importance of the legal dimension not only of the European integration process but also of current crisis resolution. The European treaties are still at the heart of the European project. Conflicts arise because there is a European legislation and because it is interpreted differently by the member states. These conflicts can only be resolved in accordance with these legal rules, otherwise the legitimacy of the European project is severely challenged. In addition, European legal rules and national legislation in the member states are (still) in conflict. Whether European integration will continue and succeed, therefore depends also on how the inherent conflict between the different legal systems can be resolved. The three chapters in this section highlight these lines of conflict and inquire whether and how they can be resolved.

Christian Joerges, in his chapter „The Overburdening of European Law through Economic and Monetary Union", traces the legal development of the European integration process from its beginning to the recent crisis. He identifies two important contributions to the constitutionalisation of the Treaty of Rome (TEEC) that established the European Economic Community in 1957: the jurisprudence of the European Court of Justice (ECJ) and the ordo-liberal project of a European economic constitution. Both added to the primacy of market-building orientations, but started to move into separate directions with the Maastricht Treaty. While the ECJ hoped for a move towards an "ever closer Union" based on the further development of European law, the ordo-liberals expected the establishment of the consummation of economic constitutionalism through a "Stability Union". Joerges argues that with the financial crisis these expectations proved to be illusionary, as the crisis overburdened the institutional framework which the Maastricht Treaty had established. Europe had to resort to an authoritarian style of crisis management irreconcilable with its commitments to democracy, the rule of law and social justice. Since the author does not believe in the availability of ready-made recipes through which Europe would overcome its present dilemma and regain legitimacy, he questions that law could serve as a substitute for democratic politics. If Europe continues resorting to the prevalent 'one-size-fits-all' philosophy of the integration project, Europeans will have to endure political contestation, social and economic conflicts. Therefore, he suggests that Europe should reorient its praxis towards recognition of its manifold diversity (similar to the 'unitas in pluralitate' vision of the EU Draft Constitutional Treaty) and learn how law can mitigate conflicts generated by that diversity and help to organize innovative and fair problem-solving.

The chapter "Legitimacy, Democracy and the Future of the Monetary Union" by Francesco Nicoli continues the discussion started in Joerges' contribution by exploring why the European crisis constitutes a turning point in the fundamental working principles and the legitimacy of the European project. He argues that with the crisis Europe has started advancing on the path of economic policy coordination and fiscal integration. With these new priorities, however, the question of the EU's alleged democratic deficit and the lack of political legitimacy arises newly. Nicoli argues that neither aspect was a major concern in the pre-crisis EU, but that since the crisis began ongoing fiscal integration has led to a 'genetic change' of the Union through the introduction of new institutions and policies at the EU level that are inherently redistributive in nature. This produces a democratic deficit today and requires democratic legitimacy. Starting from this observation, Nicoli identifies a fundamental trilemma when analyzing the relationship between democratic deficit, legitimacy and economic policy-making in the EU. Only pairs of these three dimensions can be achieved at the same time, thereby necessarily failing on the third dimension. In particular, the interactions between democratic legitimacy and fiscal integration are of some interest, given that the EU does not consist of one people with shared preferences but of twenty-eight nation states with distinct interests of their citizens. Creating a European identity among them can hardly be achieved without severe political conflict, as the recent rise of euroscepticism shows clearly.

In the final chapter of this volume, Stefan Oeter chooses to analyze a very specific variety of conflict from the series of conflicts over the adequate reaction to the various dimensions of the European financial crisis. More specifically, he analyzes the dispute between the German Constitutional Court and the political organs in Germany and the EU on the distribution of competence in the area of monetary and economic policy. The chapter highlights this conflict by analyzing in detail the line of argumentation of the Bundesverfassungsgericht in the OMT decision of 2014 – a decision which has taken a peculiar position regarding the policy measures of the European Central Bank, trying to limit rigidly the ambit of competences of the ECB. In order to do so, the Court had to take a very specific position in interpreting the relevant provisions of the European treaties, but also in reconstructing the economic rationale of the ECB's measures. The position taken by the Court, Oeter argues, can only be understood in terms of epistemic bias and cognitive dissonance as a result of the specific socialization which constitutional court judges have experienced.

Thus, the book makes an argument for the conflict theoretical perspective. Analyzing the European financial and economic crisis from this angle allows uncovering not only underlying structures and dynamics, but provides also a heuristic instrument to develop possible solutions in the economic, societal and legal realm.

Bibliography

Alesina, A./ Drazen, A.: Why are Stabilizations Delayed? American Economic Review 1991 81, pp. 1170-1188.

De Grauwe, P.: The Political Economy of the Euro. Annual Review of Political Science, 2013 1, pp. 153-70.

De Grauwe, P./ Ji, Y.: How Much Fiscal Discipline in a Monetary Union. Journal of Macroeconomics, 2014 39, pp. 348-60.

Dokko, J./ Doyle, B. M./ Kiley, T. M./ Kim, J./ Sherlund, S./ Sim, J./ Van den Heuvel, S.: Monetary Policy and the Global Housing Bubble. Economic Policy, 2014 26, pp. 237-87.

Garfinkel, M. R./ Skaperdas, S.: Economics of Conflict: An Overview. Handbook of Defense Economics, 2007 2, pp. 649-709.

Hirshleifer, J.: Competition, Cooperation, and Conflict in Economics and Biology. The American Economic Review, 1978, pp. 238-43.

Hirshleifer, J.: The Dark Side of the Force: Economic Foundations of Conflict Theory. Cambridge University Press, 2001.

Joyce, M./ Miles, D./ Scott, A./ Vayanos, D.: Quantitative Easing and Unconventional Monetary Policy–an Introduction. The Economic Journal, 2012 122, pp. F271-F88.

Landmann, O.: On the Macroeconomics of European Divergence. CESifo Forum, 2011 12(2), pp. 19-25.

Schelling, T.: The Strategy of Conflict. Second ed. Cambridge: Cambridge University Press, 1980.

Siems, M./ Schnyder, G.: Ordoliberal Lessons for Economic Stability: Different Kinds of Regulation, Not More Regulation. Governance, 2014 27, pp. 377-96.

Sinn, H.-W.: The Euro Trap: On Bursting Bubbles, Budgets, and Belief. Oxford University Press, 2014a.

Sinn, H.-W.: Austerity, Growth and Inflation: Remarks on the Eurozone's Unresolved Competitiveness Problem. The World Economy, 2014b 37, pp. 1-13.

Skaperdas, S.: Policymaking in the Eurozone and the Core vs Periphery Problem. CESifo Forum, 2011 12(2), pp. 12-18.

B. Economics

First chapter
Any Solution in Sight to Europe's Crisis? Some General Thoughts from a Conflict Theoretical Perspective*

Tim Krieger (University of Freiburg)

I. Introduction

Over six years after its outbreak, Europe's crisis lingers on. The EU member states still have not managed to work out how to return to a steady and sustainable growth path that helps to maximize welfare across the Community. While we have seen some steps towards a common response to the crisis, such as the introduction of the banking union and the European Stability Mechanism (ESM), it is undeniable that there are too few common, that is Europe-wide, measures to address this crisis with its truly European dimension.

What we instead see all too often are unspecific complaints that times are bad, that fellow member states are behaving selfishly, and that reforms – while inevitable if the crisis is to be resolved – need to be postponed until after the crisis. The dispute between the new Syriza government in Greece and the Eurogroup (in particular its German representative) is the most striking example of a large number of unresolved inner-European conflicts. Generally, the member states' response to the crisis has been disappointing. They have been, and still are, fighting the symptoms rather than the causes, while national interests remain the main drivers of policy measures, a situation that strongly calls into question the idea of European solidarity.

The crisis has revealed that Europe's institutions lack the framework required to deal with EU-internal conflict. This brief chapter sheds some light on Europe's organizational structure from a conflict theoretical per-

---

* This chapter is based on the workshop's opening address and includes arguments published previously in a blog post in German (http://wirtschaftlichefreiheit.de/wordpress/?p=13475).

spective and outlines future requirements to be placed on Europe's institutions and its conflict-solving mechanisms.

II. The Origins and Progression of the Financial Crisis

The impact of the US subprime mortgage crisis in 2007-08 infected Europe, too, abruptly terminating the exceptional economic growth that Europe's periphery had enjoyed during the prior decade. International investors that had invested heavily in Southern Europe and in Ireland suddenly realized that the convergence of interest rates in the Eurozone did not translate into a convergence in default risks across the Eurozone. The heavily concentrated and construction-dependent economies on Europe's periphery, with their oversized banking sectors and/or heavy public debt, were soon considered too risky and capital rapidly redirected to safe havens in northern Europe.

As a result, the countries on the margins of Europe came under pressure from several fronts. Their banks and construction companies collapsed, their economies shrank, and their unemployment rates skyrocketed. Their budgets groaned under the burden of the necessary bailout funds for the banking sector and increasing social spending. This development was especially severe because these countries had failed to implement structural reforms during the boom years after they entered the Eurozone.

The countries in the central Eurozone and particularly Germany that did implement structural reforms before the crisis benefited from the capital flowing back from the periphery. Although they, too, experienced some problems in the banking sector, they were reluctant to share liabilities with the peripheral countries. The countries at the core hoped to create immunity against the peripheral countries' debt and hence escape the crisis unscathed by rejecting Eurobonds, demanding a close link between liability and supervision, imposing the requirement to implement reforms *before* assistance, and demanding a stronger 'Maastricht Treaty 2.0'. At the same time, these measures aimed at preventing future moral hazard by setting clear boundaries for unilateral government actions within a common currency area that lacks common economic and fiscal policies. However, a more careful analysis of the situation in Europe reveals the impossibility of this strategy.

For one, the assumption that the countries whose debt increased should be held individually liable is anything but straightforward. Although the

European periphery was wrong to allow a set of wrongly developed incentives affect their economies and finances, international investors failed to recognize the risks. For too long, they fostered the problematic developments by sending enormous amounts of capital to the European periphery. Once the risks had become impossible to overlook, the investors started to withdraw most their capital and thus contributed heavily to the troubles these countries are currently experiencing.

For another, though commonly argued otherwise, the crisis has already spread to every economy in the Eurozone. Because of the tangled, opaque ties between securities at the beginning of the crisis, countries ring-fenced their banking systems before the effect of the crisis had become fully apparent. Other risky exposures, for which taxpayers were forced to assume liability, were pooled in bailouts and other structures. Almost every country in the EU suffered from a ratings downgrade and thus higher refinancing costs. The common monetary policy expanded, creating inflationary risks and asset bubble risks in core countries. Even if the crisis does not eventually cause the peripheral countries to default, the Eurozone countries will have assumed liability without taking into account the origins of the crisis.

III. A Conflict Theoretical Interpretation of Government Actions in the Current Crisis

Although the costs of the crisis have spread across Europe, the extent to which a country must carry the costs and risks is not predetermined and burden shifting is possible. The ultimate costs depend on the strategic behavior of a given country and its neighbors. This behavior assumes the structure of a zero-sum game in which progress is only attainable through redistribution, i.e., for any winner there must also be losers. Without coordination, progress as a whole will not be achieved; however coordination is not the players' preferred strategy.

Over the last six years – plus, in a nutshell, the first weeks of the Syriza government – we have observed a behavior that resembles a 'war of attrition' game that is often used to model the escalation of conflicts. This game involves two contestants who compete for a valuable resource. They do so by resorting to a 'wait-and-see' strategy because the country that moves first and reveals its strategy is fated to be the loser. The main problem with this game is that the players constantly accumulate costs for the entire duration of the contest. In other words, while both players individually have an incentive to wait so that they don't have to give in, this is a strategy that leads to the worst possible outcome globally.

Specifically, while countries on the periphery wait to implement structural reforms until assistance from the core arrives, the countries at the core prefer to wait for structural reforms to be implemented and the periphery to stabilize in order to minimize their own costs. Yet waiting pushes up the negative macroeconomic effects of the crisis even further. Current welfare losses, however, are distributed unequally and core countries such as Germany are much better prepared to wait. This has allowed the rich countries to exercise this strategy – rather successfully – for more than six years now.

Where negotiation has been possible, the behavior typical of power-based negotiation has become apparent. Any redistributed benefits depend on the relative power distribution across the parties involved. This explains why Greece has only been able to receive assistance subject to strict monitoring by the Troika, while the Spanish financial sector received assistance with no such strings attached. The reason for this discrepancy is the systemic relevance to the Eurozone of Spain's financial system; by contrast, Greece is considered a non-systemic risk.

Power-based negotiation mechanisms such as the one described above have significant downsides. They are selective, erratic and always dependent on time and context. That is why current problems can change and challenge the existing sets of rules, leading to enormous instability problems. A prime example of this is the breach of the Maastricht Treaty – not in the shape of Greece's accession to the Eurozone, but in the shape of Germany's and France's breaking of deficit rules in 2002-03. Through their ministers and the ECOFIN Council these countries exercised their power to avoid a penalty. Their behavior rendered the stability criteria irrelevant, turning them into no more than a tool for majority interests in the Council of the European Union. The message this sent to the other member states was that they should work less on complying with the Maastricht criteria and more on forming alliances to avoid any penalties.

The current crisis and the attempts to resolve it have not only distorted our view of problems such as these, they have also exacerbated the crisis by weakening the power of the European Commission and Parliament. Rather than taking place at Commission and Parliament level, the negotiations happened in the Council, where member state leaders are clearly on an unequal footing, an imbalance that affects the outcome of every negotiation. Following this mechanism, it is not surprising that the Council has only produced a remedy for the symptoms, rather than the causes, of the crisis. This suggests that when the next crisis arises, which may or may not originate in a then hopefully more stable banking industry, the same old conflict lines will reappear and decisions will be taken based on the same old power relations.

In light of this, and in the absence of binding and enforceable rules, it is hardly possible to predict how the Council would respond to a future crisis. What we do know, though, is that the decision-making process will be conflict-laden and very drawn out, maybe excessively so, due to built-in veto rights. In this respect, the European Union has a systematic competitive disadvantage versus other major trading blocs.

IV. Outlining the Conditions for Structural Reforms: Rule-Based vs. Power-Based Decision-Making

In the context of the situation described above, the solution to the current crisis must be a more comprehensive reform of decision-making structures within Europe. The Council's role and its decision-making process must be adjusted, without prescribing much-disliked centralization. Power-based negotiation must be replaced by a rule-based approach that incorporates clear incentives and evaluation criteria. Ideally, the rule-based approach should be self-enforcing, meaning it should be the best possible option, with power-based negotiation appearing less attractive. This can be achieved through well-designed sanctions. Creating such a mechanism is a difficult and complex task that the European political system must nonetheless tackle in order to avoid stagnation and threatening Eurosclerosis.

The following scenario (if only rudimentarily) illustrates what a mechanism to implement stability criteria could look like. The proposal emulates a mechanism that has been successfully implemented in the General Agreement on Tariffs and Trade, or GATT, and is used in the trade negotiations between GATT members. The mechanism of the GATT is self-enforcing and rests on very basic elements: voluntary participation, the principle of reciprocity, and clearly defined sanctions for member states that choose to breach the rules.

Adopting a GATT-like mechanism for the Eurozone and using the stability criteria of the Maastricht Treaty as a default could help create better incentives and conflict-solving mechanisms. Countries could pledge to respect deficit targets and/or implement structural reforms provided other countries also agree to do so or if they offer other concessions of equivalent quantity and/or quality. The member states would have to achieve a consensus on the offered concessions and would each sign an agreement to this effect. If a member state is found to be noncompliant, the rule-based sanctions would kick in. Most importantly, these sanctions would not be imposed by majority decision (as in the Council under Maastricht Treaty rules) but on a decentralized basis as under the GATT. Member states would decide individually whether to impose said sanctions unilaterally.

Suitable sanctions could facilitate compliance with the mechanism. One possible method would be to cut the agricultural subsidies (specifically, a given country's pro rata share of said subsidies) paid to the member state in question. Attaching sanctions to agricultural subsidies is an appealing option since farmers have a strong lobby and would put pressure on governments to respect the rules to ensure the subsidies keep flowing.

The rule-based sanctions would be a very clear penalty for noncompliance (in this case, loss of subsidies, domestic political conflict). Since majority-based conflict resolution mechanisms such as log-rolling could no longer be applied in the Council, the member states would be forced to carefully weigh the cost of compliance (for example, introducing austerity measures) against the cost of noncompliance (for example, becoming sanctioned for an excessive budget deficit). A predefined price tag attached to noncompliance would stabilize political decision-making in the member states and in turn across the EU as a whole. Strategic zero-sum games would have less of an impact. Importantly, the proposed mechanism includes the option to include escape and exit clauses in cases where the utility of noncompliance is greater than the sanction. Accordingly, the sanctions would have to be set at a level where they would be capable of compensating all other member states for a given State's noncompliance.

Finally, it is important to state that although the Council and its majority decisions would lose significance, the conflict-solving capacities of the EU would increase without having to centralize decision-making. This would serve the interests of the member states.

V. Conclusion

The example above, while obviously a simplification of Europe's complex reality, demonstrates the direction in which the EU's current conflict resolution mechanisms should develop. To address questions with conflict potential and those that involve redistribution, mechanisms based on voluntary participation, decentralization and reciprocity plus a set of clear rules should be the norm. They would make it possible to move from zero-sum to variable-sum games in a competitive environment in which sound legal rules apply, with interaction between states henceforth only taking place at the economic level. The implementation of such mechanisms naturally challenges the status quo in Europe. Yet when would it be more appropriate to reform EU institutions if not in times of crisis?

Second chapter
Could Exit Rules be Self-Enforcing in the EU? The Cases of
France and Germany

Robert Kappius and Bernhard Neumärker (University of Freiburg)

I. Introduction

Exit rules allow for a temporary or permanent withdrawal from international cooperative regimes. For the ongoing crisis in the European Monetary Union (EMU), such rules are seen as a desirable solution to enhance flexibility in case of economic and political shocks in member countries and to restrict fiscal externalities in the Eurozone. As the EU acts as a union of sovereign countries, politically powerful nations like France or Germany are likely to block or circumvent such a rule, if it negatively affects their interests. The underlying strategic problem of self-enforceability is largely neglected with respect to an EU exit rule. This contribution to the political economy of exit and escape rules aims at assessing conditions for voluntary adherence to an exit scheme by all parties of a common currency union such as the EMU.

In the wake of the ongoing EU crisis, several authors have proclaimed the need for codified exit rules for destabilized countries (e.g. Delors 2011; Huck and Valasek 2013; Hefeker and Neugart 2015). As an important reason, an exit rule may enhance the flexibility of an international regime to cope with economic and political shocks in individual member countries. For example, the GATT and WTO architecture allows its member countries to withdraw from specific tariff arrangements to leave room for domestic policy concerns (see Bagwell and Staiger 2005). With respect to the EU and the EMU, flexibility towards domestic issues such as financial failure looms large: Structural reforms can often be implemented only in a long term, while a departure from the Euro will result in a freely adjusting exchange rate that could possibly ease economic symptoms in the short run and alleviate structural reforms. A codified exit rule as part of the EMU regulatory framework may help to overcome costly speculation about Eurozone exits that leads to a continued flow of capital away from suspected countries. The uncertainty also affects financial movements and economic planning in the destabilized country in a negative way (Huck and Valasek 2013). Also, an exit rule may limit a destabilized countries' so called brinkmanship behavior, which is its potential to abuse the Unions' bailout-efforts (Fahrholz and Wójcik 2013). Through this channel, market discipline is strengthened once more. By strenghtening the economic discipline of relevant actors, an exit rule could even make the actual case of an actual exit less likely than in the status quo (Haidar 2014).

The political economy of implementing an exit rule in the EU is largely neglected in the literature. Proponents of an exit clause commonly appeal to an impartial economic reasoning that weighs global costs and benefits of an exit (e.g. Blankart and Bretschneider 2012). Also, troubled countries are treated as responsible for their fate and for exploiting bail-out interests of other union members, thus insinuating a just cause for an imposed exit rule (Haidar 2014). Contrary to policy recommendations towards the "common European good" (Haidar 2014: 2), actual reforms of fundamental EU regulation are oftentimes accompanied by resistance and ongoing conflicts. Specifically for the case of financial and fiscal policy, vital de jure rules were de facto barely enacted. The obligation of financial austerity decided upon in the Maastricht treaty was rarely pursued. Reversely, the so called "non-bailout"-clause (125 AEUV) did not prevent measures such as the ESM and OMT which arguably serve as concrete bailout policies (Sinn 2012). In still other cases, economically sound changes did not yet pass the reform process (e.g. Roland 2000). It is therefore by no means clear, that an economically sound reform option will pass the EU legislative process and will be effectively applied afterwards. With respect to an exit rule, strategic interests of member states may possibly be opposed. For example, formerly synchronized federal debt paths of France and Germany went in opposite direction in recent years – while Germany stabilized its debt, France significantly increased borrowing, thus failing to meet the demands from the European Fiscal Compact (EFC) that was enacted only in 2012. Also, the increase of nominal unit labor costs in France as diametrically opposed to Germany (Heise 2013) hints to a different economic and political path. These opposed economic developments may well turn into opposed interests towards the design and application of an exit rule. As both France and Germany are key veto players in the EU, their corresponding interests will have to be met for a formal exit rule to work effectively.

In order to highlight the strategic interests of quasi sovereign EU member states while challenging the effectiveness of de jure EU law, we propose to employ the theory on self-enforcing contracts to assess the feasibility of an EU exit rule. A self-enforcing contract requires that for all relevant contingencies, all contracting partners should have an incentive to act according to the contract at any time instead of reaping the short-run benefits from breach (Klein 1985: 595). The theory strand has numerous applications in international regimes, as no supranational agency may ensure compliance to a contract. Surely this approach implies a quite extreme view towards the foundations of the European community. It should be valued as a methodological counterweight against economists' "objectivism" in EU matters: An exit rule, if recommendable from an economic point of view, needs to reflect the current interest of all (powerful) member states in order to be both effective and viable.

II. Exit Rules in Self-Enforcing International Agreements

According to the theory of self-enforcement, contracts prevail in international regimes, if they lead to Pareto-improvements compared to an otherwise anarchic equilibrium (Bagwell and Staiger 1990; Rodrik 2007: 205). As a consequence, sovereign nations obey to international law and contracts even if this implies costly behavior – as long as the overall consequences of remaining in the contractual regime are beneficial. Such a regime commonly draws its benefit from solving an externality problem: In uncoordinated international interaction, self-interested national tax or regulation policy may excessively damage other countries. A contractual regime like the GATT and WTO effectively keeps single countries in the coordinated, mutually beneficial equilibrium. The idea of an exit clause serves to improve such a regime: An exit rule may enhance the flexibility of an international regime to cope with external economic and political shocks. For example, the GATT and WTO architecture allows its member countries to withdraw from specific tariff arrangements to leave room for domestic policy concerns (Staiger 1995; Bagwell and Staiger 2005). By paying a specific sum to other members, the country may still remain in and profit from the overall regime. This encourages more countries to enter the beneficial regime, while remaining flexible towards unanticipated contingencies and heterogeneity (Piketty 1996; Rodrik 2007).

Applied to the EU and the EMU, could an exit rule also be part of a superior union contract? An exit rule in this respect implies that member states as players must have an incentive to exit voluntarily when their economy is sufficiently harmful to the Union. Unfortunately, the results from the international regimes cannot be directly applied to the European case. As a reason and unlike the international regimes above, the EMU was not established to overcome a negative externality in pre-Euro Europe, but to reap additional benefits from a common currency zone. Rather, the EMU even gave birth to new externalities: Among other channels, the consequences of members' fiscal discipline are striking. Therefore, national decisions whether or not to remain in the EMU in case of a country-specific economic or political shock are assessed in the following section.

III. Modeling the Exit Decision

In order to delineate a self-enforcing exit rule, conditions must be defined under which a country that is hit by a fiscal, economic or political shock will want to leave the union in its own interest. While the ex-ante conditions for a country to join a currency union may be monitored by existing members, the reason why a country would or should leave the union are generally not known ex ante. In this respect, the question is not whether the EMU still is an optimal currency area (e.g. Petreski 2007; Tavlas 2009), but whether from the perspective of a specific country remaining in the Eurozone for at least another period is seen more beneficial than an immediate exit or not. We assess negative or positive economic shocks that result in a fiscal policy reaction, leading to either an expansion or a contraction of public debt. Compared to adjustments in wages, prices or even factor movements, fiscal compensation measures have shown to be quick and politically convenient compensatory measures in many EU instances.

A decision for or against exiting the EMU is a multifaceted assignment. Due to the highly complex decision environment, a precise model that calculates quantifiable payoffs is neither conceivable nor attractive. In order to find the elementary attributes of a self-enforcing exit rule, the basic qualitative components of such a political decision should suffice. In this respect, political motives, the benefit of the EMU, externalities as well as (optional) transfer payments are regarded as key elements of such a decision.

We assume, therefore, that in each period, countries face an economic and political sentiment a_i that translates into pressure towards enhancing or deleveraging public debt. Regarding the Eurozone, $a_i \lessgtr a_i^*$, where a_i^* stands for the EMU average condition. The choice of a fiscal debt $f_i \geq 0$ is set according to a function of the domestic political interaction, $p_i(f_i, a_i) = \min_{f_i} |a_i - f_i|$. In effect, the country will choose an f_i^*, defined as the average public debt in the EMU, whenever it faces a_i^*, otherwise an f_i close to a_i (see, for that, also Suzuki 2012). Other conceptions of $p_i(f_i, a_i)$ could be used to map different domestic politics interactions or preferences. The general form of the function that explains choice of fiscal debt is in accordance with similar international models that allow for a whole array of perceivable domestic policy objectives (e.g. Bagwell and Staiger 2002).

The benefits of a monetary union, G_i, largely consist in lower transaction costs and omission of exchange rate risks (see De Grauwe 2012). From a transaction cost perspective, a common currency also serves as a common standard (Blankart and Knieps 1993). All of this may add to market transparency, direct investments and trade volume. Also, gains pertain from the Euro as a reserve currency for foreign countries. These benefits are not to be confused with the advantages of a free internal market that affect the EU as a whole. Whether a currency regime may be viable in the long run crucially depends on a sufficient degree of economic symmetry and flexibility (Mundell 1961). Symmetrical economic development inhibits asymmetric shocks whereas flexible channels such as high factor mobility and flexible wage policy may function as shock absorbers. Departing from EMU benefit evaluations in the line of the Optimal Currency Area (OCA) theory (cf. Petreski 2007; Meier 2010), we capture consequences of asymmetric shocks not in G_i as these shocks lead to asymmetric costs, captured as externalities later on. For our purpose, qualitative gains from the common currency are captured in the term $G_i > 0$.

This does not imply that a common currency regime is always an ex-ante optimal choice for a candidate. Importantly, the loss of an independent central bank may lead even to an amplification of negative or positive shocks (De Grauwe 2012: 9-10). In a cross border currency regime, rising distrust due to a negative shock may induce investors to withdraw money from that country and to invest it – without devaluation – in a neighboring country, leading to a further increase of the domestic interest rate. In a stand-alone currency regime, investors would be inhibited from unsubstantiated capital flight due to devaluation. However, this reasoning does not play a role if a country is already part of a currency area, because debt obligations are contracted in the common currency.

Within the EMU, externalities of domestic policies may significantly influence an exit decision. In our case, the fiscal debt ratio of one country can have an effect on other countries and vice versa. A lot has been debated about the negative external effects of an excessive fiscal debt in one country with respect to that of other union members. During the first EMU decade, interest rate spreads for public bonds across the EMU were insignificant and allowed for excessive spending and investments in peripheral states. Whether to blame local governments and investors for shortsighted decisions or uninformed and overly powerful markets for greedy speculation, does not wipe out the result of an infectious 'Angst' that spread around Europe's banking and financial system and required encompassing counter-measures other than 'haircuts' for insolvent members (Heise 2013, chapter 3). For example, France feared cumulative panic and a cascade effect (Heise 2013: 20). Lack of insolvency regulations exacerbated the speculation externality on financial markets. The ECB jumped in to stabilize the Euro when southern European countries faced solvency problems. The European Stability Mechanism (ESM) as well as TARGET balances are seen as ongoing costly bailout measures (Sinn 2012). While these measures may in part be justified to make up for Greek sufferance from a self-fulfilling prophecy, it nevertheless introduced a moral hazard situation. Costs of general uncertainty and of contagion (Huck and Valasek 2013) add to the negative externalities of excessive deficits. The magnitude of these externalities crucially depends on EMU institutional settings as well as the functioning of capital markets. Among others, efforts of the ECB and the Financial Stability Board (FSB) to prevent systemic risks may dampen risk of contagious fiscal debts. Also, the financing of destabilized countries through the ESM is contingent on reform measures that limit long term debt accumulation and moral hazard behavior. Likewise, the fiscal debt shock may entail a negative externality for other countries like Germany when in spite of its fiscal austerity it has to partake in the EMU burden. On the other hand – and less echoed in the current debate on the burden sharing in the crisis – capital flight from destabilized countries like Greece may lead to falling interest rates in trusted member states. Incidents of negative interest rates for German federal bonds in 2014 can be attributed to the crisis. Net externalities, being a potential key factor in the decision whether or not to exit the EMU, are in principle endogenous to the EMU institutional arena. Generally speaking, the net externality $E_i(f_i, f_{-i})$ can be > 0, indicating a positive externality for country i when remaining in the Union (likely in case of excessive spending), and < 0 in case of a negative net externality (in case of austerity below EMU average debt).

Finally, there are payoffs X_i that appear when country i decides to leave the EMU. On a first account, a destabilized country $(f_i > f_i^*)$ will face conversion costs, a currency depreciation and capital flight (Blankart and Bretschneider 2012). Especially the magnitude of capital flight crucially depends on the design of exit (Huck and Valasek 2013). A codified exit rule can make an actual exit cheaper, as it leads to less speculation about the exit process. For a full account, economic responses to price changes and fiscal restructuring due to higher interest rates have to be included. Therefore an instantaneous devaluation will most likely induce the typical u-shaped economic development during structural reforms. X_i is assumed to be < 0 as immediate costs of an exit are obvious, while gains of a stand-alone reform compared to a guided reform process within the EMU are not evident (e.g. Kasimati and Veraros 2013). An intrinsic value of nationalism and autonomy (see Meyer 2010: 59) is ruled out. Those benefits of an exit are typically evident like reduced TARGET and reform payments in the Greek case (Blankart and Bretschneider 2012: 3) accruing to other member states. From the perspective of the destabilized country they are reversely part of the externality received when remaining in the union (thus making exit less likely). For an outperforming economy $(f_i > f_i^*)$ the opposite holds.

If a country faces an economic or political shock $(a_i \neq a_i^*)$, it is able to act upon comparing the expected payoff from remaining in the Eurozone, W_i^{EURO}, and the payoff from exiting the Eurozone, W_i^{ALONE}:

$$W_i^{EURO} = G_i - P_i^{EURO} + E_i \qquad (1)$$

$$W_i^{ALONE} = X_i - P_i^{ALONE}. \qquad (2)$$

Assuming that countries can enforce their preferred fiscal debt policy $f_i = a_i$ in both regimes (and ignoring the possibility of fiscal expenditures f_i higher than politically optimal due to externalities), $P_i^{EURO} = P_i^{ALONE}$, the decision reduces to

$$W_i^{EURO} = G_i + E_i \tag{3}$$

$$W_i^{ALONE} = X_i - P_i^{ALONE}. \tag{4}$$

Thus a voluntary exit will happen when

$$X_i > E_i + G_i. \tag{5}$$

This basic argument tells us that in case of a country profiting from externalities on a EMU level, we can never expect it to leave voluntarily, because $X_i < 0$ and $G_i, E_i > 0$. A transfer $T_i > 0$ has to make up for this inequality so that

$$T_i \geq X_i + E_i + G_i. \tag{6}$$

The transfer thus has to cover the costs of exiting plus the opportunity costs of not being in the Union anymore. Other countries will support a collectively financed payment T_i to country i if

$$-T_i + \left(G_{-i}^{i\,EXIT} - G_{-i}\right) \geq E_{-i}. \tag{7}$$

That is, subsidizing exit and facing a less encompassing Union is cheaper than suffering from negative externalities of country i as a Union-member.

Facing the constraint that a breakup of the EMU is not cheaper (assuming identical EMU members):

$$W_i^{EURO} = G_{-i} + E_{-i} + X_i + G_i + E_i \tag{8}$$

$$W_i^{i\,EXIT} = -X_i. \tag{9}$$

A voluntary exit will thus occur, if

$$-X_{-i} - G_{-i} - E_{-i} \leq X_i + E_i + G_i \leq -E_{-i} + \left(G_{-i}^{i\,EXIT} - G_{-i}\right), \tag{10}$$

stating that the effective exit costs for country i must entail less (opportunity) costs than a full union breakup (left hand side), while the remaining union is better off after the exit (right hand side).

High a_i shock and the 'downward' exit (France)

With its newly augmented fiscal debt and its power to effectively veto amendments in the EMU regulatory framework, France serves as a good example for a deficient country in this analysis. However, also small destabilized countries like Greece may arguably avert the enactment of exit rules, if the current treatise is conceived as unalterable against a member's will.

An increased a_i will induce an immediate political reaction $a_i > f_i^*$, thus leading to a positive E_i for France and negative E_{-i}. According to (5), only conditional payments will make a voluntary exit plausible, as this would entail sacrificing previous bailout-payments along with exit costs. On the side of other member states, only a sufficiently severe externality E_{-i} can incentivize this costly support. As a result, current regulatory changes that limit contagion and moral hazard behavior will make a 'downward' exit less likely. Alternatively, a full EMU breakup with its associated costs (exit costs, loss of union benefits but also lack of externalities) can even be a cheaper solution.

Low a_i shock and an 'upward' exit (Germany)

Due to a positive a_i, higher tax revenues and lower interest rates will ensure a lower fiscal debt that leads to negative E_i for Germany and positive E_{-i}. According to (5), a unilateral decision to exit the union is possible. Apart from $E_i < 0$, $X_i > 0$ is conceivable because an 'upward' exit could lead to an inverse market reaction. As there are no incentives on behalf of other member countries to subsidize this exit, it remains a self-contained action that entirely depends on the German $G_i < X_i - E_i$. Furthermore, there is no incentive for a currency union to regulate this 'upward' exit: A codified exit rule that reduces uncertainty and thus improves the payoff X_i and make an exit more likely, thus destabilizes the Union from the beginning.

IV. Discussion and Implications

The exit rule is not a cure-all for the EU crisis. With its jurisprudential justifications and economic consequences being disputed, it also faces serious headwind from a politico-economic view as the present examination suggests. While there seems to be no reason for regulating an 'upward' exit from the Union perspective, a mutually agreeable 'downward' exit hinges not only on complex issues as the current externalities and hard-to-estimate exit costs but also transfer payments that can be interpreted as exit-contingent bailout payments. Quantifiable conditions as part of a codified exit rule may not enhance market transparency or reduce market uncertainty. Refraining from these specifications on the other hand and merely specifying unified macroeconomic conditions for an automatic exit will result in political resistance.

In line with ineffective Maastricht criteria and no-bailout clauses, even a de jure regulation of EMU exits will then become incredible and cannot calm financial markets anymore. What the discussion on EMU exit rather needs is a material specification and quantification of self-enforcing exit rules or, otherwise, powerful European institutions or a Hegemon inside the group of member-states who is forcing other member nations towards upward exits. The second option would move away from the idea of a voluntary cooperation of European nations codified by unanimous decision-making and would enact – implicitly or explicitly – a new hierarchical system in the EMU.

We prefer the first option which is clearly more in the spirit of the peaceful and voluntary architecture of Europe, and it makes more centralization of political power superfluous. But then, it is a crucial requirement to transform the common European fiscal rules towards a self-enforcing European fiscal constitution. The mix of the Maastricht criteria and the no-bailout clauses is not self-enforcing. Some new mix may survive the enforcement test when the suggested exit rule is added. If Europe does not start the engine in search for truly self-enforcing (exit) rules, one has to fear that rather uncontrollable evolutionary processes will drive the decision making of the EU and EMU in the direction of involuntary, hegemonic and conflict-laden solutions.

Bibliography

Bagwell, K./ Staiger, R. W.: A Theory of Managed Trade. American Economic Review, 1990 80, pp. 779-795.

Bagwell, K./ Staiger, R. W.: The Economics of the World Trading System. Cambridge, Mass.: MIT Press, 2002.

Bagwell, K./ Staiger, R. W.: Enforcement, Private Policy Pressure, and the General Agreement on Tariffs and Trade / World Trade Organization Escape Clause. Journal of Legal Studies, 2005 34, pp. 471-513.

Blankart, C. B./ Bretschneider, S.: Nutzen und Kosten eines Austritts Griechenlands aus dem Euro. ifo Schnelldienst, 2012 65(9), pp. 12-16.

Blankart, C. B./ Knieps, G: State and Standards. Public Choice, 1993 77, pp. 39-52.

De Grauwe, P.: Economics of Monetary Union. 9th Ed., Oxford: Oxford University Press, 2012.

Delors, J.: Delors Urges Giving EU Power to Eject Nations from Euro. Reuters (Paris) 18 October 2011. <http://www.reuters.com/article/2011/10/18/eurozone-delors-idUSL5E7LI2KF20111018> (last accessed 25.3.2015).

Fahrholz, C./ Wójcik, C.: The Eurozone Needs Exit Rules. Journal of Banking & Finance. 2013 37, pp. 4665-4674.

Hefeker, C./ Neugart, M.: Fiscal Transfers in a Monetary Union with Exit Option. CESifo Working Paper No. 5244, Munich, 2015.

Heise, M.: Emerging from the Euro Debt Crisis – Making the Single Currency Work. Heidelberg: Springer, 2013.

Huck, S./ Valasek, J. M.: Institutionalizing Eurozone Exit: A Modified NEWNEY Approach. CESifo Working Paper No. 4116, Munich, 2013.

Kasimati, E./ Veraros, N.: Should Greece Adopt a Dual-Currency Regime to Resolve Its Economic Crisis? Journal of Policy Modelling, 2013 35, pp. 588-600.

Klein, B.: Self-Enforcing Contracts. Journal of Institutional and Theoretical Economics, 1985 141, pp. 594-600.

Meyer, D.: Währungsdesintegration in der EURO-Zone: Staatsbankrott und Inflation als zwei Szenarien infolge der Finanzmarktkrise. Jahrbuch für Regionalwissenschaft, 2010 30, pp. 45-70.

Mundell, R.: A Theory of Optimum Currency Areas. American Economic Review, 1961 51, pp. 657-665.

Petreski, M.: Is the Euro Zone an Optimal Currency Area? Working Paper, School of Business Economics and Management, University American College Skopje, 2007. Available at <http://ssrn.com/abstract=986483> (last accessed 25.3.2015).

Piketty, T.: A Federal Voting Mechanism to Solve the Fiscal-Externality Problem. European Economic Review, 1996 40, pp. 3-17.

Rodrik, D.: One Economics, Many Receipts: Globalization, Institutions, and Economic Growth. Princeton-Oxford: Princeton University Press, 2007.

Roland, G.: Transition and Economics: Politics, Firms, Markets. Cambridge: MIT Press, 2000.

Sinn, H.-W.: TARGET Losses in Case of a Euro Breakup. VoxEu, October 22, 2012.

Staiger, R. W.: International Rules and Institutions for Trade Policy. In: Grossman, G. M./ Rogoff, K. eds. Handbook of International Economics. Amsterdam: Elsevier, 1995, pp. 1495-1551.

Suzuki, Y.: Centralization, Decentralization and Incentive Problems in Eurozone Financial Governance: A Contract Theory Analysis. Working Paper, Hosei University, 2012. <http://repo.lib.hosei.ac.jp/bitstream/10114/7978/1/170suzuki.pdf> (last accessed 21.5.2015).

Tavlas, G. S.: Optimum-Currency-Area Paradoxes. Review of International Economics, 2009 17, pp. 536-551.

Third chapter
Debt Restructuring in Times of Crisis: A European Perspective

Maximilian Stephan (University of Freiburg)

I. Introduction

The European debt crisis centers around the Greek debt overload which became virulent from 2010 onwards. In fact, the Greek case led to severe conflicts within the Eurozone that are still unresolved today. These conflicts result from systematic difficulties related to debt restructuring and they arise not only between debtor and creditors, but also among creditors. In this chapter, the general problems of conflicts in debt restructuring are explored, before applying them to the specific crisis in Europe.

The huge public debt in Greece concerns European policy makers for more than five years now. When Greece announced its need for financial aid from the European Union in April 2010 and increasingly threatened the stability of the Eurozone, several Eurozone members and some other European Union member states introduced a first aid package to bailout Greece. These creditors of last resort linked aid to conditions, requiring the Greek government to introduce reforms to consolidate its budget. These requirements were demanded because the donor countries wanted to reduce the risk of moral hazard. They were afraid that Greece would not make the promised reforms. In order to minimize this risk the so-called Troika[1] consisting of EU, European Central Bank (ECB) and International Monetary Fund (IMF) was established. Together, these institutions monitor the agreements between the creditors, i.e., private investors and other countries, and the debtor, Greece. The disbursement of aid packages depends on positive evaluation of Greece's reform steps by the Troika. This is to ensure that the Greek government has no incentive to deviate from the announced austerity measures. Similarly important is the fact that the Troika gains access to extensive information about Greek public rev-

---

1 Since 2010, the supervisory committee of the European Commission, the ECB and the IMF have been named 'Troika' in the media.

enues and spending. This helps significantly to reduce the information asymmetry between creditors and the debtor. At the same time, the establishment of the Troika has been prone to conflict between Greece and its creditors. The Troika takes away degrees of freedom for the Greek government and weakens the country's position vis-à-vis the rest of Europa. Because of the reduced information asymmetry, the Greek threat to default at the expense of other EU members has become less alarming which, in turn, reduces Greece's threat point in the intra-European distributional conflict.

The role of the Troika is, however, also controversial from a different angle. Proponents of the Troika and of budgetary austerity among EU member states are mostly those countries that are solid in fiscal terms. Countries with larger deficits view the proposed reform policies much more critically as the fear to be pressed to fulfill similar reforms in case of own debt overload. Since all of these countries provided aid to Greece, conflicts arise between creditors as well. In addition, conservative governments are typically somewhat more willing to implement reforms than left-wing governments. Among the countries hit most severely by the crisis, Spain and Ireland have therefore enforced much deeper reforms than France and Italy.

Finally, there is a political dimension of reforms. The Troika has been intensively discussed in the Greek electoral campaign in early 2015, because the Troika tends to curtail any forms of excessive redistribution within the crisis countries. Hardly surprisingly, this gives rise to conflicts between the EU and parts of the Greek population. Those who are affected most negatively by the reforms are in strong opposition to them. The winners of the reforms, in turn, appreciate the Troika's proposals.

Unfortunately, the numerous conflicts within Europe have had a negative impact on both financial stability and the Euro exchange rate. While high public debts are a problem in general, sovereign default, or the threat thereof, poses an even bigger challenge for the international capital markets. Today's problems in Greece result in particular from the country rescheduling its debt in 2012 and even more so from the present government's wish for a new haircut of its debt. It helps to take a closer look at how sovereign insolvency is dealt with in the negotiations between creditors and the debtor and how the incentives of the relevant actors in these negotiations look like. With this, the conflict dimension of the European crisis becomes very obvious. The general line of conflict is easy to see: While the debtor nation tries to reduce its liabilities following the haircut to a sustainable level, the creditors' interests lie in attaining the highest possible repayment.

In the following, it will be explained in detail why investors differ in their behavior and their reasons for an inefficient debt restructuring. The creditors differ according to the type of bonds they acquired. Furthermore, creditors vary in their portfolio structure, their risk attitude and in the volume of invested capital. That is, heterogeneity between creditors poses a major challenge to a possible agreement. It may result in conflicts among the creditors as well as between the creditors and the debtor. These conflicts are aggravated by a high degree of asymmetric information between the relevant parties.

II. The Distinctiveness of Sovereign Debt

It is important to distinguish between private and public debt. Private debt predominantly serves to invest in production or consumption activities. In the case of insolvency due to too high private debt of individuals or enterprises, insolvency proceedings in accordance with national legislation will be opened. This will typically comprise the right of direct access to all property that can be liquidated to cover the existing liabilities. All concerned parties know ex-ante the insolvency mechanism related to private debt. The insolvency legislation differs widely between nations and pursues various goals. In contrast, sovereign debt serves to smooth consumption and to stabilize the economy. There is no insolvency proceeding for states as they are sovereign.

Since the present chapter focuses on the economic problems related to foreign debt restructuring, it is instructive to examine the structure of sovereign debt of the European countries. Table 1 shows that around half of the national debt is held by foreigners (Andritzky 2012). Approximately half of the foreigners holding European sovereign bonds stem from the EU. The other stem from the rest of the world. In the USA and in Great Britain, the share of foreign investors is less than a third. Taken together, this makes the EU less dependent on foreign (i.e., non-EU) investors than the two Anglo-Saxon states.

In the post-World War II period until well into the 1990s, sovereign debt was mainly characterized by syndicated loans. Since the 1990s, states have emitted mainly bonds as shown in Table 1. Central government financing by issuing bonds is distinctly more frequent than on a local level. Because of issuing bonds and the resulting diversified holdings, the number of creditors has risen.[2]

Table 1: Structure of sovereign debt in % for 2013

	Allocation of sovereign debt by the way of finance			Issue denomination		Structure of creditors
	Securities	Loans	Rest	National currency	Foreign currency	Foreign investors
Belgium	86.8	12.9	0.3	99.8	9.2	49.9
Bulgaria	62.5	37.5	0	29.0	71	44.2
Czech Republic	89.7	10.3	0	80.8	19.2	33.8
Denmark	81.4	16.8	1.8			
Germany	72.5	26.9	0.6	96.8	3.2	56.1
Estonia	13.7	86.3	0	100.0	0	64.9
Ireland	55.3	35.2	9.5	87.4	12.6	61.9
Greece	24.9	74.9	0.2			
Spain	79.6	20.0	0.4	99.6	0.4	41.7
France	84.1	13.8	2.1	97.4	2.6	57.3
Croatia	70.6	29.4	0	25.5	74.5	36.5
Italy	83.9	8.5	7.6	99.9	0.1	31.8
Latvia	43.5	53.9	2.6	76.5	23.5	80
Lithuania	77.9	20.3	1.8	23.3	76.7	69.9
Luxembourg	57.6	40.1	2.3	100.0	0	1.5
Hungary	82.1	17.7	0.2	57.9	42.1	57.7
Malta	91.8	7.1	1.1	100.0	0	7
Netherlands	78.5	21.4	0.1	97.6	2.4	52.8
Austria	81.2	18.8	0			71.6
Poland	82.9	17.1	0	70.5	29.5	32.7
Portugal	51.2	43.9	4.9	88.1	11.9	66.4
Romania	65.5	32.8	1.7	43.4	56.6	26.9

---

2 Most countries do not publish the number of creditors. But it is known that, for example, Argentina has about 61.000 different creditors.

	Allocation of sovereign debt by the way of finance			Issue denomination		Structure of creditors
	Securities	Loans	Rest	National currency	Foreign currency	Foreign investors
Slovenia	87.0	12.7	0.3	99.9	0.1	
Slovakia	85.9	13.8	0.3	92.9	7.1	61.3
Finland	80.5	19	0.5			81.6
Sweden	77.8	18.8	3.4			38.2
United Kingdom	89.5	1.8	8.7	100.0	0	30.4

Source: Andritzky 2012, Eurostat (http://epp.eurostat.ec.europa.eu/portal/page/portal/government_finance_statistics/data/database)

Bonds are issued in various currencies and in different places, with the Eurozone members and Great Britain issuing their bonds almost exclusively in domestic currencies. The advantage is that there are no currency fluctuations. The currency risk can cause a rise in the debt burden if the domestic currency is devalued relative to the currency of debt payment. Some EU member states, such as Poland, Romania, Croatia, Lithuania and Hungary have large foreign currency debts because they issue debt contracts denominated in Euro.

Typically, bonds are issued according to the legal rules of the issuing country. Different legal systems vary with respect to the conditions for issued bonds. For instance, collective action clauses (CAC) are included in bond issuing contracts according to British and Luxemburg legislation. Since January 2013, they are also included in bond contracts according to German law. Japanese and U.S. bonds usually do not include CACs (Eichengreen and Mody 2004). The Greek sovereign debt restructuring was made easier because most of the bonds were issued under Greek law. The Greek Parliament introduced collective action clauses in retrospective. According to these clauses, debt restructuring is mandatory when a predefined majority of bondholders accepts the restructuring offer. In the case of Greece, creditors were divided into different groups, which helped to exclude bonds held by the ECB from the restructuring.[3] Finally, bonds have varying maturities. For instance, the diversity of bond types can be

---

3 The IMF traditionally has a priority above other creditors in its operations.

increased by collateralization. With the total amount of sovereign debt, the variety of instruments expands.

The resulting problems related to sovereign debt restructuring depend largely on the factors described above. In the following section, the focus will be on the specific problems of external debt.

III. Economic Problems of Sovereign Debt

Their governments represent debtor nations, and governments can be exchanged during the period of debt restructuring. For instance, no longer being able to meet its obligations Ireland announced the need of a bailout package from the EU, ECB and IMF on November 21, 2010. On February 21, 2011, elections took place and a new government came into office. In the case of Greece, state insolvency was announced in August 2011 despite receiving financial aid since May 2010. Elections followed one year later.

The elections in both countries took place in the wake of debt crisis. Typically, there are distributional conflicts among different groups in society that shape the electoral outcome. As part of the debt restructuring, the debtor is required to align government revenues and spending. Economic growth is usually low in these times, leading to declining tax revenues. In this situation, net taxpayers advocate spending cuts while transfer recipients prefer tax increases. That is, there arises a fundamental conflict between these two groups which is in a democratic society resolved through majority decision in the elections. However, the creditors, most notably the Troika, tend to interfere in these conflicts by strengthening the advocates of spending cuts. This is why the perceived losers of austerity measures rebel against the Troika in the first place and it explains why Syriza won the Greek elections in 2015.

Asymmetric information

Sovereign debts concern a variety of conflicting interests and may result in a number of economic problems. Each actor, or player in a game-theoretic sense, is trying to maximize his return. Generally, coordination problems among the creditors may arise. The relationship between the creditors and the debtor is characterized by asymmetric information, with the debtor disposing of a superior knowledge of his financial situation. The debtor could provide information to the creditors in order to reduce the information asymmetry, but if the debtor nation is not willing to do so the creditors have practically no chance of receiving information on its financial status. Cornelli and Felli (1995) argue that no insolvency regulations for states would be required in case of complete information, no negotiation costs and perfect contracts. Obviously, these assumptions are unrealistic. Therefore, intervention of the international community in negotiations on public debt can be justified. In the case of Greece, it is the responsibility of the Troika to gather information about the debtor and to inform the creditors. Hard surprisingly, the new government prefers not to cooperate with the Troika.

Lack of security and asymmetric information both lead to strategic behavior and premature liquidation of bonds. In case of premature bond selling the advantage lies with the creditor who is the first to sell. Such a behavior may cause herd behavior among the creditors. Many creditors sell their bonds and do not subscribe for new ones, regardless of whether the country was solvent or insolvent prior to the divestment. Due to this self-fulfilling prophecy the debtor will be rendered illiquid and thus insolvent. This can be the consequence of asymmetric information and poses an incentive for the debtor to provide information to the creditors. As a result, many creditors behave like free riders and refuse monitoring (Eichengreen and Portes 1995).

Willingness-to-pay problem

The willingness-to-pay problem arises from asymmetric information combined with reduced costs of state insolvency. Increasing costs of state insolvency can prevent such a behavior. Sovereign default is often a consequence of an unwillingness to meet a country's obligations and not of its inability to serve sovereign debts. In the case of debt restructuring, it has to be ensured that a country restructures because of financial need and not in order to acquire a competitive advantage (Eichengreen and Portes 1995). The competitive advantage arises from a haircut without need when the interest burden is reduced, thereby freeing financial resources to support the economy. Therefore, the willingness-to-pay problem is the consequence of a lack of creditor protection and the immunity of states (Borensztein and Panizza 2009). The creditors will hardly be able to have a debtor state's assets seized abroad. Default because of opportunistic reasons has been called a rush to default (Roubini 2002). Often a state will meet its liabilities in good times, while preferring to default in a recession and thereby avoiding reform efforts and austerity measures.

The debtor must take the costs of debt restructuring into account (Eaton and Gersovitz 1981; Sachs and Cohen 1982). Rose (2005) names three arguments for debtors to repay their debts. On the one hand, trade with a country that does not meet its obligations is reduced. On the other hand, such a country will be excluded from the international capital markets. Finally, assets of the debtor state can be seized abroad. Panizza et al. (2009) also consider different default costs. Costs will òccur due to lower economic growth, a deteriorating reputation and less trade. A banking crisis may occur in the event of a sovereign default (Borensztein and Panizza 2009). This is in line with Kaminsky and Reinhart (1999). They identify the problem of twin crises, i.e., simultaneous crises in banking and currency (e.g., in Mexico 1994, Asia 1997 and Russia 1998). De Paoli et al. (2006) show the interaction between sovereign debt, banking and currency crisis.

An interesting point in case is Ecuador that refused to pay its interests on external debt because of alleged 'illegitimacy' in 2008. With its oil fields, Ecuador is in a position to finance itself by selling crude oil and is not dependent on obtaining funding on the financial markets, making it difficult to penalize the country. More generally, the challenge is to find the right mixture rendering defaults neither too difficult nor too easy (Eichengreen 2003).

From the debtor's perspective the willingness-to-pay problem is a sequential game, in which the debtor decides whether to pay the debt or not (see the decision tree in Figure 1). In case of default, the creditors may react to this decision with sanctions. If the debtor nation meets its obligations, the creditors have no reason to sanction the debtor.[4] In this case, the debtor receives the payoff A. Payoff C is the optimal solution available for the debtor nation, since it is not sanctioned for its non-payment. If it is assumed that the sanctions are effective and will hurt the non-paying debtor, payoff B is the worst scenario for the debtor. This means that the decision in favor or against payment depends on the debtor's expectation

---

4 This applies to both the first game and a repeated game, as the latter do not profit from sanctions.

to be sanctioned or not. If the debtor does not expect to be sanctioned, non-payment is more favorable. In case the debtor disposes of raw materials or other tradable assets, it is possible for a debtor country not to meet its obligations without having to fear sanctions or reduced capital inflows too much. In addition, the debtor should not possess pledgeable assets abroad. It may therefore be advantageous for a small country rich in raw materials not to meet its obligations for opportunistic reasons. For countries that dependent on access to the capital markets and on trade, an opportunistic non-payment is disadvantageous. They must fear to be sanctioned by the other market players posing them into an unfavorable position. For those debtors who really are not in a position to meet their obligations, there will be another consequence. In this case, the debtor must plausibly assure the creditors that the haircut is not due to opportunistic reasons. To make it credible, it is in the strongest interest of the debtor to provide information and reduce the information asymmetry.

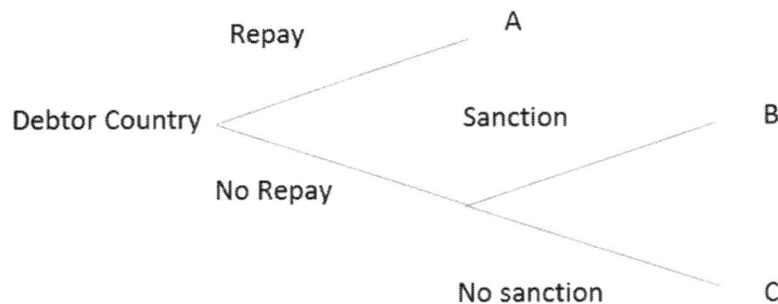

Figure 1: Sequential game of sanction

This reasoning can be applied to the situation of Greece in the spring of 2015. The Greek government is aiming for a haircut that is, however, rejected the EU, the ECB and the IMF. According to the statutes of the ECB and the IMF debt cannot be deferred. The creditors will therefore have to react to Greece not servicing its debt. The possible penalties or exclusion of Greece from the international capital markets can be worse than repaying the debt. This depends on how credible the EU's threats are and whether the EU will ultimately enforce sanctions.

Uncertainty during debt restructuring

Asymmetric information creates uncertainty for all concerned participants causing debt restructuring to take an unnecessarily long time. All the parties stand to lose, but it is ex ante uncertain who will be the losers and how large the losses will be. Borensztein and Panizza (2009) describe a negative and a positive effect arising from the uncertainty related to state insolvencies. The positive effect is due to a reduced willingness-to-pay problem as uncertainty drives up costs. This increases the inhibition threshold for a country to restructure its debt. A debt restructuring takes time and all the creditors must agree unless there is a collective action clause. Furthermore, it will be hard for the debtor to return to the capital markets as risk premiums are increasing. This is one reason why some states show a history of state insolvencies. The negative effect is that there will be speculations about the terms of repayment due to asymmetric information. There is no rule stating at which point a state is bankrupt and of what size a haircut should be in such a case. A strategic game of asymmetrical information for the terms of repayment may emerge. While the payout for creditors and debtors is reduced with each round of the game, they still cannot agree on the terms because they expect a higher payout. All conflicting parties lose with the increasing duration of negotiations. Welfare is maximized in case of a fast negotiation, but creditor and debtor may prolong the negotiation time for debt restructuring in order to increase the pressure on the negotiation partner and to improve their own position. While the debtor will have difficulties to refinance when debt restructuring is prolonged, the creditor will suffer from a longer period without payments. In this scenario, a prisoner's dilemma arises.

During the negotiations, the creditors will have difficulties to anticipate the necessary size of the haircut to guarantee state solvency in the future. The debt restructurings of Pakistan (1999), Ukraine (1998), Ecuador (2000), Uruguay (2003) and Russia (1999) demonstrated that restructuring is possible with a high degree of consent. The reason is that a state's main creditors are typically financial institutions that must depreciate their assets in a mark-to-market valuation as soon as there is a value reduction in bonds. For institutional investors it might therefore be favorable if a bond value does not change, rending depreciations unnecessary. In addition, creditors fear a disorderly insolvency. Furthermore, restructured bonds have a higher liquidity (Eichengreen 2003). These are additional reasons for a creditor to agree to a restructuring. The lack of a definition when a state is insolvent poses an information problem for the creditors. Typically, the insolvency of a state is not identifiable from economic figures. Yeyati and Panizza (2011) describe that it is rational for a debtor to default as soon as the market players assume the debtor to default.

The run-for-the-exit problem

Among a state's creditors there will arise a coordination problem as soon as the state announces to be in financial difficulties. After the shock of this announcement, there is usually a panic on the market that leads to the selling of assets and a lack of liquid funds, making it impossible to rollover the debt (Pedersen 2009). In Europe, in order to prevent contagion of other countries, aid funds were established at the EU level. A run from an indebted country can lead to fragile prices and liquidity spirals (Brunnermeier and Pedersen 2009). In this case, creditors have the incentive to be the first to sell their assets in order to avoid possible costs of restructuring or devaluation (Roubini 2002). When the first creditors sell their assets, the price drops. Further asset sales cause a downward spiral with declining prices. Prices on the market are becoming fragile and the risk of default or exchange losses rises. The first-mover-advantage causes a classic problem of collective action in sales, with all the participants wishing to sell their shares resulting in a run-for-the-exit phenomenon. Again, a prisoner's dilemma arises for the creditors. The dominant strategy for every creditor is to be the first to sell his bonds, as soon as a country encounters liquidity problems. Nevertheless, it would be advantageous for all the creditors to agree on a standstill in order to avoid a run with all its consequences (Helleiner 2008). A standstill signifies that no payments are made and that all parties involved get time to find a solution. Some economists argue in favor a standstill mode in which the creditors are provided with all available information by the debtor, allowing them to coordinate their actions. But a standstill itself creates further incentives to run for the exit as it induces creditors to sell their bonds before the standstill becomes effective (Pedersen 2009). However, it has to be distinguished between long-term and short-term investors. While a standstill is more favorable for long-term investors, it can cause a run of short-term investors (Batra 2002). This may result in conflicts among the different types of creditors.

Holdout

The number of investors in sovereign debt is usually high and their investments are often small. The creditors do not constitute a homogeneous group as the investors pursue different interests and are characterized by different economic preconditions and interests. Difficulties arise because these heterogeneous creditors have to agree to consistent terms. The larger the number of creditors, the more likely that some of them refuse to accept the debtor's offer. These investors will try to achieve a higher payout and therefore chooses to prolong the negotiations and the debt restructuring process. This is not at all in the interest of those creditors who consented to a debt restructuring. The coordination problem among the creditors can be exemplified by actual approval rates during debt restructuring negotiations. For example, the approval rates were 76% in Argentina (2005)[5] and 85.8% in Greece (2010).

These approval rates illustrate the potential for conflict between the creditors. If all the creditors agree, the most profitable strategy for a single creditor is not to agree and to push for a full payout of the obligations. If others follow this strategy, it is still better not to agree to prevent other creditors to benefit from one's renunciation. This creates the incentive for all the creditors not to consent to a debt restructuring (Roubini 2002; Daniels and Ramirez 2007). In fact, it is the dominant strategy in this prisoner's dilemma not to agree (Tamura 2002; Daniels and Ramirez 2007). Pitchford and Wright (2011) establish a holdout to be a strategic behavior, while Engelen and Lambsdorff (2009) described the problem by modelling a strategic stag hunt game. The player is said to consent if all the others consent, too. If the other players do not consent, the first player cannot share the costs. This makes it profitable for the first player not to agree.

In a holdout an investment decision is considered. The investor has a choice between a secure payout in case of consenting and an uncertain payment in case of a holdout. If investors decide for a holdout, they suffer additional costs from pushing for a higher payout. Those costs can arise from court proceedings or from seizing assets abroad. Here, the investors' decisions depend on their risk attitude as well as the variance, return and

---

5 Interestingly, two US investors (NML Capital and Aurelius) lodged a legal claim against Argentina before a US court that ruled that Argentina is to pay the creditors 1.33 billion US dollars representing the full payout.

portfolio structure of the creditors' investments. Should there be no agreement, uncertainties will occur concerning the payout. These uncertainties can be less desirable for the investor than to renounce on part of his debt claim. As a result, different investors come to different decisions. Large banks often have an interest in continuing business relations with the debtor and they will consider this in their decisions (Miller and Thomas 2007). Roubini (2002) mentions reasons why the holdout problem is irrelevant in banking practice, pointing in particular to the high costs an investor faces in case of a holdout. Agreement rates were lower in the two largest (Argentina 2005, Greece 2012) debt restructurings than in other debt restructurings, as these bonds constituted a large part of the portfolio. The investor is prepared to bear higher costs in order to receive a higher payout than in the case of debt restructurings that constitute a small part of the portfolio. According to Yeyati and Panizza (2011), the GDP reaches its local minimum during a haircut and rises again afterwards. Should the creditors expect a quick improvement of the economic situation, they may speculate for a holdout. Tomz and Wright (2007) disagree with this argument, however, as their analysis shows an economy's minimum not to appear during debt restructuring but with delay.

Due to holdout behavior, the negotiations between debtor and creditors become more time-consuming and cost-intensive for all concerned parties. This becomes particularly evident when considering the debt restructuring of Argentina (2005). In the worst case there will be a disorderly insolvency. Haldane et al. (2005) show that CACs could solve inefficiencies arising from a holdout (Eichengreen and Mody 2004; Eichengreen and Portes 1995). CACs solve the conflict among creditors by majority decision. The Greek debt restructuring was facilitated by the ex-post introduction of a CAC. However, such a decision is discriminating for those investors who do not consent with the debt restructuring because of their different risk attitudes and diversification strategies. Only if a merely destructive behavior is at play, CACs may solve the problems arising from holdout behavior. Nevertheless, CACs lead to a discrimination of certain investors. Furthermore, CACs improve the position of the debtor in the negotiations because it suffices to have the consent of a critical mass. Therefore, the debtor makes an acceptable offer only to those creditors who are pivotal.

IV. The Economic Debt Crisis in Europe

In the wake of the debt crisis in Europe a number of measures have been taken. They aim at restoring the solvency of countries and reducing the economic problems discussed in the previous sections. Table 2 summarizes some of the most relevant measures to counter the crisis.

Table 2: The development of the European crisis and its countermeasures

Date	Event
April 23, 2010	Greece officially announces the need for financial aid from the EU.
May 2, 2010	EU finance ministers decide to grant Greece emergency loans totaling €110 billion in exchange for reinforcing austerity measures. Only ten days later, the first tranche flows to Athens.
May 3, 2010	ECB accepts Greek government bonds at face value as collateral.
May 9, 2010	ECB starts Securities Markets Program (SMP).
May 7-10, 2010	European Financial Stability Facility (EFSF) is agreed upon.
May 10, 2010	European Financial Stabilisation Mechanism (EFSM) is introduced as an emergency funding program (it is raised from the financial markets and guaranteed for by the European Commission using the EU budget as collateral).
June 10, 2010	EFSF officially launches with €750 billion in guarantees. It can lend up to €440 billion.
November 10, 2010	Ireland receives financial aid totaling €67.5 billion.
November 28, 2010	The finance ministers of Eurozone agree upon a permanent €700 billion crisis fund, the European Stability Mechanism (ESM) that may payout a maximum of €500 billion to distressed countries (the rest serves as a security deposit). In 2013, the ESM replaces the EFSF.
May 11, 2011	Portugal receives a €79.5 billion promise from EFSF, ESFM and IMF. €76.9 billion are disbursed.
July 21, 2011	Second Greek bailout package. Greece receives a €163.7 billion promise from EFSF and IMF. €162.8 billion are disbursed.
July 28, 2011	Greek parliament approves further billion Euro budget cuts and austerity measures. Greece has come a step closer to the disbursement of the second rescue package.
November 11, 2011	Elections in Greece, Italy and Spain lead to changes of governments.

Date	Event
December 21, 2011	ECB announces measures to support bank lending and money market activities.
March 12, 2012	Sovereign debt restructuring of Greek debt with an approval rate of 86% and an effective haircut of 70%.
June 12, 2012	ESM is confirmed by the national parliaments. It starts its activities on September 27, 2012, with a share capital of €702 billion.
July 12, 2012	ESM can now also be used for bank bailouts.
September 6, 2012	ECB approves OMT program. The ECB Council is allowed to buy government bonds without limit but subject to several conditions.
November 7, 2012	Despite protests, the Greek Parliament votes for an austerity package totaling €13.5 billion.
December 3, 2012	Spain requests the disbursement of €39.5 billion for the recapitalisation of the banking sector from the ESM.
December 12, 2012	Greece needs to extend the deadline for its debt buyback program.
December 13, 2012	EU finance ministers agree upon a centralized banking supervision starting in 2014.
January 13, 2013	European Fiscal Compact comes into force.
March 16, 2013	Cyprus is guaranteed €10 billion by the ESM and IMF. Until October 31, 2014, €5.8 billion are disbursed.
November 14, 2014	ECB takes over the European banking supervision.
January 15, 2015	Change of government in Greece. The new government immediately stops reforms and announces to cooperate no longer with the Troika.
February 4, 2015	ECB cancels special rule on Greek government bonds.
Febuary 15, 2015	The Euro group approved Greece an extension of the aid for 4 months.

The Greek debt restructuring led to a conflict between the creditors because of the ex-post introduction of a CAC for some bonds. By early March 2012, 86% of the creditors had accepted the exchange offer. This provided the necessary majority for a remortgage and rescheduled all bonds. The Greek government had threatened the holdout investors with a total failure. A coalition of the EU and Greece was formed to the detriment of private creditors. These had to bear the entire burden of the 2012 debt restructuring. Due to the change in loan contracts, the bonds held by investors who had not agreed were rescheduled as well. Both in Greece and in Germany there are lawsuits filed against this form of forced conversion. The Greek government wants to lead the processes in Greece while the creditors prefer to sue in their home countries. The investors had to give up 53.5% of the original value. Furthermore, the maturity of the bonds was stretched. Sturzenegger and Zettelmeyer (2008) calculated a haircut of 70%. The duration of the Greek debt restructuring was short compared to other restructurings. The EU played the role of a mediator and the EU member states were able to put pressure on their financial institutions because most creditors of Greece were European financial institutions.[6]

In the previous section, the run-for-the-exit problem was discussed. Investors fear that a country is unable to meet its obligations so they will not lend capital to it anymore. For this reason, the debtor country cannot refinance and becomes illiquid, which ultimately can end up in bankruptcy. During the Greek crisis, there was a risk of contagion to other peripheral European countries. In addition, a restructuring of Greek sovereign debt was feared to lead to a banking crisis in the Eurozone (Siebert 2010). This is why EU member states awarded loans to Greece in the early times of crisis. In June 2010, the European bailout mechanisms European Financial Stability Facility (EFSF) and European Financial Stabilization Mechanism (EFSM) were established. They were replaced by the European Stability Mechanism (ESM) in June 2012. These funds help countries in financial need to fulfill their payment obligations (Table 3 shows the commitments and disbursements to the European crisis countries). This procedure helps to counteract the self-fulfilling prophecy of a sovereign default. The capital from the EU partners made the participating countries less dependent of the capital markets, which gives them time to reform. Public institutions replace private creditors. The default risk of bonds decreases and yields decline. Therefore, the aid packages from EFSM, EFSF and ESM were in the interest of the recipient country, potential other recipient countries and private investors. This approach is, however, not beneficial to the liable taxpayers in the rest of Europe.

---

6 Barclays Capital estimates the exposures of European banks to periphery states. More than 90% of the banking exposures in Greece come from the Eurozone and 4.4% come from the British banking sector.

Table 3: Overview of various programs in billion Euro

	Disbursed					Promised				
	EFSF	EFSM	ESM	IMF	bila-teral	EFSF	EFSM	ESM	IMF	bila-teral
Greece, first bailout				20.1	52.9				30	80*
Greece, second bailout	130.9			11.8		144.5			28.7	
Ireland	17.7	22.5		22.5	4.8**	17.7	22.5		22.5	4.8**
Portugal	26.0	24.3		26.6		26.0	26.0		27.5	
Spain***			39.8					41.4		
Cyprus			5.7	0.4				9.0	1.0	

* The amount decreased because Slovakia did not participate in the Greek loan facilities. Ireland and Portugal also did not participate because they applied or received financial aid themselves.
** United Kingdom €3.8 billion, Sweden €0.6 billion and Denmark €0.4 billion. €17.5 billion were own resources.
*** Spain has repaid €1.6 billion. The amount was used to capitalize banks.

Source: Bundesministerium der Finanzen (2015)

The ECB policy was supported by the fact that market participants did not expect an insolvency of any European country. In May 2010, the ECB reduced the requirements for collateral, so that commercial banks could store all Euro government bonds at the ECB as collateral. Moreover, in May 2010, the Securities Markets Program (SMP) was started, which was replaced in 2012 by the Outright Monetary Transactions (OMT). The two programs have reduced uncertainty and ensured that yields on government bonds declined. Private creditors know that they expect to have their debt paid under all circumstances.

The over-indebted countries are rescued by the European Community. The various rescue measures and funds provide the applicants with urgently needed capital, giving them time to consolidate their budgets. However, these financial constructs are characterized by strong incentives for adverse selection and moral hazard (Bratis et al. 2013). The Troika has access to information, which reduces the information asymmetry between creditors and debtors. However, especially the current Greek government prevents the Troika from doing their work. As a result, information asymmetries cannot be reduced and the conflict between creditors and the debtor intensifies.

The Troika counteracts the willingness-to-pay problem by setting conditions for reform. The bailout countries must undertake reforms. The requirements of EU, ECB and IMF ensure that no country requests financial aid from the European funds for opportunistic reasons. In the case of Spain, which applied exclusively for banking sector funds, the EU support reduced the uncertainty and a possible contagion in the banking sector. The government in Madrid therefore had to fulfill fewer conditions than the other states in crisis. At the same time, there is a conflict between states like Spain on the one hand, that cooperates with the EU, and Greece on the other hand, that is not willing to pay back its debt. The cooperating states acknowledge the advantage of reforms and therefore demand stronger sanctions against Greece. This is because governments fear that the domestic political opposition wants to behave similar as in Greece. Sanctions against Greece are a credible strategy since the cost of a haircut are most likely greater within the monetary union than outside. If the EU would support the reforming countries and would not tolerate an opportunistic default, this would strengthen the position of the reformers and would be an important signal to Greece to fulfill its obligations.

V. Conclusion

In this chapter, economic problems in sovereign debt restructuring were illustrated. Moreover, it was explained how the EU tried to resolved this issue. The difficulties are characterized by asymmetric information, uncertainty during a restructuring, willingness-to-pay problems, a run-for-the-exit behavior of investors and holdout strategies. The EU provides financial aid to stumbling countries and forces these countries to undertake reforms. The financial aid leads to moral hazard, which is reduced by the supervision of the Troika. Furthermore, the Troika provides information about the financial situation of the debtor countries. The EU should punish uncooperative behavior in order to reduce conflicts among the European member states.

Bibliography

Andritzky, J.: Government Bonds and Their Investors: What Are the Facts and Do They Matter? IMF Working Paper WP/12/158, 2012.

Batra, A.: Sovereign Debt Restructuring. Indian Council for Research on International Economic Relations, 2002.

Borensztein, E./ Panizza, U.: The Costs of Sovereign Default. IMF Staff Papers, 2009 56, pp. 683-741.

Bratis, T./ Laopodis, N./ Kouretas, G.: Creditor Moral Hazard during EMU Debt Crisis. Working Paper, 2013, available at SSRN: <http://ssrn.com/abstract=2604909>.

Brunnermeier, M./ Pedersen, L.: Market Liquidity and Funding Liquidity. Review of Financial Studies, 2009 22, pp. 2201-2238.

Bundesministerium der Finanzen: Europäische Finanzhilfen im Überblick. 28.2.2015.

Cornelli, F./ Felli, L.: The Theory of Bankruptcy and Mechanism Design. In: Eichengreen, B./ Portes, R. eds. Crisis? What Crisis? Orderly Workouts for Sovereign Debtors. London: Centre for Economic Policy Research, 1995, pp. 69-86.

Daniels, K./ Ramirez, G.: Debt Restructuring, Holdouts and Exit Consents. Journal of Financial Stability, 2007 3, pp. 1-17.

De Paoli, B./ Hoggarth, G./ Saporta, V.: Cost of Sovereign Default. Financial Stability Paper No. 1, Bank of England, 2006.

Eaton, J./ Gersovitz, M.: Debt with Potential Repudiation: Theoretical and Empirical Analysis. Review of Economic Studies, 1981 48, pp. 289-309.

Eichengreen, B.: Restructuring Sovereign Debt. Journal of Economic Perspectives, 2003 17, pp. 75-98.

Eichengreen, B./ Mody, A.: Do Collective Action Clauses Raise Borrowing Costs? Economic Journal, 2004 114, pp. 247-264.

Eichengreen, B./ Portes, R.: Crises? What Crisis? Orderly Workouts for Sovereign Debtors. London: Centre for Economic Policy Research, 1995, pp. 1-68.

Engelen, C./ Lambsdorff, J.: Hares and Stags in Argentinean Restructuring. Journal of International Economics, 2009 78, pp. 141-148.

Ghezzi, P./ Garcia, P. A./ Fransolet, L.: Greece: The (Long) Countdown to Restructuring. Barclays Capital Economic Research, 11.5.2011.

Haldane, A./ Penalver, A./ Saporta, V./ Shin, H.: Analytics of Sovereign Debt Restructuring. Journal of International Economics, 2005 25, pp. 315-333.

Helleiner, E.: The Mystery of the Missing Sovereign Debt Restructuring Mechanism. Contributions to Political Economy, 2008 27, pp. 91-113.

Kaminsky, G./ Reinhart, C.: The Twin Crises: The Causes of Banking and Balance-Of-Payments Problem. American Economic Review, 1999 89, pp. 473-500.

Miller, M./ Thomas, D.: Sovereign Debt Restrukturing: The Judge, the Vultures and the Future of Creditor Rights. World Economy, 2007 30, pp. 1491-1509.

Panizza, U./ Sturzenegger, F./ Zettelmeyer, J.: The Economics and Law of Sovereign Debt and Default. Journal of Economic Literature, 2009 47, pp. 651-698.

Pedersen, L.: When Everyone Runs for the Exit. International Journal of Central Banking, 2009 5, pp. 177-199.

Pitchford, R./ Wright, M.: Holdouts in Sovereign Debt Restructuring: A Theory of Negotiation in a Weak Contractual Environment. Review of Economic Studies, 2011 79, pp. 812-837.

Rose, A.: One Reason Countries Pay Their Debts: Renegotiation and International Trade. Journal of Development Economics, 2005 77, pp. 189-206.

Roubini, N.: Do We Need a New Bankruptcy Regime. Brookings Papers on Economic Activity, 2002 1, pp. 321-333.

Sachs, J./ Cohen, D.: LDC Borrowing with Default Risk. NBER Working Paper No. 925, 1982.

Siebert, A.: The EFSM and the EFSF: Now and What Follows. European Parliament – Policy Department: Economic and Scientific Policies, 2010.

Sturzenegger, F./ Zettelmeyer, J.: Haircuts: Estimating Investor Losses in Sovereign Debt Restructurings, 1998-2005. Journal of International Money and Finance, 2008 27, pp. 780-805.

Tamura, K.: The Problem of Sovereign Debt Restructuring: How Can We Deal with Holdout Problem Legally? Harvard Law School, 2002.

Tomz, M./ Wright, M.: Do Countries Default in "Bad Times"? Journal of the European Economic Association, 2007 5, pp. 352-360.

Yeyati, E./ Panizza, U.: The Elusive Costs of Sovereign Defaults. Journal of Development Economics, 2011 94, pp. 95-105.

Fourth chapter
Two Level Reform Game Problems of Greece

Martha Kontodaimon and Bernhard Neumärker (University of Freiburg)

I. Introduction

Contracts, may they be bilateral or multilateral, are formed with contemporary facts in mind. The contracting parties, aiming at an agreement and wanting to cover their needs, define rules that define the essence of the relationship that is to be formed. Aiming for maximum utility they cover as many aspects of affiliation and any respective cooperation. Still, no matter how well thought or mapped, a contract may become nuanced over time or by an unexpected event. This contingency may lead towards inefficiency of its rules and the need of its reform. The social contract of a nation – otherwise known as its constitution –, is incomplete by nature, and will be the first institution to face the need of a reform if the existing variables change. Within the framework of constitutional economics, which identifies the social contract rules that have been built under unanimous agreement, the tools and guidelines for this initial contract reform are provided by the institution itself. Still, even if the knowledge exists, and the elasticity or inelasticity of a law is predefined, reforms that may be seen, by the impartial observer, as an improvement on the society's welfare are not immediately realized.

The focus of this chapter is to map the timing of an already delayed national reform, recognized as publicly beneficial, and how it can be affected by external influence under negotiation. As an external influence we identify the provision of aid coming in the country from the international sector, who by assumption here aims to support the national reform. The actors of this conflict game are heterogeneous social, national and international groups of power, influenced by their respective utilities and the negotiations occurring, simultaneously, by the two sides.

On a theoretical basis this work combines the "war of attrition" model, presented by Alesina and Drazen (1991), with the "two level game problems" theory, presented by Putnam (1988). The Alesina and Drazen model is used as the explanatory base of delayed stabilization occurring from the side of the nation. Putnam's theory is used to show the connecting links between domestic and international sectors, how national problems can become international ones, and how international intervention can influence a national reform procedure.

The literature on the political economy of reform has studied deeply the subject of delayed stabilization. Alesina and Drazen (1991) and Drazen and Grilli (1993) approached the concept of delayed reforms as a distributional conflict. Fernandez and Rodrik (1991) and Rodrik (1993) explained the stabilization delay on the basis of information uncertainty, and Drazen (1998) combined these works into a single framework coming to the conclusion that "inherited conflict of interests in allocating the net benefit or cost of reform is a crucial factor in the failure of countries to enact reform" (Drazen 1998). International help is considered as an effective reform-delaying factor, especially by Casella and Eichengreen (1994), Orphanides (1996) and Hsieh (2000) who, respectively, make the point that international help can be a factor that increases the time period of resistance to reform. In the aforementioned theories, the provision of international help comes exogenously pre-defined – by the international sector – in time and proportion. This chapter has a different view. Here, through negotiation, the international players become active in the stabilization game played by the national sector which has the possibility to bargain on the levels of the provision provided.

The motivation of this chapter is derived from the recent Greek economic crisis. A European mass wave of negative reactions rose when on April 23rd, 2010, the Greek Prime Minister G. Papandreou asked for international help in national economics, in order to avoid the country's bankruptcy. Apart from the huge amounts of money that had to be contributed in order for the country to stabilize, Greece had been already one of the main receivers of economic support from the European institutions in order to upgrade its national institutions and economy to the European standards. Therefore, it was hard to grasp the level and need of the international support in order for the country's economy to be stabilized. This study provides, as an applied example of its theory, an analysis of the game played by the Greek social groups, the Greek government and the international community during the time of Greece's economic convergence towards EU and the recent crisis. Specifically, it focuses on State Owned Enterprises (S.O.E.s) and their long unsustainable path, maintained through public funding and the European support programs. The model highlights the hidden reasons for failures in the past and shows why the negotiations and the timing of the help offered by the international side influenced, negatively, successful stabilization.

II. The Theoretical Background

This chapter constitutes the first attempt to unite the model of the "war of attrition" with the "two level game theory", by modeling one of Putnam's elements, the soon to be presented win sets, and to deliver an aspect of the game where the international sector is active through negotiation, managing to directly influence the national stabilization game. Within our framework the international conflict game is played simultaneously with the national dynamic "chicken" game influencing the reform, the so called "war of attrition". In the vast majority of related models, the international provision of support for a successful reform to happen is discussed as an exogenous factor. Drazen and Grilli (1993) and Orphanides (1996) identify the fact that international aid influences, mostly negatively, the timing of the reform. Hsieh (2000) clearly states that the international aid increases the delay of reaching an agreement and reforming, and Casella and Eichengreen (1994) distinguish even three possible reactions of the social groups on the timing of stabilization depending on the timing of the aid provision before the reform is initiated. In the aforementioned theories, the provision of international aid comes exogenously defined – by the international sector – in time and proportion.

We combine the "war of attrition" with the "two level game theory" in order to explain how the international support provided to Greece in accordance to its integration in the European Economic Union helped to delay stabilization actions within the country. On the one hand, the Alesina and Drazen (1991) model of the "war of attrition" is utilized to explain the national conflict of sustaining the sub-optimal regulations of the S.O.E.s. On the other hand, Putnam's (1988) theory on the "two level game problems" is employed to explain the reasons and ways the international sector managed to become part of this domestic conflict and how its participation influenced the turn of the game. The importance of the S.O.E.s for the Greek society and governments does not lie only in the fact that they provided the citizens' common wealth benefits (Law of 2005). Their size and number is such that they can still influence the direct macroscopic elements of the Greek economy. The fact that these companies have been supported in an unstable path during the whole convergence period of Greece to the Maastricht criteria and real actions took place only when the austerity measures were voted in, was what motivated us to connect the latter mentioned theories.

Delayed reforms: The Alesina/Drazen model of the "war of attrition".

The theory and model developed by Alesina and Drazen (1991) deviates from the usual literature since the key actors of the economic game are socioeconomic groups and not the usual policymaker. The groups are heterogeneous, with different levels of lobbying power, different welfare losses when remaining in a non-stabilized economy and conflicting distributional objectives.

The background condition for a "war of attrition" to emerge is an unexpected economic shock that hits a national economy. The governmental income collected through taxation is reduced because of the shock and this forces the government to use inefficient methods of public finance, i.e., debt and distortionary taxation, in an attempt to cover the developing deficit. The groups recognize the necessity to reform after the shock but still do not do it on time.

In the original model, this reform is a levy in taxation that will eliminate the deficit produced and stabilize the debt. The nature of the reform is that of a public good and bears costs, economic, political or both, for the stabilizer, i.e., the group that stabilizes. The other group(s) that operate within the society and are not the initiator(s) of reform (but still pay a small share of the reform costs) are non-stabilizer(s). When deciding to reform all groups face a trade-off. On the one side lay their losses, in capital or power, if stabilizing, and on the other side their gains of remaining in a non-stabilized economy. Then, under information uncertainty about the other groups' power, they calculate their costs if they are the stabilizers or not. Using their groups' time paths of consumption, they derive a concession time when they will have to reform and raise the share (α) of taxes if no other group has committed already. This share (α) is an exogenously given parameter that depicts the degree of polarization in the society. In a highly polarized country the more unequal the distribution of the burden, the longer the concession time of the groups will be. A group will stabilize when the costs of delaying the reform even further exceed the benefits of not stabilizing. The stabilizer is considered to be the loser of the game, since he is the one who will carry a disproportionate share of the tax increase necessary to stabilize. The non-stabilizer, or winner, will assume a smaller burden.

In the "war of attrition" model the debt before stabilization increases linearly and stops increasing thereafter, whilst the taxes after the stabilization are non-distortionary. The groups have their own lifetime utility functions which are calculated according to their given conditions and expectations in the future. In order to obtain an endogenous timing of the reform, Alesina and Drazen (1991) derive the optimal utility paths of each group and their independently decided concession time optimizing the following trade-off function between the group's gains and losses:

$$\left[\frac{f(\theta)}{F(\theta)}\frac{1}{T'(\theta)}\right]\frac{2\alpha - 1}{r} = \gamma\left(\theta + \frac{1}{2} - \alpha\right)$$

Here, θ shows the losses of remaining in a non-stabilized economy, α the share of the stabilization burden the stabilizer will have to assume, r the constant international interest rate and γ the fraction of the deficit of the economy covered by distortionary taxation. When the above function equalizes, the optimal time of stabilization, $T'(\theta)$, is decided for each group according to its group specific losses, ω_i. The game is finite when it is assumed that at least one group exists in the society for which the costs of reforming are, at some point, less than the costs of remaining in a non-stabilized economy. If there exists no group with such features then the groups will continue to play infinitely or until the point at which an exogenous actor such as the government will intervene and stabilize.

Entangled domestic and international policies: Putnam's two level game model

Putnam (1988) developed the "two level game" theory in order to explain when and how the international sector will find an "opening to intervene in the domestic politics and influence regulations and rules formation, [and] when from the other side the national sector will find a stepping stone which can help them develop policies that were beforehand beyond its possibilities" (Putnam 1988) depicting in that respect how "the domestic politics of several countries became entangled via an international negotiation" (Putnam 1988). Using the Bonn summit conference of 1978 as his starting point, he researched similar cases and found general patterns that develop similarly in most of the cases.

In Putnam's framework there are three main categories of actors present. On the national level there are domestic groups, such as political parties or lobbying groups, and each of them pursues own interests and policies. On the international level there are national governments, seeking to maximize own gains by international co-operation and to satisfy domestic pressures. The third actor is the "chief negotiator", an individual player, who operates in both tableaus, and whose aim is to help the two levels reach a mutually attractive agreement. The former actors operate in two levels. In Level I, the bargaining stage, the international negotiations occur between the national and international actors. In Level II, the ratification stage, the domestic groups decide on whether to ratify the international treaty emerging through the negotiations or not.

Putnam's underlying assumptions are the following: A nation exists where the necessity of policy actions arises, and they turn to the international arena to seek support. The links that connect the different actors with each other increase the higher their economic interdependence is. Through negotiation the different parties try to reach a feasible agreement on a policy by forming a mutual "win set". A "win set" according to Putnam is the set of "all possible Level I agreements that would 'win' the necessary majority among the Level II constituents when simply voted up or down" (Putnam 1988). During this period each side makes different attempts to alter coalitions, perceptions of costs or gains of an agreement. The treaty that is to emerge after this game of negotiation will be applied only after ratification at the national level. The chief negotiator, rising from each side, national and international, is the connecting link that controls the flow and the distribution of information among the negotiating parties and can support the sides in order to reach an agreement or not. Once the sides have formed a plausible "win set", the game moves from Level I to Level II, in other words from the bargaining phase to the ratification phase. Here each side has to ratify the agreement on the national level, if it is a country, and a binding contract, if it is an institution.

This chapter utilizes four key ideas from Putnam's theory in order to explain the game played for the initiation or hindering of a feasible reform. The bargaining phase, the ratification phase, the chief negotiator, here as a mere "honest" information broker without a personal utility aiming for an optimal solution, and the "win sets", as "any set of potential international agreements that could be simply voted up or down" (Putnam 1988) when the time for ratification comes. It is very important to note that the size of the win sets may differ and can define the course of negotiations and plausible agreements. A big win set offers more possibilities to come to an agreement but reduces the negotiation power of the party who holds it. Respectively, a small win set provides high negotiation power but less agreement possibilities. Additionally, strategic reasons may lead the parties act to understate the size of their win sets in order to pursue a better deal, or even more present them as "kinky" win sets. A "kinky" win set, according to Putnam (1988), is one that can be presented as a feasible one, but that with a slight difference towards its opponent's interest would not be likely to be ratified. In Level I the size of the win set may vary according to the strategies taken and information shared by the chief negotiator. In Level II the size of the win set may vary according to the social groups' preferences and coalitions or according to domestic institutions' coercive power. Reverberation can be positive, expanding the domestic win sets and aiding agreement on the international level, or negative, shrinking the win sets and hindering agreement.

III. Reform Delay in the Two Level Game

The presented models are combined in order to illustrate how international aid affects national stabilization and public debt reduction. The war of attrition in this setting occurs simultaneously with the Level I negotiations. The national and international negotiators in Level I act in accordance with their win sets which are clearly defined by their utility paths, and they reach out to find the point at which they intersect. When the common point of the stabilization time is found, international aid is provided. The chief negotiator is assumed to be an information broker for reasons of simplification. Thus, no explicit utility function is modeled for him and there are no transaction costs.[1] The national and international sides eventually reach an agreement that needs to be ratified in Level II. If this agreement is ratified, the game ends, but if not, it starts again, until an end solution to the game is found.

The nation's state of nature and initial assumption of the following model is the need of a change in the existing status quo. The necessity of reform is recognized and accepted by the national social groups, the

---

1 In the case of the Greek crisis, the European Commission could be in the position of the chief negotiator.

domestic government as well as the international sector entities that the nation at hand cooperates with.

The actors of the two level reform game problems are the following. On the national side are the domestic social groups and the government. The national social groups can be civic society organizations, lobbying groups, political parties or any other kind of group that could coordinate aggregate behavior. These actors can be plenty. For simplification this chapter complies to Alesina and Drazen's (1991) assumption of only two groups or two political parties operating in the domestic level. The second actor rising from the national side is the chief negotiator. This chapter assumes him to be acting as a mere broker of information between the two sides. On the international side, we find entities connected with the nation through multilateral or bilateral agreements. These could be other nations, international institutions whose welfare and gains are connected and influenced by the nations' respective domestic problems, or even unions of nations with which the nation at hand has some connection.

The type of the reform may vary. It could be economical, e.g., a change in the tax or redistribution system, or political, e.g., a change in the voting system or decision making mechanisms, or both, as it was the case in the working regulations in the S.O.E.s. However, the nature of the reform is the same for any case: It is a public good. This means that once the change is made, it bears both the characteristics of jointness of supply and non-excludability by its provision (e.g. Mueller 2003).

According to their utility levels, the groups calculate an optimal time of stabilization. In their setting the groups derive the optimal stabilization under a trade-off between the gains of remaining in a non-stabilized economy and the gains of waiting one more moment to concede. Until here the framework follows the simple model of the "war of attrition" at the national level. This game would veritably end with one of the groups conceding and bearing a disproportionate share of the reform.

The twist of this chapter is that a further step is introduced before concession. This is active international participation in order for a solution to be found. Now the international actors become active within the national problem solving arena and can negotiate with the national actors their share of the reform burden. This point is important, because the failure of one country to implement the necessary changes could create disproportionate welfare problems to the other countries connected with it and we need to model the ways nations would try to hinder this from happening. Putnam classifies the economic interdependence between countries under the term of "synergistic linkages". This describes the cases where the "economic interdependence derived through the current globalised world can multiply the opportunities for altering domestic coalitions by expanding the set of feasible alternatives in this way – in effect, creating political entanglements across national boundaries" (Putnam 1988). Synergistic linkages allow the international side actors to intervene in an arena which before was beyond their reach. Evidently, the increasing economic relations among countries raise their economic interdependence. From an international perspective, they stand to gain by taking on part of the economic burden rather than leaving the country in its economic stalemate. From the national perspective, this means that "policy possibilities rise that beforehand were beyond domestic control and that the national groups will not have to change their preferences when deciding on a reform since they are offered a greater span of policy possibilities" (Putnam 1988). When the international sector enters the game described above, a change in dynamics occurs. The two levels are introduced in accordance with Putnam's ideas.

The starting point $t_1 = 0$ of this game is the moment the national actors enter the bargaining phase, or Level I. At this moment the state of the country is a "nation in need of a reform", with heterogeneous social groups suffering different losses from not reforming and a fixed level of polarization α which will affect the distribution of the national burden. The international actors enter the game interested in carrying, under negotiation, a share of the burden of the national reform in order for this reform to happen. Their motivation stems from their economic interdependence with the respective nation. At point t_1 each group, indexed by the letter i, has already calculated its own losses and gains from not reforming and has optimized in a point in time to reform $T_i = T(\omega_i)$ (Alesina and Drazen 1991). The chief negotiator distributes the information provided to him by the two national and the international sides and has no personal utility function. The win set of the national side is (T_i, ω_i, α) and it includes the optimal time of the stabilization according to each group (T_i), its respective costs of not stabilizing (ω_i), and the fixed share of the stabilization burden the stabilizer will have to assume which is common knowledge (α). As mentioned before, the costs of not reforming and the gains of remaining in a non-stabilized economy form a trade-off.

On the other hand, the win set of the international sector (T_{intern}, ζ) includes the optimal stabilization time according to their optimal utility path (T_{intern}) and the share of the national burden they will agree to carry at that point in time, shown by ζ. This share can effectively be defined as the optimal amount of burden the international society will bear upon the possibility of the reform taking place. The international sector decides on the level of ζ under a trade-off. This trade-off constitutes the gains of providing a public good in their respective countries as opposed to the gains from promoting a reform in another country. This means that the gains coming from ζ being distributed on supporting the other country have to be higher than their gains of providing this ζ to their own public good. This chapter assumes that ζ has been calculated by the international sector within its respective utility function and holds under the optimality condition mentioned above. The goal of the chief negotiator in this phase is to find the group with ω_i that would agree to stabilize at time $T_i = T_{intern}$ while the international sector will assume a share of the burden equal to ζ.

When a plausible international agreement is reached the game enters the ratification phase or Level II. In this phase, the treaty that has been agreed upon at the international level is voted in or out. If the agreement is ratified, its clauses come into effect at the national level with the national institutions monitoring its implementation. If, on the other side, the treaty is voted out, the agreement is broken and negotiations start from the beginning. The international game can be repeated as long as it is necessary to come to an acceptable agreement. This chapter focuses on the point in time that an agreement will be ratified and applied by the national sector. Under the games observed here the aid offered by the international sector may either postpone further or force it to happen faster. This chapter identifies the two main ways how this will happen.

IV. International Aid before Stabilization Policies

In this approach the burden share ζ by the international sector is distributed in the nation in need of a reform before the reform has happened in order to accelerate it. Therefore, international support is calculated as a share of the total burden falling to the non-stabilized economy. This means that aid received from the international side will be deducted equally from the total burden of the economy, affecting the utilities of all the groups operating under the non-stabilized economy.

The utility function of operating under a non-stabilized economy and sharing an equal part of the burden is adopted from the Alesina and Drazen model:

$$u^D(t) = -\gamma r(\tfrac{1}{2} + \omega_i)\overline{b}e^{(1-\gamma)rt}$$

The notation follows their own. Here, u^D is the utility any national group will have under a non-stabilized economy, γ is the fraction of the deficit of the economy covered by distortionary taxation, r is the international constant interest rate and $\overline{b}$ the share of the deficit covered by debt. Furthermore, ω_i are the group specific costs and $\tfrac{1}{2}$ is the assumption that if only two groups exist in the economy. They will have to equally pay the burden of the reform not happening in equal shares.

Introducing ζ to the former utility function yields

$$u^D_{new}(t) = -\gamma r(\tfrac{1}{2} + \omega_i - \zeta)\overline{b}e^{(1-\gamma)rt}.$$

ζ enters negatively the utility function because it is subtracted from the losses the groups have to suffer when operating under the non-stabilized economy. Its subtraction leads to a positive effect in the utility function before stabilization. The levels of utility under the non-stabilized economy rise. The international sector delivers ζ with the expectation that the reform will be realized at a point equal to T_{intern}. The problem with the implementation of the reform is that it will have to occur through the national instruments which the international sector cannot officially control or influence. On the other side, with their utilities increasing, the groups will recalculate their expected utilities and the optimal time of concession according to the level of ζ. This means that their span of life in the "war of attrition" will expand.

The expected utility function $EU(T_i)$ in this model is drawn from Alesina and Drazen (1991) where $1 - H(T_i)$ is the probability that a group will be the stabilizer, $h(x)$ the probability that it will be the non-stabilizer, u^D the utility of the group living under an un-stabilized economy, $V^L(T) = -\alpha\overline{b}e^{(1-\gamma)rT}$ the utility of the loser, $V^W(T) = -(1-\alpha)\overline{b}e^{(1-\gamma)rT}$ the utility of the winner and T_i the optimal time of stabilization of the group i. Again, α is the share of the burden the stabilizer will assume, $1-\alpha$ the share of the non-stabilizer, $\overline{b}$ the share of the economic deficit covered by issuing debt and $e^{(1-\gamma)rT}$ the discounted constant interest rate to the stabilization date, so that expected utility is

$$EU(T_i) = [1 - H(T_i)] \left[\int_0^{T_i} u^D(x)e^{-rx}dx + V^L(T_i)e^{-rT_i} \right]$$

$$+ \int_{x=o}^{x=T_i} \left[\int_0^x u^D(z)e^{-rz}dz + V^W(x)e^{-rx} \right] h(x)dx$$

Substituting in this function the condition $T_i = T(\omega_i)$ means that each group will choose its optimal concession time according to its individual losses. Deriving with respect to ω, equalizing to zero and solving for the optimal $T'(\omega)$ we receive

$$T'(\omega_{new}) = \frac{f(\omega)}{F(\omega)} \frac{2\alpha - 1}{\gamma r(\omega_{old} - \zeta + \frac{1}{2} - \alpha)}$$

where $\omega_{old} > \omega_{new} = \omega_{old} - \zeta$ and $T_{i\,new} = T(\omega_{i\,new})$
such that $T_{i\,new} > T_{i\,old}$. This means that the optimal time of stabilization will be postponed in time for each group with the $T_{i\,new}$ being their adjusted optimal concession time. Thus the social groups will not stabilize so fast because it becomes cheaper for them to remain in a non-stabilized economy. This seems to be a dynamic version of the well-known moral hazard effect of aid.

V. When International Aid is Provided upon Stabilization

Here, the support coming from the international actors is to be provided directly to the stabilizer. The actors come into negotiations in order to decide the share of the stabilizer's burden that will be carried by the international side. The government plays the role of the chief negotiator reaching out for the common optimal share of the burden/time of stabilization win sets proposed. In this case, the share of the burden to be covered by the international sector is to be deducted after the initiation of the reform. Therefore, this share's size varies between the fixed level of the burden the stabilizer will have to assume and zero, i.e., $\alpha \geq \zeta > 0$. In order for the reform to happen relatively fast, the share that the international sector will carry will need to be relatively large, compared to that of the stabilizer. During the negotiations, the groups now calculate their optimal time of stabilization incorporating the share proposed by the international sector in their expected utilities. The utility function of the stabilizer described above is applied again. Thus, in the national "chicken" game an international coordination game is introduced. If the national groups manage to negotiate effectively, they can happen to be the stabilizer and still pay a smaller amount of the burden than the non-stabilizer.

Under this premise, the share subtracted by the international sector will be deducted from the expected utility of the stabilizer, $V^L(T) = -(\alpha - \zeta)\bar{b}e^{(1-\gamma)rT}$. Consequently, deriving again their optimal utility paths incorporating the international support in their probability of being the stabilizer themselves they recalculate their optimal timing of stabilization under their costs of remaining in a non-stabilized economy. This would yield

$$T'_{new}(\omega_{old}) = \frac{f(\omega)}{F(\omega)} \frac{2\alpha - 1 - \zeta}{\gamma r(\omega + \zeta + \frac{1}{2} - \alpha)}$$

where $T_{i\,new} > T(\omega_{i\,old})$. This means that with the same costs and a given help, once they are the stabilizers, their costs of waiting one more time to concede, $\gamma(r\omega + \zeta + 1/2 - \alpha)$, increase and their gains of waiting one more time to concede, $2\alpha - 1 - \zeta$, decrease. This makes $T_{i\,new} < T_{i\,old}$ and the timing of the reform closer.

In this case, the groups aim at finding the best agreement under which complying would mean that they are having gains from this agreement, or not losses of the same size. Thus, the group stabilizing will try to negotiate a position where most of the share it will have to carry would be the share that the international sector will carry in the end. In order for a reform to happen under these conditions, ratification of the treaty has to occur. After the agreement is ratified, the international side will assume the set share of the burden while the other social groups operating in the nation will have to bear a smaller share of the burden equal to $1 - \alpha$, similar to the "winner" in the Alesina and Drazen model.

VI. Stabilizing the Greek S.O.E.s

Following the logic of the two different approaches two main consequences may be derived. First, the international aid provided to a nation creates the tendency for the groups to postpone even more stabilization. Second, the international sector could implement an efficient change at the domestic level only under effective negotiations and directed contracting.

The S.O.E.s were part of Greek economy's negative growth (Petrakis 2011) for the last quarter of the 20th century. Their power in the Greek economy is vast and that is because their investments' influence the growth rate of the economy, as well as the inflation, through their pricing policies; the government deficit through their operating results; the policy implications on the government debt through their funding; and, finally, the terms and conditions of the respective industry where they operate through their business strategies (Law of 2005). These companies operated for almost thirty years producing debt, under the national funding and international support, before effective policy changes and reforms were made in their operating regulations. The change of the S.O.E.s working regulations and establishment of accountability rules would influence their efficiency and productivity levels. The nature of the companies, their size and number of employees, as well as the fact that they utilized state funding to operate whilst being in debt would make any reform applied on them to have a public good effect. It also would not only affect the deficit levels of the Greek economy but the power of the political party that would try to enforce it and the distribution of the capital injected into the Greek economy through the Community Support Framework. Utilizing the former presented framework we will identify how their regulatory reform game was played and ended.

On the national side we find the political parties of Greece, as the main actors, and as the chief negotiator each government's respective Prime Minister. The reason for choosing the political parties as the main actors is the fact that in Greece the parties are the main source of influence and decision making within the different operating sectors of the nation, as well as the hard core of any societal organization (Petrakis 2011). On the other side, the international sector includes all actors that are united through agreements or coalition formations with Greece such as the European Union and its constituting countries, and their international interests are influenced by the Greek domestic problems.

From the explanatory statement of the law 3429/2005 it emerges that the former governments and the Greek parties supported the fact that the S.O.E.s operating regulations needed to be changed in order for them to function efficiently and not produce further deficits in the Greek economy. Any political party could promote the change of the S.O.E.s regulations. However, the political costs of reforming were considered higher than the economic ones when remaining in the non-stabilized economy. The government of 1993, which wanted to sell the then state owned telecommunications company, was thrown out of power and the party that had proposed this operational reform was stigmatized under the label of "extreme market liberalization".

A clear and recent example of how the game is played can be found in the S.O.E.s' activities in the last years before the crisis. In 2003, the borrowing of the S.O.E.s from the Greek state was raised to the level of 2.3 billion Euros, when at the same time their revenue fell by 43% (Voultepsi 2013). From 2003 to 2004, their deficits rose by about 20%, with the outstanding loans reaching 30% and in 2005, only for the debts of the 13 ailing S.O.E.s, the state paid about 4.5 billion, which is half the costs of the Olympics (Voultepsi 2013).

The reports of the European Court of Auditors in 2002-2003 testified as well great mismanagements in the S.O.E.s. More specifically they recorded: Overtime that exceeded weekdays. Payments of graduate benefits to employees before even taking the title and payment of bonus to employees for performance while on holiday. Hiring contractors to fill positions of employees who were on leave and then keeping them in position when the latter returned. The debt created in the economy by the support to S.O.E.s became unsustainable over time.

The social groups did not promote reforms earlier because of the economic support flowing into the Greek economy from the international side. If the international sector was out of the game, the reforms necessary would have happened at time $t_x = T'(\omega_i)$, where ω_i would have been the losses of a group that could not remain in the non-stabilized economy and support the capital flow anymore. If no group would undertake the reform the government would have to intervene and distribute the shares of the burden. The funding coming to the public budget through the international support sustained the operation of these companies until recently. The economic support from the European Union equal to ζ helped the groups update their utility levels and optimal stabilization time. The new optimal time of stabilization was more distant in time than the one the groups would have had if the international sector was out of the game. This provided the different groups in the Greek society with the opportunity to pass on the "hot potato" of reforming the S.O.E.s operating regulations for almost 30 years.

The "new governance" model with "permanent control administrations" was applied in supervised S.O.E.s (Voultepsi 2013) and stable budget schedules were made, when the international support was directly provided to the stabilizer. In the Greek case, Prime Minister Papandreou was the first chief negotiator and the political group implementing the reform PASOK. On the international side the main actor was the Troika of lenders constituted by the European Central Bank, International Monetary

Fund and European Commission. Under the direct negotiations with the groups that were to vote on implementing the reforms, Troika imposed on Greece the integration of the S.O.E.s finances to the general government data (Galiatsatou 2010). In 2010 the Troika set, for the first time of the operation of the S.O.E.s, a plan on downsizing them. This was a move that carried a huge economic and political cost. This cost the domestic parties were able to renounce by pointing out that is was "the Troika that was pushing them to do these changes" and they did not chose to. The Troika support was provided under directed contracting and the regulations on efficiency controls, permanency and non-accountability of the S.O.E.'s employees were finally reformed.

VII. Policy Implications and Conclusions

The investigation of the model results corroborates that the direct intervention of the international sector can lead to an immediate application of a reform through international help. Otherwise the money introduced to the economy will further delay stabilization. This rises from the fact that the incentives presented to the loser, instead to all of the interest groups, can promote the kind of the bilateral contract between the domestic social group and the international sector which will exhilarate the time of the reform. Problems of information uncertainty that may rise can be overridden by the liability ties created by this type of a contract.

Following this line of argumentation we suggest that a reform can be effectively applied with the support of international aid when this aid is directed to the social group that will promote it, and after its provision, and not to all the groups operating in the society. A statement as such could raise ethical dilemmas based on lobbying activities of the groups and their power to information holding. This result would not infringe any legal rules or personal freedom but may be frowned for its explicit favoritism towards the group that would be the stabilizer. Also unintended consequences may rise from the fact that the stabilizer may improve its social position relative to the other social groups. Following utilitarian argumentation the main counterargument would be that if the aggregate society's welfare rises by this reform which is considered to be a public good, directing the help to the stabilizer will indirectly support the whole society's welfare.

Altogether, we discussed the question of how the provision of international aid influences national reforms. In this respect, the timing of the international aid and the negotiation processes followed appear to have a great influence when deciding on the implementation of a reform. The main topic investigated was the ways that Greek reforms in the S.O.E.s were influenced in the last years by the European stabilization support. The timing of the international aid as well as the contracting between the players could both exhilarate and postpone stabilization plans. This research comes to the conclusion that international support may exhilarate the timing of reform only when it is provided under a contract with the stabilizer group and upon its application. Aid that is intentioned to enable stabilization and is provided before any stabilization actions to have taken place is proved mainly to provide the opposite results. The importance of the results stems from the fact that they can guide the international player to apply more effective help when its intentions are actually to efficiently help and enable stabilization.

The limitation of the chapter is that on the international level it focuses only on the implications produced by one country. It is not only the problems coming from Greece that influence the game. There are other domestic policies that have the same connectivity with the international game played. Also entities exist within the international side that will try to implement their own private or domestic policy on the international game in order to delay or to transfer the burden of the reforms to the other countries. Interesting expansions of this model would be the modeling of the self-interest of the chief negotiator, the modeling of the reformers' burden in the national level as negotiable among the social groups, the mathematical derivation of the international utility functions defining the levels of the share ζ and the international sectors utility path.

Bibliography

Alesina, A./ Drazen, A.: Why are Stabilizations Delayed? American Economic Review, 1991 81, pp. 1170-1188.

Casella, A./ Eichengreen, B.: Can Foreign Aid Accelerate Stabilisation? Economic Journal, 1994 106, pp. 605-619.

Dornbusch, R.: Credibility and Stabilization. Quarterly Journal of Economics, 1991 106, pp. 837-50.

Drazen, A.: The Political Economy of Delayed Reform. In: Sturzenegger, F./ Tommasi, M. eds. The Political Economy of Reform. Cambridge, Mass.: MIT Press, 1998, pp. 39-60.

Drazen, A./ Grilli, V.: The Benefit of Crises for Economic Reforms. American Economic Review, 1993 83, pp. 598-60.

Fernandez, R./ Rodrik, D.: Resistance to Reform: Status Quo Bias in the Presence of Individual-Specific Uncertainty. American Economic Review, 1991 81, pp. 1146-1155.

Galiatsatou, P.: Πληρώνουμε «αμαρτίες» 30 χρόνων στις ΔΕΚΟ. Ποιες κυβερνήσεις και πώς τις μετέτρεψαν σε κομματικό «φέουδο» και ελλειμματικές. Kathimerini, November 7, 2010. <http://news.kathimerini.gr/4dcgi/_w_articles_politics_1_07/11/2010_421553>.

Hsieh, C.: Bargaining Over Reform, European Economic Review, 2000 44, pp. 1659-1676.

Kamaras, I. D.: Το χρονικό διόγκωσης του δημόσιου χρέους, 1980-2005. Kathimerini, December 15, 2005. <http://news.kathimerini.gr/4dcgi/_w_articles_economy_1_15/12/2005_166904>.

Karanikas, H.: Το χρονικό ενός προαναγγελθέντος εκτροχιασμού: Τα άλματα του χρέους από το 1974 μέχρι σήμερα. Kathimerini, July 31, 2010. <http://www.tanea.gr/news/economy/article/ 4587246/? iid=2>.

Law of 2005: Printed in the Tribune of the Government FEK. Issue 1, Serial Number 314, December 27, 2005, pp. 5733-5740.

Mouzelis, N.: Γιατί αποτυγχάνουν οι μεταρρυθμίσεις. To Vima, Jun 29, 2003. <http://www.tovima.gr/ opinions/article/?aid=152249>.

Mueller, D. C.: Public Choice III. Cambridge: Cambridge University Press, 2003.

Orphanides, A.: The Timing of Stabilizations. Journal of Economic Dynamics and Control, 1996 20, pp. 257-279.

Petrakis, P.: The Greek Economy and the Crisis: Challenges and Responses. Berlin: Springer 2011.

Putnam, R.: Diplomacy and Domestic Politics: The Logic of Two-Level Games. International Organization, 1988 42, pp. 427-460.

Rodrik, D.: The Positive Economics of Policy Reform. American Economic Review, 1993 83, pp. 356-361.

Stergiou, D.: Τα οικονομικά εγκλήματα των κυβερνήσεων στο χώρο των ΔΕΚΟ. Antibaro, November 22, 2010. <http://www.antibaro.gr/article/2486>.

Velasco, A.: A Model of Endogenous Fiscal Deficits, and Delayed Fiscal Reforms. NBER Working No. 6336, Cambridge/Mass., 1997.

Voulgaris, J.: Η Ελλάδα απο την Μεταπολίτευση στην Π(α)γκοσμιοποίηση, Πόλις, Αθήνα 2008.

Voulgaris, J.: Η Μοιραία Πενταετία. Η Πολιτική της Αδράνειας. Πόλις, Αθήνα 2011.

Voultepsi, S.: ΔΕΚΟ: Οι πολιτικές ευθύνες. Eleftheri Zoni, Jun 25, 2013. <http://www.elzoni.gr/html/ent/210/ent.35210.asp>.

C. Political Science and Sociology

Fifth chapter
The Eurozone Crisis and Party Conflicts in Greece and Germany – Discursive Struggles about Responsibility

Moritz Sommer (Freie Universität Berlin), Jochen Roose (University of Wrocław), Franziska Scholl (Freie Universität Berlin) and Dimitris Papanikolopoulos (University of Crete)

I. Introduction

Rather than being a social pathology, conflict is intrinsically rooted in society (Dahrendorf 1967). Controversies about diverging interests and opinions are to be expected; the lack of such conflict is extremely unusual. These assumptions mark the starting point and the common denominator of conflict theories in the social sciences. Analysing the ways people deal with conflict and find procedures to handle opposing perspectives is at the core of understanding society.

One central arena for dealing with these conflicting interests is politics. In the Federalist Papers Madison famously claimed that while it is impossible to cure the causes of faction among people, "relief is only to be sought in the means of controlling its effects" in the political process (Hamilton et al. 2008: 51). Along these lines, the democratic system is the one institutional configuration to come to terms with the multiplicity of conflicting interests.

The core arena for political conflict in democracies is party conflict. Competing parties offer their propositions to modify legal structures, to distribute public money and to influence the general design of society. This continuous dispute provides alternatives and arguments to the voters. The questioning of these arguments implies a continuous validation process (Habermas 1988) which extends to interest groups, social movements and other actors in the political arena. Understood as this permanent debate, the party conflict is part and parcel of a dynamic democratic system (Dahl 1989; Sartori 1987).

While conflict is inherently grounded and omnipresent in party politics, the emergence of salient issues and controversial topics in society fuels this tension. The Eurozone crisis is such an issue. It not only holds the potential to intensify the party conflict, but even to change the party system altogether. In Germany, for instance, the *AfD* (Alternative für Deutschland) emerged as a single-issue party focused on the criticism of the bailout loans for the south of Europe. In Greece, the rise of *SYRIZA* at the political left and the successes of the radical right party *Golden Dawn* (*Chrysí Avgí*) cannot be explained without the Eurozone crisis, its management, austerity enforcement and the disastrous social consequences (Karyotis and Rüdig 2013). However, while in Germany the changes in the party system have not been fundamental and lasting, in Greece a formerly well-established party practically vanished (i.e. *PASOK*) while a formerly marginal party became a major player now forming the government (*SYRIZA*). We want to look at the public debate on the Eurozone crisis in both countries to find indications at which point these different paths have been taken.

A change in the national party system is by no means self-evident as the crisis is European in its very core. The monetary union and the fear of its collapse have brought Europe together. This strained European interconnectedness sets the scene for a new constellation of the political conflict, involving a national and a European dimension and therefore opening up discursive opportunities for crisis interpretations. Different processes and actors have contributed to the current situation. Consequently, in order to identify culprits or to seek assistance, stakeholders in the political process can point to a broad range of possible actors ranging from European Union institutions and the Troika, to the German government and Merkel *ad personam*, to current and former Greek governments, to corrupt Greek elites or to an unproductive national economy. The crisis issue holds the potential to extend the conflict arena to a transnational level. The use of this potential by the actors in the discourse is another step, though.

The core of our analysis is the evaluated attribution of responsibility. An attribution of responsibility is the (reconstructed) answer to the question "Who makes whom responsible for what?". Attributions of responsibility are particularly interesting because they link actors in the sense that someone is made responsible for an action or outcome by someone else. It is this attribution of responsibility which transforms the description of a situation into a conflictive statement. Attributions of responsibility form the core of a contentious debate.

The party conflict was traditionally fought in parliaments and other institutionalized settings of the political system but the mediatisation of politics has transformed the media and the wider public sphere into the central stage for party contention. This mediatized party competition is at the core of this chapter. Political discourses related to the Eurozone crisis have been subject to multiple analyses (e.g. Antoniades 2012; Mylonas 2012). It has been described, which arguments were used and which more general 'frames' have been applied to the crisis and its protagonist countries. From a conflict theoretical perspective, however, these studies are unsatisfactorily as they lose actors out of sight. In our analysis we choose a different approach which is focused on actors and actor relations.

Our analysis is focused on two countries: Greece and Germany. Greece is certainly the most prominent case among the crisis countries. The country has been hit most severely and the political programs to deal with the crisis, namely austerity and economic liberalization, provoked heated debates and popular resistance. Germany, on the other hand, grants the largest amount of guarantees and has most strongly pressured for strict austerity and reforms. It is the most prominent case on the other side of this European cleavage.

In this chapter we want to analyze the public debate under the lens of the conflict structure. Especially we are interested in whether we can find a conflict pattern which paved the way to a reconfiguration of the conflict structure, i.e. the party system. Therefore, we ask to which extent political parties are involved in the interpretation of responsibility in this debate. Secondly, we want to know how confrontational the debate in both countries is. Thirdly, we look at who has been made responsible and especially to which extent the addressees are found within the national party system (or political system) and to which extent responsibility attributions are directed beyond the domestic arena. We ask these questions to find hints for a more party centered, conflictive, nationally confined conflict in Greece than in Germany. We assume that this conflict pattern in Greece contributed to the structural change in the party system.

II. The Attribution of Responsibility – Conceptual Considerations

In politics, the questions of who is to blame, who is in charge of acting and who may claim to lift the burden are crucial and omnipresent. In the social movement literature these questions have been covered by the framing approach (Benford and Snow 2000; McAdam et al. 2001). Weaver (1986) and others discussed these questions with respect to administration design and accountability (c.f. Bovens 1998; Hood 2011). Especially in situations of crises, in which fundamental uncertainty and insecurity are pervasive, the demand for interpretation and sense making – and as a consequence the quest for responsibility – is pressing.

An attribution of responsibility is a statement of an actor (attribution sender) who ascribes responsibility for an issue (attribution issue) to another actor (attribution addressee). Figure 1 illustrates this relation. It is important to note that attribution sender and attribution addressee can be identical (self-attribution).

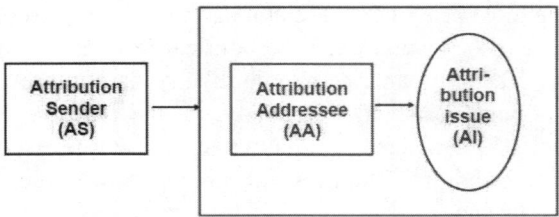

Figure 1: Attribution Trias (adapted from Gerhards et al. 2007: 111)

This attribution of responsibility for outcomes, issues, and even social change or for its absence is a social construction. Every situation and phenomenon has multiple necessary conditions and is, hence, the product of many different actors and actions. To mark one actor as responsible is therefore always a specific selection which – *in principle* – could be different. The same applies for improvements and successes. Which actor is responsible for initiating change and solving a problem is again a selection which can be made otherwise. Obviously, there are multiple conventions of who is regarded as responsible. Often the attribution of responsibility is taken for granted.

More interesting are those attributions which are contested, debated and taken to a wider audience. In these cases, it seems necessary to make explicit claims to indicate matters of responsibility distribution. Being part of a public debate, these attributions become discursive, explicitly linking issues or outcomes and evaluated actors. It is these discursive attributions our analysis focuses on.

Attributions can appear in different forms. Blame establishes a negatively evaluated causal link between the attribution addressee and the issue. The addressee is blamed for having caused the attribution issue and its consequences. In analogy, credit implies a positive evaluation of this link. Again, the addressee has caused the attribution issue but in this case the result is regarded as a success. These two forms are causal attributions as they regard the attribution addressee as the causal agent of the issue or outcome. Causal attributions can relate to past events (*diagnostic*) but they can also be a prediction of future consequences (*prognostic*).

Next to these causal attributions, responsibility attributions can take the form of request attributions, which call others to action or competence attributions, which ascribe factual competence to others. In this analysis, these two forms are taken together.

In societal crises such as the current Eurozone crisis, responsibility attributions are omnipresent in multiple forms and directions. Obviously, we can expect parties to contribute to this process of public sense making. However, other actors will be involved, too. Civil society actors and social movements are classic challengers who take part in this interpretation process but also economic interest groups, legal actors or academics can be expected to raise their voices. Hence, the question is not *whether* party actors are involved in this discursive struggle but *to what extent*. Our first question is to what extent party actors contribute to the crisis debate and the public attribution of responsibility compared to other actors in Greece and Germany. We expect that an intense conflict among a specific category of actors is associated with the likeliness of a reconfiguration of the involved actors altogether. In our case, more party involvement in the debate could be expected rather in Greece than in Germany due to the reconfiguration of the Greek party system we have found.

Discourses can be more or less conflictual in various ways. Attributions can be stated in neutral language or as personal assaults; they can be dramatic or distanced. Our instrument is intentionally insensitive to most of these stylistic dimensions of conflict intensity (see Section III). We do not intend to represent the debate's style or tone but its core (actor) structure. Still, the types of attribution as presented above differ with regard to their conflictual nature. The most conflictive form is the blame attribution as it involves a direct negative evaluation of the addressee. The least conflictive attribution is credit granting as it links the addressee to success. Intermediate types are request and competence attributions. At least in principle, the call for action and competence attributions imply the addressee's general ability to contribute to positive outcomes. At the same time, requests imply an implicit form of criticism since the addressee is obviously unable or unwilling to see the correct choice by herself/himself. Our second question is how conflictual the attribution pattern in both countries is. We expect a link between a more conflictual debate and developments leading to a reconfiguration in the party system.

Attributions of responsibility are highly consequential. The attribution of success or failure defines the quality of an actor and therefore is of central importance for party competition. The public perception of responsibility is expected to influence voting behaviour (Hobolt and Tilley 2014). Accordingly, party actors will be determined to attribute success to themselves and failure to others. While this holds generally for all actors[1], in the party competition parties have two options. They either could try to accuse the competitor of misdoings and underline the own competence. This would be a conflictive strategy which aims at delegitimizing the competitor and gaining support. Or party actors could try to calm down the conflict and address responsibility to actors beyond the national arena. The complexity of the Eurozone crisis opens up a multitude of possibilities for attributing responsibility. For our focus on party conflict, we are particularly interested in whether attributions are part of the domestic party conflict or whether attributions refer beyond national borders, addressing European institutions or institutions from other EU member states. The third question is to what extent party actors address the national arena and to what extent they address actors beyond national borders. We assume that a debate prior to a reconfiguration of the party system we will find less attributions beyond the domestic arena (Greece) than in a situation which did not change the party system (Germany). This would be the case even though the EU institutions and the Troika were highly influential for the developments in Greece and would therefore be an apparent addressee.

III. Method and Data: Discursive Actor Attribution Analysis

The Discursive Actor Attribution Analysis (DAAA) is a tool for the standardized measurement of the backbone of a controversial discourse: the attribution of responsibility. Its unit of analysis, an actor attribution, is the reconstructed answer to the question: Who makes whom responsible for what? The actor attribution consists of an attribution sender, an attribution issue and an attribution addressee, including an evaluation. In the following analysis, sender, addressee and attribution type are central.

---

1 For an analysis under non-crisis conditions, see Gerhards et al. (2013).

The actor attributions are reconstructed in newspaper reporting on the Eurozone crisis. Based on this material, we looked for actors who attribute responsibility to others, in direct or indirect quotes. Actors are not necessarily individuals; also collective actors such as institutions and organizations can be senders or addressees. Journalists are only regarded as senders when they get actively involved in the debate by explicitly evaluating others (category *Domestic Media* in Table 1). For each attribution of responsibility, we coded a case with information on the sender and addressee, the issue at stake, the attribution type and some further information.

The sample is taken from quality newspapers between September 2009 and September 2013. The data for this chapter stems from the German *Süddeutsche Zeitung* and *Frankfurter Allgemeine Zeitung* as well as the Greek *Kathimerini, Eleftherotypia* and *Ta Nea* (for 2012, the year that *Eleftherotypia* stopped operating). We sampled every seventh issue resulting in a rotating week design with changing week days. The selected days are covered by each newspaper in turn. For this chapter, we coded a total of 6631 attributions. The coders are instructed to include only those articles and attributions containing relevant information connected to the Eurozone crisis.[2]

IV. Party Involvement in Greek and German Crisis Debates

Not surprisingly, the Eurozone crisis evoked many different actors to participate in the responsibility debate. In both countries, the debate exceeds beyond the domestic party conflict and involves a broad range of actors.

In the German newspapers, German parties and party actors – including party spokespeople and individual parliamentarians with no further role in the government – are responsible for 10% of all crisis related attributions which is slightly more than the share of German government officials. If we take these two categories together only 18.7% of all attribution senders are directly or indirectly connected to the domestic party conflict. Other domestic actors form the realm of economic governance, science, the judiciary, culture and others make up another 12.1%. Nearly half of all

---

2 A detailed description of the sampling procedure, the crisis definition and the coding instruction can be found in our codebook which is online on www.ggcrisi.info. See also Roose et al. (2014).

senders are found beyond the national arena, mainly on the European level or in other EU member states.

Table 1: Attribution senders in German and Greek newspapers; in %.

	Germany	Greece
Domestic government	8.7	9.8
Domestic parties	10.0	21.9
Other domestic actors	12.1	14.2
Domestic media	23.2	18.9
Government EU Member state	8.2	6.8
Parties EU Member state	3.2	2.0
Other actors EU Member state	10.3	4.9
EU actors/Troika	12.7	9.5
EU parties	1.1	0.9
Other non-dom. actors	10.5	11.2
N	2462	4169

In Greece, the situation is different. Here the sender structure is more nationally biased with higher numbers for all domestic actors (apart from the media) in absolute and in relative terms. Overall, more than 65% of all attributions are 'sent' by domestic actors. The share of domestic party actors is 21.9% and government actors add another 9.8%. Overall, domestic party actors play a much greater role in the crisis debate than in Germany.

Foreign party actors rarely appear as attribution senders in either country. Parties from other EU member states represent 3.2% (German newspapers), respectively 2% (Greek newspapers) of all senders. Whereas EU actors account for a considerable share of 12.7% (German media) and 9.5% (Greek media), European parties and European parliament members are almost absent in the debate (1.1%, respectively 0.9%). On the supranational level, it is clearly the executive and technocratic actors who make their voices heard while the parliament remains silent. Other studies on the European public sphere confirm this marginal role of the European parliament and its party groups (Koopmans 2014).

To reflect the actual party conflict, we take a closer look at the activity of individual parties, including the government coalition for all those cases in which we cannot link government statements to single parties (Figures 2 to 4).

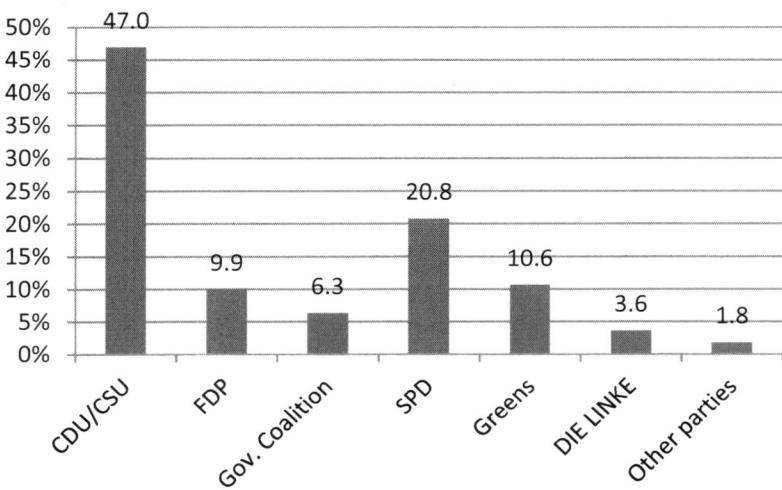

Figure 2: Parties as attribution senders in German newspapers during the CDU/CSU-FDP-government period, 09.2009 – 09.2013; in %. N=443.

In Germany, the party conflict about the Eurozone crisis is to a very large majority dominated by the government parties and in particular by party actors from the conservative *CDU* and its Bavarian sister party (*CSU*) (47.0%, Figure 2). Of course, this is partly due to the strong presence of Chancellor Merkel and *CDU*-finance minister Schäuble. The liberal coalition party *FDP* is responsible for 9.9% of the attributions and another 6.3% goes to the coalition government. Altogether, the oppositional parties account for only 36.8% of all attributions within the party conflict (6.6% of all attributions in German newspapers). While the share of 20.8% for the main oppositional party at that time (the social-democratic *SPD*) is quite low, the overall order of the party involvement largely reflects the actual vote shares in the 2009 national elections. This can be interpreted as a first hint that at least between 2009 and 2013 the Eurozone crisis has not fundamentally changed the German party constellation when it comes to discursive mobilization.

In Greece, the importance of the party conflict is significantly higher. Table 1 showed that the share of attribution senders with direct party affiliation is significantly higher than in Germany (31.7% vs. 18.7%). Moreover, the number of parties involved in the debate is larger.

The Greek government constellations between 2009 and 2013 are more complex than in Germany. The one-party *PASOK*-government Papandreou lasted from October 2009 until November 2011 (Figure 3). It was followed by the technocratic cabinet Papadimos until May 2012.[3] After that and extending beyond the analysed timespan, the three-party *ND-PASOK-DIMAR*-coalition under the leadership of Prime-Minister Samaras (*ND*) was in power (Figure 4).

During the years of the Papandreou government, his social-democratic *PASOK* is by far the most active sender with 44.6% of all attributions. However, the oppositional parties are much more involved in shaping the crisis discourse than in Germany. Attributions from the opposition account for more than 52%. The conservative *ND*, the leftist *SYRIZA* and the communist *KKE* are active attribution senders in this period.

In the later stages of the crisis during the Samaras government, the party conflict looks different. Having lost its position in a one-party government, *PASOK* declines by 38 percentage points whereas its long-time rival *ND* remains stable (19%) despite occupying the Prime-Minister's seat. Altogether, the share of the government parties (including unclassified statements by the coalition) is 48.4%. This is almost identical to the former *PASOK*-government which is remarkable given the change from a one-party government to a three-party coalition. Compared to the early crisis years, *SYRIZA* massively gains in public visibility. With a change from 13% to more than 30%, the leftist oppositional party was the most visible single party in this timespan. While the share of the communist *KKE* remains identical, the rightist *LAOS* loses 1.9 percentage points. At the same time, the share of other fringe parties and independent politicians doubles.

Overall, the analysis of the sender dimension of the crisis debate showed that the party conflict in Greece is broader, more heterogeneous and more intense than in Germany. Especially the role of the opposition is a clear indicator of this difference; on average, the opposition parties' share in Greece is about 15 percentage points higher than the respective share in Germany. The strong visibility of the Greek opposition is not even affected by the establishment of a three-party government due to the increased presence of *SYRIZA*. While the government-opposition ratio

---

3 Due to the limited timespan and the technocratic character of this government, we refrain from a detailed analysis of this period in this chapter.

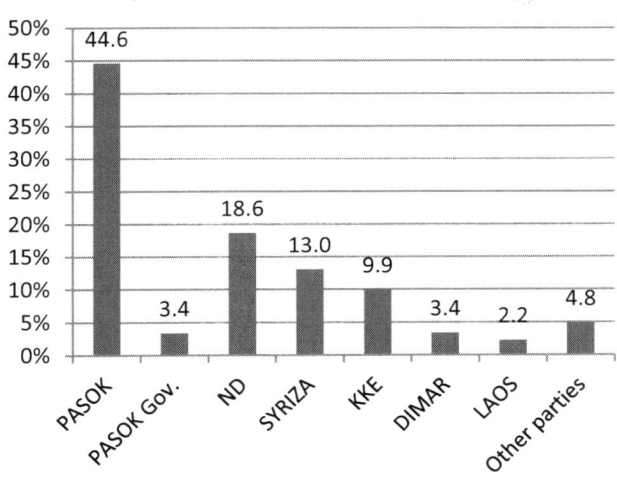

Figure 3: Parties as attribution senders in Greek newspapers during the PASOK-government period, 10.2009 – 11.2011; in %. N=805.[4]

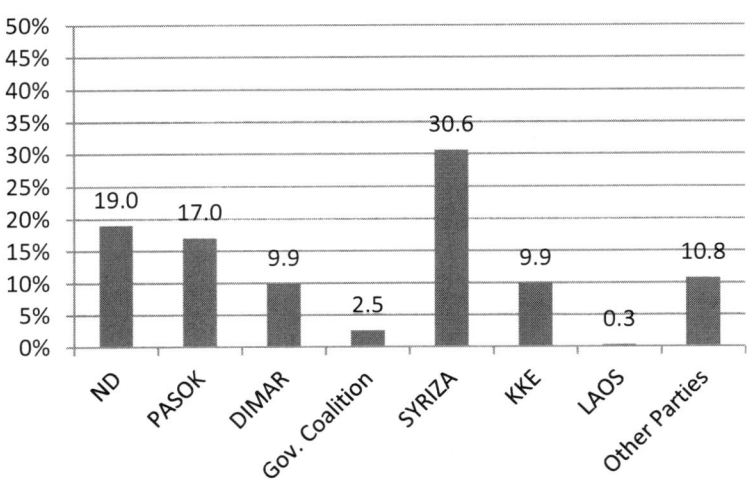

Figure 4: Parties as attribution senders in Greek newspapers during the ND-PASOK-DIMAR-government period, 06.2012 – 09.2013; in %. N=353.

---

4 In the Greek case, the category Other Parties includes a considerable share of inde-pendent politicians.

remains balanced, the particular party composition in the later phases of the crisis illustrates the transformative power of the crisis on the Greek party system. As the main oppositional voice against the grand *ND-PASOK-DIMAR* coalition and the dominant austerity policy, *SYRIZA* seems to profit most from the crisis while the relative importance of the former governing parties declines (*PASOK*) or stagnates (*ND*). The pattern of senders involved in attributing responsibility is in line with the expectation that a higher share of party actors with a wider spectrum of parties involved is found in Greece where we find major shifts among the actors later on.

V. Attribution Types in the Party Conflicts

As mentioned in Section II, attribution senders can attribute credit, they can request others to act or attribute competence and they can blame others for misconduct. The different attribution types hint to the degree of conflict with blames being more conflictive than requests / competence attributions, and requests / competence attributions being more conflictive than credit granting.

Credit granting is not the dominant attribution type we find in the public discourse (Figures 5, 6 and 7). Considering the negativity bias of news reporting, this is not surprising.[5] Only government parties are active in granting credit. Oppositional parties are much more hesitant in this regard. Overall, blames and request / competence attributions are by far the two dominant attribution types.

The country comparison reveals a striking difference between blames on the one side versus requests / competence attributions on the other. In Greece, blames clearly dominate. In the earlier years of the crisis, only for politicians directly linked to the *PASOK*-government (Figure 6), credit-granting is a common strategy. All other Greek parties dominantly blame with shares between two thirds and three quarters of all their attributions. During Samaras' prime-ministership (Figure 7), the overall picture is similar with blames being the most common strategy (51.5% for all parties on average). Again, it is predominantly the opposition parties who blame

---

5 For a conceptual overview with multiple references see Lengauer et al. (2011), for results in attribution analysis see Gerhards et al. (2009).

(*SYRIZA* 70.4%; *KKE* 80%), whereas the government parties show a stronger inclination to engage in credit granting. But even among the coalition, the gap between *ND* (44.8% credit attributions) and *PASOK* (10%) is remarkable. It mirrors *PASOK*'s strategy to present itself as the progressive pillar in the government in order to preserve its electoral center-left constituency. Consequently, it tried to avoid applauding its party rival *ND* and its leader Samaras.

The situation in Germany is different (Figure 5). Only for the left party *DIE LINKE* (87.5%) and to a lesser extent for the oppositional *SPD* (54.4%) blames make out more than half of the attributions. Requests and competence attributions are more present when compared to the Greek debate (41.4% on average vs. 28.3% on average in Greece). In particular, the governing party *CDU/CSU* uses request and competence attributions in almost half of all cases.

All in all, the strong blame-game in Greece reflects a much more conflictive debate during both periods under investigation. While the Greek party debate is primarily focused on the identification of culprits, the larger share of request and competence attributions among German parties points to an equally important focus on crisis management. Again, we find support for our assumption that a more conflictive debate is a precursor of changes in the actor configuration (see next section).

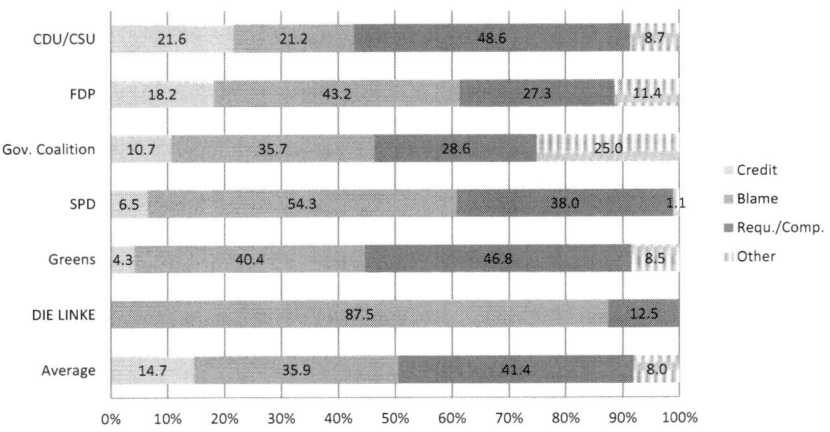

Figure 5: Attribution patterns of German parties during the CDU/CSU-FDP-government period, 09.2009 – 09.2013; in %.

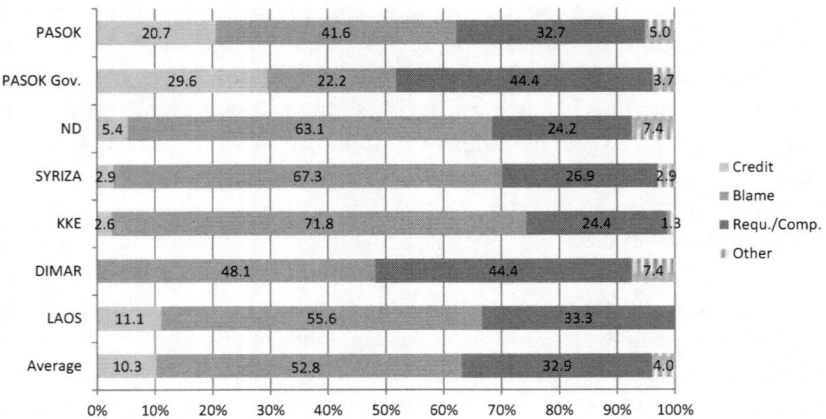

Figure 6: Attribution patterns of Greek parties during the PASOK-government period, 10.2009 – 11.2011; in %.

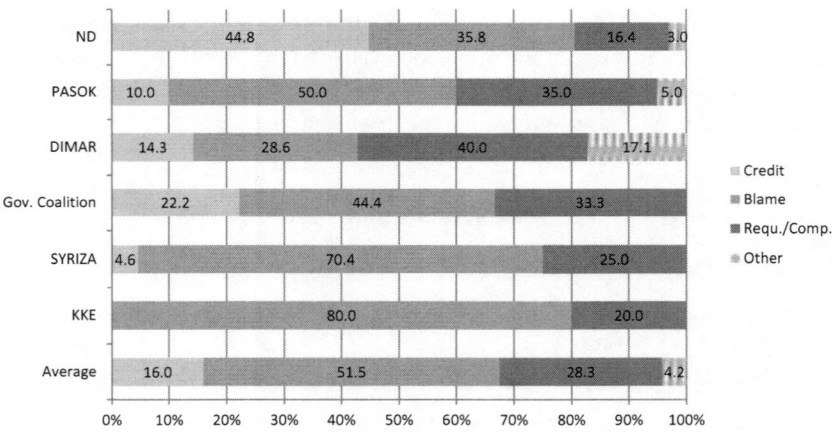

Figure 7: Attribution patterns of Greek parties during the ND-PASOK-DIMAR-government period, 06.2012 – 09.2013; in %.[6]

---

6 Since the rightist party LAOS is almost absent in this period, we refrained from including it in Figure 7. Other fringe parties and independent politicians are excluded as well.

VI. Attribution Addressees in the Party Conflicts

The conflict constellation of a national party competition within a Europeanized setting opens opportunities for either addressing actors and particularly competing party actors within the national polity, or addressing attributions to the European level or other EU member states, implying a redirection of the conflict to external actors. To grasp the general direction of the debate we calculated an index indicating the extent of domestic attributions or *internal attributions* in comparison to European and international attribution or *external attributions* (short, *I-E-Index*).[7] An index score of -1 points to a purely transnational/European selection of addressees, a score of +1 indicates a purely domestic framing.

We focus on attributions sent by party actors only, again distinguishing government and opposition parties. We start with attributions sent by the German government coalition parties *CDU/CSU* and *FDP* (Table 2). Table 3 shows the attribution addressees of the oppositional parties, *SPD*, *BÜNDNIS 90/DIE GRÜNEN* and *DIE LINKE* for the same period.

Table 2: Addressees of German coalition parties during the CDU/CSU-FDP-government period, 09.2009 – 09.2013; in %[8].

	Gov.	Opp.	DEU other	EU MS	EU/ Troika	int./ global	I-E-Index
Credit	31.6	33.3	23.8	19.1	10.5	5.9	
Blame	23.7	66.7	19.0	21.3	31.6	52.9	
Requ./Comp.	34.2	0.0	52.4	53.2	43.4	35.3	
Other	10.5	0.0	4.8	6.4	14.5	5.9	
N	76	6	42	47	76	17	-0.061
% of all	28.8	2.3	15.9	17.8	28.8	6.4	

---

7 *Calculation*: I-E-Index (A) = (Internal Attributions, A – External Attributions, A) / (Internal Attributions, A + External Attributions, A); -1 ≤ x ≤ 1. See: Adam (2008:188).

8 In Tables 2-7, the category *Government* refers to the government at that time. Former governments either appear in *Other* actors or, in the case of single politicians and clearly identifiable party actors, in the category *Opposition*. The values at the bottom line indicate the relative share for each group of addressees.

Table 3: Addressees of German opposition parties during the CDU/CSU-FDP-government period, 09.2009 – 09.2013; in %.

	Gov.	Opp.	DEU other	EU MS	EU/ Troika	int./ global	I-E-Index
Credit	2.0	25.0	3.8	3.3	21.7	0.0	
Blame	74.0	50.0	34.6	20.0	21.7	25.0	
Requ./Comp.	23.0	25.0	50.0	73.3	52.2	75.0	
Other	1.0	0.0	11.5	3.3	4.3	0.0	
N	100	4	26	30	23	4	0.390
% of all	53.5	2.1	13.9	16.0	12.3	2.1	

In Germany, the government parties seem to have very little interest in addressing the opposition and in engaging in a contentious exchange of arguments with their domestic rivals. Only 6 attributions (equalling 2.3% of the government's attributions) are directed at the opposition. Much rather, the ruling parties are concerned with themselves (76 attributions or 28.8%), with other European member states (47 / 17.8%) and with European Union institutions (76 / 28.8%). Overall, the negative score on the *I-E-Index* (-0.061) shows the transnational framing of the government's crisis discourse. 53% of all attributions are directed at actors outside of Germany. Concerning the actual evaluation, among the self-attributions the relatively high share of the self-directed blames stands out (23.7%). In general, it is assumed that when entering the public stage, actors are interested in a positive self-presentation which translates into external blaming and self-ascribed successes (Gerhards et al. 2009; Weaver 1986). Interestingly, global and international actors beyond the EU are the most negatively evaluated actor group but also EU institutions receive more blames than credits (31.6% vs. 10.5%).

The opposition on the other hand is much more focused on domestic politics. The *I-E-Index* value of 0.390 illustrates the strong domestic bias. 53.5% of all attributions are directed at the government and the evaluation is extremely negative with 74% blame attributions. European and transnational addressees are less present and in these cases requests are more present than blames.

Overall, the crisis led to a weak and rather one-sided party conflict in Germany, where a comparatively silent opposition attacks the government which, on her part, abstains from the domestic party struggle and rather focuses on its own role and the grand questions of European politics. The crisis debate is only partly one between government and opposition. Only some dissenting voices within the coalition contribute to partial disputes. It were parts of the market liberal *FDP* and namely the parliamentarian Frank Schäffler who publically criticized the government's policy of massive market interventions and bail outs. Overall, however, the German party conflict is limited at best. Apart from occasional opposition attacks and some inner-governmental quarrel, the government's crisis policy remains relatively uncontested.

Again, the Greek crisis debate looks different. The addressees chosen by Greek parties in the time of the *PASOK*-government show a surprising similarity for government and opposition parties (Tables 4 and 5): for both, European actors only play a minor role as addressees of responsibility attributions. The *I-E-Index* scores of 0.738 for the government party *PASOK* and 0.808 for the opposition point to a very strong domestic bias. Given the earlier discussed involvement of European Union actors in the crisis management and the German government's tough line on austerity in the country, this is an astonishing outcome. Rather than Europeanized, the party conflict is fought out in the domestic arena. Both, government and opposition are much more focused on national politics than their German counterparts. For the *PASOK*-government, scapegoating to the European Union as a means of blame avoidance is no common strategy. The *PASOK*'s traditional pro-EU stance and its close cooperation with EU-institutions help to explain this comparatively minor importance of blame-shifting to the EU. Not even for the opposition, targeting the EU is the dominant strategy. In contrast to the government, however, the attributions directed at EU-institutions and the Troika are predominantly negative (61.8% blames).

The large majority of all oppositional parties' attributions are directed at the government and most of them are blames (72.3%). Again, addressing European actors is the exception rather than the norm.[9] The government responds, though to a much lesser extent, with blames addressed at the opposition (81.3% blames). Predominantly, however, the government focuses on its own role in the crisis. 54.6% of all attributions (208) are self-attributions. Among these, self-directed blames are even more common than credit-claiming. This mirrors the fierce controversies about the

---

9 This does not necessarily imply that transnational actors are regarded as irrelevant. Rather the Greek government is interpreted as a close ally of the transnational institutions and addressed as such implying a domestication of the conflict with transnational actors.

austerity measures which led to severe inner-party conflicts. *PASOK*-members of parliament and less high-ranked *PASOK*-politicians harshly criticized both Papandreou and finance minister Venizelos for the unjust implementation of public cuts. After each austerity package the government faced new massive popular mobilizations and new deputies' defections.

The Greek opposition neither speaks with one voice. Opposition parties exchange 14.7% of their attributions (208) among each other and blames are by far the most important type (67.2%). In this case, it is predominantly the conflict between left and right and in particular the left parties' attacks on the conservative, former ruling party *New Democracy* (*ND*) which shapes this conflict.

Table 4: Addressees of the government during the PASOK-government period, 10.2009 – 11.2011; in %.

	Gov.	Opp.	GRC other	EU MS	EU/ Troika	int./ global	I-E-Index
Credit	26.4	4.7	18.6	35.7	14.8	44.4	
Blame	30.8	81.3	39.0	35.7	25.9	22.2	
Requ./Comp.	37.5	12.5	37.3	28.6	48.1	33.3	
Other	5.3	1.6	5.1	0.0	11.1	0.0	
N	208	64	59	14	27	9	0.738
% of all	54.8	16.8	15.5	3.7	7.1	2.4	

Table 5: Addressees of Greek opposition parties during the PASOK-government period, 10.2009 – 11.2011; in %.

	Gov.	Opp.	GRC other	EU MS	EU/ Troika	int./ global	I-E-Index
Credit	3.1	8.2	6.8	0.0	2.9	0.0	
Blame	72.3	67.2	25.4	50.0	61.8	50.0	
Requ./Comp.	21.5	19.7	66.1	0.0	29.4	25.0	
Other	3.1	4.9	1.7	50.0	5.9	25.0	
N		61	59	2	34	4	0.808
% of all	256 61.5	14.7	14.2	0.5	8.2	1.0	

Tables 6 and 7 display the addressees during the *ND-PASOK-DIMAR*-coalition period. The earlier pattern of a predominantly domestic orientation of the party conflict is underlined (*I-E-index* scores of 0.845 for the coalition and 0.717 for the opposition). Due to the change from a one-party to a three-party government, the share of inner-governmental attributions even increases to now 61.3% and again, self-directed blame accounts for more than one quarter (Table 6). Again, attributions directed at the opposition are rather limited but with 88% blames extremely negative. As for the opposition (Table 7), 58.7% of the attributions are directed at the government and the evaluation is predominantly negative (77.8%). Again, inner-oppositional dispute plays a role (57.1% blames).

Table 6: Addressees of coalition parties during the ND-PASOK-DIMAR-government period, 06.2012 – 09.2013; in %.

	Gov.	Opp.	GRC other	EU MS	EU/ Troika	int./ global	I-E-Index
Credit	34.0	0.0	25.9	50.0	0.0	0.0	
Blame	27.2	88.0	44.4	0.0	33.3	0.0	
Requ./Comp.	31.1	8.0	29.6	50.0	44.4	100.0	
Other	7.8	4.0	0.0	0.0	22.2	0.0	
N	103	25	27	2	9	2	0.845
% of all	61.3	14.9	16.1	1.2	5.4	1.2	

Table 7: Addressees of opposition parties during the ND-PASOK-DIMAR-government period, 06.2012 – 09.2013; in %.

	Gov.	Opp.	GRC other	EU MS	EU/ Troika	int./ global	I-E-Index
Credit	8.3	19.0	27.6	9.1	7.7	0.0	
Blame	77.8	57.1	17.2	54.5	61.5	50.0	
Requ./Comp.	13.9	23.8	51.7	36.4	30.8	50.0	
Other	0.0	0.0	3.4	0.0	0.0	0.0	
N	108	21	29	11	13	2	0.717
% of all	58.7	11.4	15.8	6.0	7.1	1.1	

In Greece, we find a full-fledged, multi-dimensional party conflict with oppositional parties blaming the government and, to a lesser extent, the government blaming oppositional parties. European and international actors are secondary in the debate. The controversy is focused on blames directed across the party cleavage. Remarkable though is the additional inner-governmental conflict, at first in the form of an inner-party conflict within the government party *PASOK* and later in the form of an inner-coalition conflict between *ND*, *PASOK* and *DIMAR*. In Germany, we find a similar pattern, though much less dramatic, with some dissenting voices from within the government coalition. The crisis situation itself seems to contribute to these inner party conflicts.

In respect to addressing non-domestic actors, the debate in Greece is more nationally confined than the German debate. On the one hand, this is a surprise as the developments in the Greek society are dramatic and transnational actors are directly involved in this. Therefore, we would expect more attributions directed towards transnational actors and especially more when compared to the German case. On the other hand, the findings correspond to the intense party conflict in Greece as a precursor of a structural reconfiguration of the party system.

VII. Discussion and Conclusion

In this chapter we analysed party conflicts in the Eurozone crisis in two very distinct national settings, Germany and Greece. Our focus was on publically stated responsibility attributions as the core of a contentious debate. The crises in both countries are fundamentally different and so are the party conflicts. In Greece, the party structure has been turned upside down five years after the beginning of the crisis while in Germany the structure remained more or less stable with one party (*CDU*) remaining continuously in power, even though with changing partners. We wanted to know whether the structures of the debate in the respective countries resemble these different paths.

In crisis-ridden Greece, we find an intense party conflict. Both governing parties and the opposition are actively involved. Conflictual blame attributions dominate when compared to requests, competence attributions or crediting. The party conflict is complex and multifaceted. Surprisingly, however, one dimension is almost absent: European actors only play a minor role as addressees in the party blame-game. By far the most important addressees are other party actors within the domestic domain. These are partly equated with EU and Troika due to their joint memoranda but still the transnational actors as such remain in the second row. This domestic conflict is polarized on several dimensions: We observe mutual blame-shifting between opposition and government as well as visible inner-governmental quarrels and disputes among oppositional parties. While this conflictive pattern of the party conflict equally applies to the earlier (*PASOK*-government) and to the later stages of the crisis (*ND-PASOK-DIMAR*-government), the party composition changes; the rise of *SYRIZA* and the relative decline of *PASOK* are a strong indicator of the transformative power of the crisis. The structure of the discourse in fact seems to correspond to a change in the party system. Closing ranks, also a typical pattern in case of external threat, cannot be found among Greek parties in spite of the tough demands from the Troika.

In Germany, in contrast, the party conflict is limited. Parties, in particular from the opposition, are less active in the debate. The less conflictive request and competence attributions are predominant; crisis management is central. This implies a less contentious character of the party debate when compared to the Greek blame-game. A large share of addressees are found beyond national borders. Especially coalition parties abstain from accusing their domestic rivals. Apart from some oppositional attacks on the government, only the limited inner-government dispute on behalf of the *FDP* adds some controversy to the by-and-large consensual debate.

This pattern corresponds to the reconfiguration of the party system in Greece and a relatively stable party system in Germany. This correspondence should not be regarded as the debate causing the change in the system. A causal analysis would need to go more into the details of both party systems and electorates, and also consider historical developments. Rather the patterns of the debates in both countries are pieces of the larger picture which lead to a broad shift in Greece and not in Germany.

Several factors explain the greater intensity of the party conflict in Greece. First, the crisis has hit the Greek society much harder than any other country. While Germany is marginally affected, Greece has suffered severely. The social, economic and political insecurity evokes a strong need for public sense making which contributes to a higher crisis salience and hence more crisis-related attributions than in Germany. The high share of blame attributions illustrates the public demand to identity culprits and to clarify matters of causal responsibility. This results in a contested and confrontational party debate.

Second, in Greece, our analysed time frame covers electoral campaigns and the prospects of changing majorities contributed to the domestic orientation of the crisis debate. Even for parties which are very critical of the European crisis policy such as *SYRIZA*, the arising opportunities to gain power "entailed that it would primarily target its domestic competitors" (Vasilopoulou et al. 2013: 11).

Finally and maybe most importantly, political culture and path dependency play a role. The political culture in Greece is more conflict-oriented than in traditionally consent-oriented Germany. Among others, this explains the broader political spectrum in the Greek parliament with parties on the far left and the far right. Part of this political culture is that leftist parties such as *SYRIZA* consider themselves as parliamentary spokes-people for extra-parliamentary protest and lawyers of popular resistance. This includes anti-austerity protests and consequently movement claims entered the Greek party debate. In general, the overall left-wing bias of the Greek party conflict – in particular the strong presence of *SYRIZA* and the communist *KKE* – is noteworthy. At the same time, the relative silence of right-wing parties is surprising given that in recent years the populist right has been the most active player in mobilizing on European integration topics in party systems all over Europe (Kriesi et al. 2012). However, the literature on party politics has pointed out that these right-wing parties predominantly focus on cultural and identity-related issues such as immigration while falling short on socio-economic topics and redistribution (Kriesi et al. 2012). Concerning these latter issues, it is the parties left of center, which are strongest. The Eurozone crisis and its disastrous impacts on the socio-economic situation in Greece put economic justice and redistribution on the top of the party agenda. In Germany, the evolving cleavage of national closure against globalized openness (Kriesi et al. 2012) – which includes contentious arguments about the costs and benefits of European integration – has up to now gained little prominence.

With these explanations in mind, it still remains surprising how little EU institutions are addressed in Greece. Despite the important role of European actors in the crisis management, the answer to the prevalent question of "Who is to blame?" is predominantly found in the national arena, among the political adversary and sometimes among the coalition partners or even the very own party officials. Against the expectations, in Greece the party conflict remains a domestic conflict.

In Greece, the party system has been shaken by the crisis. The *PASOK* has been a major player and became marginal. The formerly marginal *SYRIZA* gained power. This development is fundamentally different to what we find in Germany. The leading government party has remained identical throughout the crisis. An emerging EU-critical party, the *AfD*, was not able to stabilize and had only few small successes. The comparison of the political debates in both countries, the patterns of responsibility attribution, correspond directly to these developments. The public debate as the core arena of competition on the party system directly mirrors these structural changes which are emerging during the time span under surveillance. To further investigate this close link of debate, actor involvement and changes of actor configurations during a conflict in crisis situations remains a task for social sciences – a promising task.

Bibliography

Adam, S.: Medieninhalte aus der Netzwerkperspektive. Neue Erkenntnisse durch die Kombination von Inhalts- und Netzwerkanalyse. Publizistik, 2008 53(2), pp. 180-199.

Antoniades, A.: At the Eye of the Cyclone: The Greek Crisis in Global Media. Athens: ACIPE, 2012.

Benford, R. D./ Snow, D.: Framing Processes and Social Movements. An Overview and Assessment. Annual Review of Sociology, 2000 26, pp. 611-639.

Bovens, M.: The Quest for Responsibility. Accountability and Citizenship in Complex Organizations. Cambridge: Cambridge University Press, 1998.

Dahl, R. A.: Democracy and its Critics. New Haven: Yale University Press, 1989.

Dahrendorf, R.: Zu einer Theorie des sozialen Konflikts. In: Zapf, W. ed. Theorien des sozialen Wandels. Köln: Kiepenhauer & Witsch, 1967, pp. 108-123.

Gerhards, J./ Roose, J./ Offerhaus, A.: Die öffentliche Zuschreibung von Verantwortung. Kölner Zeitschrift für Soziologie und Sozialpsychologie, 2007 59(1), pp. 105-124.

Gerhards, J./ Roose, J./ Offerhaus, A.: Die Rekonfiguration von politischer Verantwortungszuschreibung im Rahmen staatlichen Wandels. In: Zürn, M./ Ecker-Ehrhardt, M. eds. Die Politisierung der Weltpolitik. Frankfurt/M.: Suhrkamp, 2013, pp. 109-133.

Habermas, J.: Theorie des kommunikativen Handelns. Frankfurt/M.: Suhrkamp, 1988.

Hamilton, A./ Madison, J./ Jay, J./ Goldman, L.: The Federalist Papers. Oxford: Oxford University Press, 2008.

Hobolt, S./ Tilley, J.: Who's in Charge? How Voters Attribute Responsibility in the European Union. In: Comparative Political Studies, 2014 47(6), pp. 795-819.

Hood, C.: The Blame Game. Spin, Bureaucracy, and Self-Presentation in Government. Princeton: Princeton University Press, 2011.

Karyotis, G./ Rüdig, W.: Blame and Punishment? The Electoral Politics of Extreme Austerity: The Case of Greece. Political Studies, 2013 63(1), pp. 2-24.

Koopmans, R.: How Advanced is the Europeanization of Public Spheres? Comparing German and European Structures of Political Communication. In: Risse, T. ed. European Public Spheres. Politics is Back. Cambridge: Cambridge University Press, 2014, pp. 53-83.

Kriesi, H./ Grande, E./ Dolezal, M./ Helbling, M./ Höglinger, D./ Wüest, B./ Hutter, S.: Political Conflict in Western Europe. Cambridge: Cambridge University Press, 2012.

Lengauer, G./ Esser, F./ Berganza, R.: Negativity in Political News: A Review of Concepts, Operationalizations and Key Findings. Journalism, 2011 13 pp. 1-24.

McAdam, D./ Tarrow, S./ Tilly, C.: Dynamics of Contention. Cambridge: Cambridge University Press, 2001.

Mylonas, Y.: Media and the Economic Crisis of the EU. The 'Culturalization' of a Systemic Crisis and Bild-Zeitung's Framing of Greece. 2012 triple C 10, pp. 646-671.

Pappas, T.: Populist Democracies: Post-Authoritarian Greece and Post-Communist Hungary. Government and Opposition, 2014 49, pp. 1-23.

Roose, J./ Kousis, M./ Sommer, M.: Discursive Actor Attribution Analysis. A Tool to Analyze How People Make Sense of the Eurozone Crisis. Paper presented at the ECPR General Conference, Glasgow, 2014.

Sartori, G.: The Theory of Democracy Revisited. Chatham: Chatham House, 1987.

Vasilopoulou, S./ Halikiopoulou D./ Exadaktylos, T.: Greece in Crisis: Austerity, Populism and the Politics of Blame. Journal of Common Market Studies, 2013 52(2), pp. 1-15.

Weaver, K.: The Politics of Blame Avoidance. Journal of Public Policy, 1986 6(4), pp. 371-398.

Sixth chapter
Increasing Winners-Losers Gap? Increasing Euroscepticism?
Exploring the Economic Crisis' Conflict Potential

Karsten Mause and Bernd Schlipphak (University of Münster)

I. Introduction

Identifying 'winners' and 'losers' in certain respects and settings is a classic theme in the political economy literature. As early as in the 19th century, Marx and Engels ([1848] 2002) and writers inspired by their thoughts
have argued that the 'working class' is exploited by business firms and
their owners ('the capitalists') in capitalist societies. While social scientists are still interested in themes connected to Marx and his followers –
analysing, for example, the winners and losers of "turbo-capitalism"
(Luttwak 1998) – the way in which winners and losers are identified and
further examined has obviously changed to some extent since the times of
Marx and Engels. For instance, social scientists interested in inequality
and (re)distribution have for quite some time used statistical methods to
divide the populations of societies – more or less explicitly – into individual 'winners' and 'losers' as measured by their position in society in terms
of individual levels of income, wealth or education (c.f. OECD 2008,
2011; and the much-debated recent books by Stiglitz 2012 and Piketty
2014). In this context, researchers also focus on the dynamic aspect of
whether changing contextual factors (e.g. economic crises; transformations of the political/economic system) are responsible for interesting
moves of (groups of) persons up or down the income distribution within a
society over time (e.g. Silverman and Yanowitch 1997; Birdsall and Nellis
2003; Burkhauser 2007; Hisnanick 2011).
   The identification and analysis of gaps between beneficiaries (or winners) and victims (losers) of economic developments has been of interest
to social scientists as the consequences of such winner-loser gaps and their
widening (e.g. through economic crises) have been interpreted as causes
of social unrest or the rise of anti-democratic parties and rulers (c.f. Houle
2009; Ponticelli and Voth 2011; Caruso and Schneider 2011; Baten and
Mumme 2013). Recent research focussing on the individual level has indi-

cated that being or at least identifying oneself as an economic winner or loser crucially shapes not only one's attitudes toward the domestic political system but also one's perception of the European Union (EU) and European integration (Herzog and Tucker 2010; Kuhn et al. 2015). Such research has been connected both to the literature on euroscepticism and to literature interested in the effects of globalisation on inequality.

Regarding the latter, as '*the* globalisation' is often presumed and/or perceived to be a major driving force of societal transformations, it is not surprising that in recent years many social scientists have been trying to identify the winners and losers of globalisation (for surveys of this literature, see De la Dehesa 2006; Williamson 2008). Dreher and Gaston (2008), for instance, find that globalisation (as measured by the KOF Index of Globalisation) has increased household income inequality and industrial earnings inequality over the period 1970-2000 in OECD countries. Other empirical studies have demonstrated that specific forms of globalisation – firms' international outsourcing activities, offshore outsourcing, variation of labour market regulations across countries, etc. – significantly but divergently affect the situation of different subgroups of the workforce such as high-/low-skilled workers, ethnic minorities and part-time workers (c.f. Paus 2007; Geishecker and Görg 2008).

Within the Euroscepticism literature, studies have shown that individual self-perception as being an economic winner or loser crucially shapes citizens' attitudes toward the EU (Gabel 1998; Tucker et al. 2002; Herzog and Tucker 2010). Whether one identifies oneself or one's country as being in a positive economic status or as developing positively in economic terms, positively shapes an individual's stance on the EU. Speaking to both of the literatures sketched above, Kuhn et al. (2015) recently demonstrated that macro-economic indicators such as the development of the Gini index and the level of unemployment within a country led to an increase in euroscepticism among citizens; this effect is strongest among the lower (educated) strata of society. However, their investigation period ends in 2009 when the European financial, fiscal and economic crises (hereinafter simply denoted as 'the' economic crisis) actually set in.

As this crisis might not only shape the future of European integration (Giddens 2014) but might even lead to domestic social unrest, in this chapter we use more recent public opinion data to analyse the effects of this crisis on citizens' economic and EU attitudes. More specifically, we take a first look at aggregate developments between time points prior to and during the economic crisis (i.e. the years 2006 and 2012) in order to get answers to three related questions. First, did the crisis actually increase the number of citizens perceiving themselves as economic losers? Second, did the crisis result in a growing gap between self-perceived economic winners and losers, making winners more confident and losers feeling more deprived? Third, and finally, did the crisis – as an indirect effect via the (potential) increase of the number of self-perceived economic losers – increase citizens' euroscepticism in the aggregate? The latter is to be expected in light of the individual-level findings reported by Kuhn et al. (2015) and others for the pre-crisis period.

The chapter proceeds as follows. Drawing on theories and insights from the fields of political economy and European studies, Section II develops a number of hypotheses with respect to the issue of how the recent economic crisis might have affected (a) the mix between economic winners and losers at the national level, and (b) winners' and losers' attitudes towards the EU. Subsequently, Sections III, IV and V present our empirical strategy (i.e. data and methods), the empirical results, and some robustness checks, respectively. Using various statistical techniques to compare 2006 and 2012 data from the European Social Survey and from Eurostat reveals that the degree of severity of the crisis in a country positively influences the likelihood of a country's citizens perceiving themselves as being economically in a situation of loss. Also, the harder the crisis hits a country in terms of increasing debt and unemployment levels, the more a country's self-perceived economic losers are likely to demonstrate EU-sceptical attitudes. Finally, Section VI provides a concluding discussion of the implications and significance of the empirical results.

II. Hypotheses: The Winners-Losers Divide and Europe's Economic Crisis

Accompanying the process of European integration, a large social science literature has investigated citizens' attitudes towards this process. An interesting pattern reported in this literature is that there is a gap between citizens who perceive themselves as economic 'winners' and those who consider themselves to be 'losers' (e.g. as measured by their financial situation) – with the former being more likely to show positive, and the latter negative, attitudes towards the EU. More specifically, starting with Gabel and Palmer (1995) and Anderson and Reichert (1995), a large part of the EU public opinion literature has argued that citizens' satisfaction with the economy positively influences their attitudes towards actors and ideas at the European level. The empirical findings demonstrate that feeling like a winner in economic terms – which is again influenced partly by the coun-try's economic performance and also by citizens' levels of education, income, etc. – actually makes you feel more positively towards the EU (c.f. Gabel and Whitten 1997; Gabel 1998; Tucker et al. 2002; Herzog and Tucker 2010; Boomgaarden et al. 2011; Teney et al. 2014). In contrast, perceiving oneself as a (future) economic loser of (globalised) economic developments makes citizens much more likely to become sceptical or even cynical towards European integration and more favourable towards nationalist actors (De Vries and Edwards 2009; Lubbers and Jaspers 2011).

The aforementioned EU public opinion studies focus on the winners-losers divide *before* the recent European economic crisis; that is, they do not take into account the developments in the EU since the late 2000s. While some recent studies include aggregate macroeconomic data such as the development of a country's GDP, Gini coefficient, or unemployment rate to investigate whether the crisis (i.e. a worsening of a country's eco-nomic situation) has influenced citizens' EU attitudes (Kuhn and Stoeckel 2014; Ritzen et al. 2014; Gomez 2015), to our knowledge there is no research on the actual effects of the crisis on (i) the divide between *self-perceived* winners and losers (our argument A1/2; see below) and (ii) the extent to which this winner-loser gap influences EU attitudes (argument A3). In what follows, we will argue that both of these aspects are relevant to social scientists and policy makers analysing the crisis.

The gap between winners and losers within society – as measured by, for instance, the degree of 'social inequality' – is often expected to lead to social unrest and political instability. The probability of the latter may rise with the increase of the former: i.e. the more inequality, the higher the potential for social protest (for recent empirical studies on this topic, see Houle 2009; Caruso and Schneider 2011; Ponticelli and Voth 2011; Baten and Mumme 2013). However, for a growing divide between winners and losers to result in actual social conflict, all actors need to be aware of their status and perceive themselves as winners or losers. In other words, eco-nomic slump, increasing unemployment, rising public debt levels, or decreasing public expenditures might not in itself lead to public dissatis-faction. Only when citizens perceive themselves as being losers and others as being winners, public protest does become more probable. Interesting-ly, we are not aware of any study which analyses whether the macro-economic effects of a crisis (such as Europe's current multi-faceted crisis) have led more citizens to feel as economic 'losers' (argument A1) or to a society more polarised regarding the distinction between economic winners and losers (A2).

Yet, both arguments should be of great interest as they may give us the causal and direct explanation for an increasing EU scepticism. While some authors have proposed thinking about whether the macro-economic conditions make citizens have less trust in their national governments and, therefore, – via extrapolation – in the EU (Anderson and Tverdova 2001; Armingeon and Ceka 2014), we argue that the crisis may have influenced citizens' attitudes towards the EU. More specifically, by making more people perceive themselves as economic losers – people who are more likely to hold eurosceptic positions – the crisis may directly influence EU attitudes (A3).

The above arguments lead to three empirically testable hypotheses. All arguments focus on the national level. Following A1, which argues that the crisis affects citizens' self-perceptions of being economic winners or losers, we expect the share of self-perceived losers to more strongly increase in countries that have been hit harder by the crisis (H1). Argument A2 expects the gap between self-perceived economic winners and losers to widen as a function of the severity of the crisis and its effects. That is, the intensity of the conflict should increase due to the crisis (H2). Turning to the nexus of citizens' economic perceptions and their EU attitudes, argument A3 claims that the economic crisis makes citizens more likely to perceive themselves as economic losers *and*, as a result, to demonstrate eurosceptic attitudes (H3). Our three hypotheses can be summarised as follows.

H1. The more a country is hit by the economic crisis, the more citizens perceive themselves as economic losers.

H2. The more a country is hit by the economic crisis, the more intense the conflict between citizens perceiving themselves as winners or losers.

H3. The more a country is hit by the economic crisis, the more citizens perceive themselves as economic losers and *as eurosceptic.*

These three hypotheses, which are empirically tested by means of three different dependent variables (see below), are linked insofar as they allow to shed light on the overall context sketched above. The crisis is expected to increase the number of citizens perceiving themselves as economic 'losers'. This may result in a growing gap between self-perceived economic winners and losers at the national level, increasing the potential for social conflict within EU member countries. And if such developments take place at the national level, then this – within the EU multi-level system – may also have an impact on citizens' attitudes toward the EU and future European integration (i.e. on the level of euroscepticism). Whether these rather pessimistic mechanisms are really at work during Europe's current crisis is, of course, an empirical question to which we turn now.

III. Data and Research Design

To test our hypotheses, both (a) individual-level data for EU citizens (i.e. perceptions of economic situation, EU attitudes, etc.) that can be aggregated on the country level, and (b) official data with information on the economic situation of a country (economic growth, unemployment, public debt) has to be analysed. In so doing, we take into account that citizens' attitudes may be influenced by both objective (macro)economic indicators discussed in the media *and* subjective feelings (Gabel and Whitten 1997). The country-level data is provided by Eurostat (more details below), the individual-level data is taken from the European Social Survey (ESS) 2006 (wave 3; fieldwork: winter 2006/2007; i.e. prior to the crisis) and the ESS 2012 (wave 6; fieldwork: winter 2012/2013). The latter is the most recent ESS wave, measuring citizens' attitudes several years after the 'outbreak' of the crisis in 2008. Taking into account all EU member states that participated in both ESS waves leaves us with a dataset consisting of 29,098 (wave 3) and 32,078 (wave 6) citizens in the following 16 EU countries: Belgium (BE), Bulgaria (BG), Cyprus (CY), Denmark (DK), Estonia (EE), Finland (FI), Germany (DE), Great Britain (GB), Ireland (IE), Netherlands (NL), Poland (PL), Portugal (PT), Slovakia (SK), Slovenia (SI), Spain (ES) and Sweden (SE).[1]

Following a fundamental distinction in the literature on economic voting (for surveys, see Lewis-Beck and Stegmaier 2000; Kiewiet and Lewis-

---

1 Note that we use the ESS data because of its higher degree of data quality (particularly regarding our variables of interest) compared to the Eurobarometer (EB) data. There are several authors discussing the methodological weaknesses of the EB (see, e.g., Nissen 2014), while the ESS has recently been called the gold-standard of comparative survey research due to its methodological rigor (Heath et al. 2009; Ceobanu and Escadell 2010).

Beck 2011), we take into account that citizens may not only be concerned about their personal economic situation (wage, household income, assets, etc.), denoted as 'pocketbook' or 'egotropic' behaviour, but also about the economic situation of the country they are living in ('sociotropic' behaviour). Applied to the context under investigation, it could be the case that EU citizens perceive themselves to be economic winners or losers of the recent crisis because their personal economic situation – and/or the subjective perception thereof – has been positively or negatively affected by the crisis (i.e. pocketbook or egotropic winners/losers). At the same time, EU citizens may see themselves as economic winners or losers of the crisis as they are under the impression that they are currently living in a country that is benefitting or suffering economically from this crisis (i.e. sociotropic winners/losers). To disentangle these dimensions, we use a sociotropic measure but control for an egotropic indicator in the section on robustness checks.[2]

The sociotropic measure is based on the following ESS question: "On the whole, how satisfied are you with the present state of the economy in [your country]?" Answer options range from 0 ("extremely dissatisfied") to 10 ("extremely satisfied"). We recoded this variable 'sateco' into the three-step ordinal variable 'sateco_ord', distinguishing between citizens with the perception of living in a 'winner' (3 = original values 7–10) or 'loser' (1 = original values 0–3) country in view of the economic situation at the time of the interview; respondents somewhere in-between (i.e. original values 4–6) were coded with a 2. Subsequently, the dummy variable 'disssateco_dum' was created that divides the population into self-perceived economic losers in the above sense (=1) and all other respondents (=0). This dummy variable allows us to measure the development of a country's share of citizens feeling like economic losers between 2006 and 2012 (H1). Returning to the original variable ('sateco'), we were moreover able to calculate the country mean and its respective standard deviation ('std_sateco'). The latter allows us to control for the extremity of positions and hence for the intensity of conflict between the differing economic perceptions within a society. A country's standard deviation of citi-

---

2 Note that we do not try to include retrospective and prospective measures (i.e. respondents' assessments of their personal and/or their country's *past* and *future* economic situation; see, e.g., Lewis-Beck and Stegmaier 2000; Tucker et al. 2002) as we are exclusively interested in the change of EU citizens' assessments of their personal and their country's *current* economic situation between 2006 and 2012.

zens' economic perceptions, therefore, is used as the dependent variable for testing H2.

As we want to be sure of not missing the effects stemming from citizens' perceptions of themselves as being a beneficiary/winner or sufferer/loser of the economic crisis, as a robustness check we also control for citizens' satisfaction with their "life as a whole" as an egotropic measure (see Hessami 2011 for a similar approach to identify the winners and losers of globalisation). The ESS answer options range from 0 ("extremely dissatisfied") to 10 ("extremely satisfied"). This variable 'satlife' was further recoded in the way explained above for the sociotropic measure.

To analyse citizens' EU (or eurosceptic) attitudes (hypothesis H3), an ESS item measuring citizens' degree of trust in the European Parliament (EP) is used. Based on the answers ranging from 0 ("no trust at all") to 10 ("complete trust") the dummy variable 'distrustep_dum' is calculated, separating those respondents that do not trust the EP (1 = original values 0–3) – and, hence, are understood to be eurosceptic – from all other respondents (=0). Trust in the EP is the only EU-related question contained in an ESS item battery that also surveys attitudes towards the national parliament, legal system, police, politicians, political parties, and the United Nations. Hence, in our view, here trust in the EP is a good proxy for a respondent's overall EU attitude. To test hypothesis H3 in its expectation of a developmental effect (i.e. economic developments influencing the development of the share of citizens with specific attitudes), we then calculated a composite variable measuring for each country and each year (i.e. 2006 and 2012) the share of citizens simultaneously demonstrating economic-loser attitudes ('disssateco_dum' = 1; as defined above) *and* eurosceptic attitudes ('distrustep_dum' = 1). Finally, we subtracted a country's share of citizens showing such attitudes in the year 2006 from the respective 2012 shares. This resulting country-level variable gives us the development in the share of citizens which – after several years of crisis in Europe – demonstrate both economic-loser *and* eurosceptic attitudes, and is therefore appropriate for testing H3.

The severity of the crisis' effects in a country is the main independent variable in H1, H2, and H3. To measure the extent to which a country is economically affected by the crisis, the development of the macroeconomic standard variables GDP and unemployment rate, which are frequently discussed in the media, is considered. The unemployment rate presumably reflects the most direct effect an economic crisis might have on the life of citizens (i.e. lay-offs, money worries, and so on). In addition, the development of the level of public debt is taken into account as it reflects the development of a country's economic situation in terms of the state's fiscal performance (e.g. the leeway for public spending that benefits certain groups of citizens). Moreover, it can be expected that the EU-wide public debate about 'debt-sinner' countries and fiscal austerity has influenced citizens' evaluations of their country's economic situation. In this study, the development of a country's GDP is measured by the percent change of the absolute level of GDP (in EUR; Eurostat data) from 2006 to 2012. In the case of public debt and unemployment, we also rely on Eurostat data and subtracted a country's debt-to-GDP ratio (based on general government gross debt; Maastricht definition) and unemployment rate in 2006 (seasonally adjusted; ILO definition) from the respective rate in 2012. The resulting variables measure the development of public debt and unemployment between 2006 and 2012 in percentage points.

IV. Empirical Findings

Before presenting empirical evidence regarding H1 through H3, we first turn to the descriptive statistics presented in Table 1 that show some interesting findings. First, and confirming previous studies focussing on other contexts (e.g. Gilley 2006; Mansfield/Mutz 2009), citizens distinguish between their own (economic) well-being – measured by their degree of life satisfaction – and their evaluation of the state of the country's economy. Many citizens are obviously much more satisfied with their life (variable 'satlife') than with the nation's economy ('sateco'). This difference can be observed both in the pre-crisis period (i.e. in the ESS survey 2006) as well as in the ESS survey 2012 conducted after the 'outbreak' of the economic crisis (fieldwork: winter 2012/2013). Moreover, it turns out that citizens' life satisfaction remains relatively stable in the course of the crisis. In contrast, and as expected, citizens become more disappointed in the country's economic situation. This picture of negative developments is consistent for individual means and aggregate shares of citizens. In addition, more people seem to consider themselves as winners or losers after the crisis than they did before. Also, EU citizens' trust in the European Parliament decreased during the crisis.

Table 1: Descriptive statistics of independent and dependent variables

	Mean	Median	Range	N
2006				
Satisfaction with economy (variable 'sateco')	4.3	5	0 / 10	28,109
Share of economic losers per country (in %; based on variable 'disssateco_dum')	23.6		4.2 / 61.9	29,098
Satisfaction with life (variable 'satlife')	7.0	7	0 / 10	28,943
Share of citizens dissatisfied with life per country (in %)	8.4		2.1 / 33.1	29,098
Trust in European Parliament (variable 'trustep')	4.7	5	0 / 10	25,547
2012				
Satisfaction with economy (variable 'sateco')	4.0	4	0 / 10	31,593
Share of economic losers per country (in %; based on variable 'disssateco_dum')	43.0		8.8 / 80.6	32,078
Satisfaction with life (variable 'satlife')	7.0	8	0 / 10	31,966
Share of citizens dissatisfied with life per country (in %)	9.5		1.4 / 38.5	32,078
Trust in European Parliament (variable 'trustep')	4.3	5	0 / 10	29,312
Development between 2006 and 2012				
Difference in share of economic losers between 2006 and 2012 (in percentage points)	20.7		-21.3 / 57.3	
Difference in share of citizens having Trust in European Parliament between 2006 and 2012 (in percentage points)	-6.7		-22.1 / 6.8	
Difference in GDP per country between 2006 and 2012 (as % of GDP 2012)	14.6		-8.3 / 33.3	
Difference in debt per country between 2006 and 2012 (in percentage points)	24.4		-7.1 / 92.8	
Difference in unemployment per country between 2006 and 2012 (in percentage points)	3.3		-4.8 / 16.5	

Note: The variables and data sources are explained in Section III of this chapter.

Looking not only at the effects of the crisis but also at the aggregated changes in public opinion in the single countries, the descriptive statistics reveal some interesting cross-national differences. Figure 1a shows that – with the exception of Germany (DE), Poland (PL) and Sweden (SE) – the number of citizens perceiving their country to be in economic downturn considerably increased between 2006 and 2012, with the increase being strongest in those states that are hit hardest by the crisis (the country codes are explained in Section III). And, as Figure 1b indicates, in the majority of countries the share of citizens trusting the European Parliament decreased considerably during the crisis. An obvious conjecture is that these cross-national differences in public opinion to some extent are driven by cross-country differences in terms of economic performance. While some countries even managed to reduce their debt between 2006 and 2012 (e.g., Sweden), the debt level of others rose by over 90 percentage points (e.g., Ireland). In addition, the economy of some of the countries strongly decreased, whereas it actually increased in other countries. Finally, some countries were able to cut their unemployment rates, while countries hit hardest by the crisis witnessed an increase in unemployment, with Spain being left to deal with 25 percent of citizens without paid work in 2012 (compared to 8.5 percent in 2006).

The results of bivariate OLS regressions[3] reported in Table 2 suggest that there is indeed a correlation between the actual economic performance of countries and citizens' perceptions of their national economies (i.e., sociotropic attitudes). Regressing the development of a country's share of citizens who perceive their country as being in a state of loss on the development of either GDP, public debt or unemployment after 2006 (see regression models 1–3) shows substantial and statistically significant effects for unemployment and debt levels. The regression models 2 and 3 in Table 2 indicate that the more the levels of unemployment and debt increased in a country, the more citizens perceived their country as being on the losing end economically. The regression coefficients of the variable capturing cross-national differences in GDP development between 2006 and 2012 have the expected negative sign (i.e., a GDP increase is accompanied by a *decreased* dissatisfaction with the economic situation, and

---

3 Due to the limited number of countries/cases, we are restricted to using bivariate instead of multivariate regression models to gain reliable and solid regression results. Including all three economic indicators in one (unreliable) multivariate model, however, yields results very similar to the bivariate ones.

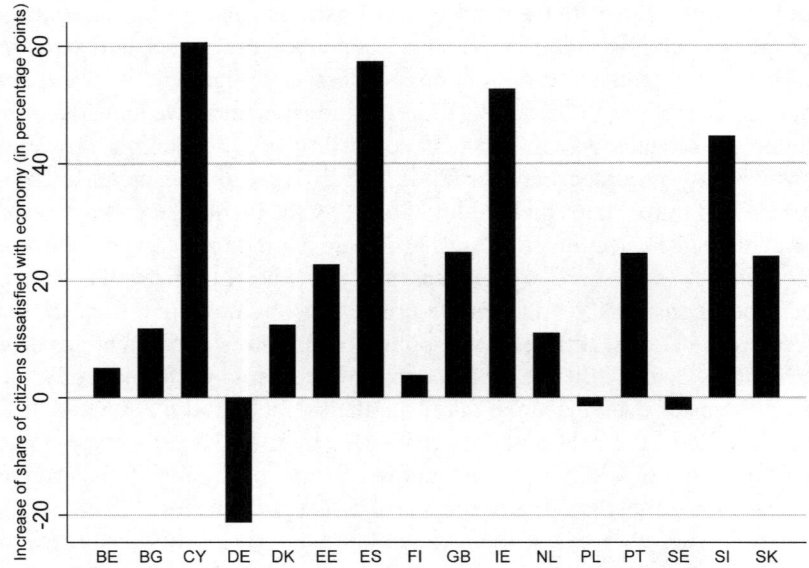

Figure 1a

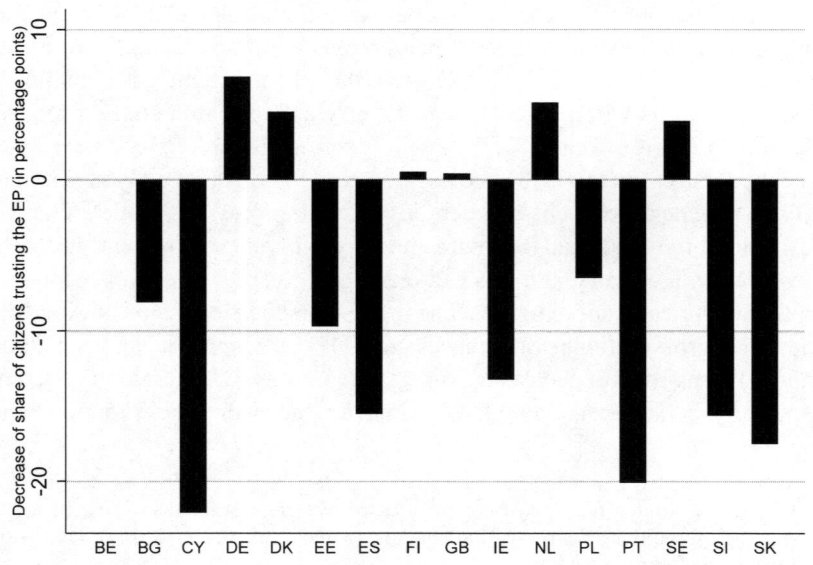

Figure 1b

vice versa) but do not reach conventional levels of statistical significance. Still, our basic hypothesis H1 – which expected the crisis to negatively affect citizens' perception of the economy – can be considered confirmed. This 'as expected' result is by no means trivial as it suggests that citizens' perceptions of the economy in fact reflect the actual economic conditions in the various EU member states – in other words, citizen-voters seem to be not as uninformed and ignorant as Downs (1957) and other political economists assume them to be.

Turning to our second hypothesis that expects the crisis to affect the conflict intensity between economic winners and losers, the regression results in Table 2 (models 4–6) obviously do not empirically support H2. This suggests that the crisis has led most citizens to become equally more sceptical towards the economic status of the country, thereby making citizens more similar in their economic perceptions.

According to hypothesis H3, the crisis is expected to increase the share of citizens that (a) feel like losers economically *and* (b) simultaneously show negative attitudes towards the EU. Again, bivariate regression models were run to test the effects of the three objective crisis indicators (i.e., GDP, public debt, unemployment rate) on the development of a country's share of citizens having negative attitudes towards the economy *and* the EU. Table 2 (models 7–9) presents the regression results which, again, demonstrate the substantial and significant effect of unemployment development on the developments of citizens' attitudes in the aggregate: the higher the number of people losing their jobs in a country between 2006 and 2012, the higher the share of citizens becoming sceptical towards the economy *and* the EU. Moreover, the deeper a country ran into public debt after 2006, the higher the share of citizens becoming sceptical towards the economy *and* the EU. These findings empirically support the expectation formulated in H3.

V. Robustness Checks

Before moving to a concluding discussion of our findings, we present the results of some robustness checks. As previous research on EU attitudes has focussed more on egotropic than on sociotropic feelings of being in a win/lose situation (Tucker et al. 2002; Herzog and Tucker 2010), we re-ran the regression models including citizens' satisfaction with their own life as an egotropic alternative to the sociotropic measures used as depen-

Table 2: Bivariate regressions: Severity of crisis and citizens' economic perceptions (H1/H2) and EU attitudes (H3)

	DV: Difference in share of economic losers between 2006 and 2012 (in percentage points)			DV: Difference in standard deviation of citizens' satisfaction with economy between 2006 and 2012			DV: Difference in a country's share of citizens' dissatisfied with economy *and* not trusting the EP between 2006 and 2012		
	Model 1	Model 2	Model 3	Model 4	Model 5	Model 6	Model 7	Model 8	Model 9
Difference in GDP per country between 2006 and 2012 (as % of GDP 2012)	-.68 (.34)			-.00 (.00)			-.21 (.19)		
Difference in debt per country between 2006 and 2012 (in percentage points)		.57*** (.12)			.00 (.00)			.27** (.08)	
Difference in unemployment per country between 2006 and 2012 (in percentage points)			3.63*** (.57)			.00 (.00)			1.62*** (.34)
_cons	30.55** (7.57)	6.76 (5.68)	8.62* (3.42)	.00 (.04)	-.01 (.05)	-.02 (.04)	14.39** (3.95)	4.70 (3.00)	5.93* (2.30)
Number of Cases	16	16	16	16	16	16	16	16	16
R² (in %)	13.0	38.3	69.6	0.2	0.2	3.3	5.5	36.6	59.0

Notes: Own calculations based on ESS (waves 3/6) and Eurostat data. Robust standard errors in parentheses.
*** p <= .001; ** p<= .01, * p<= .05.

dent variables above. As in the cases of citizens' sociotropic considerations, country differences in the share of citizens becoming more dissatisfied with their life during the crisis can partly be explained by economic indicators such as the development of a country's unemployment rates. Yet, the size of the economic effects on the aggregated life dissatisfaction of citizens is much weaker than for the sociotropic attitudes. This again is maybe due to the stability of citizens' degree of life satisfaction. However, these empirical findings also lend credibility to our theoretical expectations.

In addition, one may wonder whether the standard deviation of citizens' economic perception – and its development – provide a valid measurement of the dependent variable in H2. Hence, as an alternative measure we calculated a dummy variable that separates all citizens perceiving themselves either as winners or as losers (=1) from those identifying themselves as neither nor (=0). We then subtracted the share of winner/loser citizens in 2006 from the share of winner/loser citizens in 2012. The resulting variable demonstrates an increase or decrease of winners and losers in a country, with an increase representing a growth of the economic gap between citizens. In descriptive terms, there actually is variance across the development of countries. Regarding the percentage of citizens feeling like either an economic winner or a loser, the range is between -29.5 percentage points (i.e., fewer citizens identifying as winners or losers between 2006 and 2012) and +32.7 percentage points (in Spain). We then regressed the resulting variable again on the indicators representing the crisis' effects: the development of a country's GDP, public debt and unemployment rate, respectively. As in the original Table 2 (models 4–6), however, the economic indicators do not exert a substantial effect on the dependent variable.

Finally, as the increase of a country's unemployment rate seems to be the strongest factor for explaining the growing numbers of self-identified losers as well as the increase in a country's economic divide among citizens, we included all three crisis factors (development of GDP, public debt and unemployment rate) into multiple regression models explaining the aggregate development of citizens' economic self-perceptions. Here, only the variable measuring the development of a country's unemployment level turned out to be statistically significant and of substantial strength.

VI. Conclusion

This study has shed light on the issue of whether the recent economic crisis has widened the gap between economic winners and losers in EU countries and, if so, whether this has had an effect on citizens' attitudes towards the EU. Our empirical findings indicate that the degree of an economic crisis' severity positively influences the likelihood of a country's citizens to perceive themselves as being economically in a situation of loss (=H1). Also, the harder the crisis hits a country in terms of increasing debt and unemployment levels, the more a country's self-perceived economic losers are likely to demonstrate EU-sceptical attitudes (=H3). Our findings therefore empirically confirm the theoretically expected connection between macroeconomic indicators and citizens' attitudes which has been found in individual-level analyses investigating this relationship in the time prior to the recent crisis (c.f. Herzog and Tucker 2010; Kuhn et al. 2015). Our findings also speak to evidence from single-case studies, such as literature showing that Irish and Greek citizens' opinions during the crisis are dependent on the amount of governmental social welfare provision (Pappas and O'Malley 2014).

As noted above, however, our statistical analysis does not provide empirical support for hypothesis H2. Remember, we hypothesised that the more a country is hit by the economic crisis, the more intense the conflict between citizens perceiving themselves as winners or losers should be. One interpretation for the finding that the crisis did not affect the conflict intensity between (self-perceived) economic winners and losers may be that most citizens became equally more sceptical towards the economic status of their country during the crisis – in other words, the crisis may have made citizens from different socio-economic strata more similar in their economic perceptions. Of course, our statistical analysis of citizens' perceptions as expressed through public opinion polls does not allow to draw conclusions regarding the conflict-theoretical issue of whether the crisis has indeed incited (more) economic 'losers' in crisis-ridden countries to protest against those society members perceived as economic winners (such as 'the rich' or 'the capitalists'). While demonstrations and social unrest in Greece and other countries point in this direction, it must not necessarily be the economic 'losers' who protested during the recent economic crisis (see Rüdig and Karyotis 2014 for evidence in this respect from Greece). Moreover, (perceived) social inequality, or even hatred towards 'the winners', may only be one factor or 'enemy' among many others (e.g. 'fighting against fiscal austerity') that motivated citizens to protest.

However, the empirical results presented in this chapter demonstrate that this crisis and its consequences actually changed citizens' economic perceptions and EU attitudes. For Europe's political leaders, the results imply that they have to take into account that Europe's recent crisis has increased the group of discontented citizens who are both (a) perceiving themselves as economic 'losers' and (b) holding eurosceptic attitudes. Hence, it cannot be ruled out that these citizens may (continue to) vent their anger (i) at the ballot box, (ii) by entering extremist and/or anti-EU political parties, or (iii) by participating in demonstrations and social unrest. This group of discontented citizens may even get larger in the future, if the EU is perceived to be a community plagued by fiscal, financial, and economic 'crises' (e.g., Giddens 2014 and Offe 2015 for a deeper analysis of the political economy of Europe's multi-faceted crisis). This outlook might be too pessimistic. And our analysis of public opinion data admittedly does not indicate an intensified conflict among economic 'winners' and 'losers' within the societies of the EU member states in the period between 2006 and 2012 (see H2 above). In this context it should be clear that – despite considerable cross-country differences in terms of economic wealth – all EU member states are relatively affluent compared to many countries in other parts of the world. Still, even in the relatively rich European Union there is at least the danger that the increased group of citizens who perceive themselves as economic 'losers' (see our above results) may lead to social tensions and conflicts between 'winners' and 'losers' which, possibly, become manifest in (i) political protests, (ii) a growing support for 'anti-system' groups and political parties, or (iii) social unrest in the future.

Given such potential for conflict, at this point some may argue that there are simple solutions to reduce the shares of economic 'losers' and eurosceptics in certain countries: implementing public investment programs to stimulate economic growth, hiring more public employees, increasing social spending, and so on. The implementation of such costly measures, however, has to be financed somehow. And the heated debates about 'austerity' indicate that it is by no means clear that all political leaders and citizens in Europe are willing to run further into public debt in order to publicly finance measures that (i) possibly improve the economic situation in certain countries and that (ii) possibly counteract the recent rise of euro-/EU-sceptic political parties and their supporters.

In any case, the findings presented in this chapter are still not fully able to grasp what is going on in citizens' minds during economic crises. As we – like all other researchers dealing with this topic – lack appropriate panel data (i.e., asking the *same* citizens at several points in time), identifying what makes citizens actually change their mind during a crisis is not possible here. Therefore, at this point in time our analysis remains – theoretically and empirically – at the aggregate level. Future research is clearly needed and might be successful by (a) focussing more on the actual effects of the crisis by looking at panel data sets for single countries (such as, for instance, the Socio-Economic Panel in Germany) or (b) turning to experimental research in which the severity of a crisis is framed differently to participants. This would allow us to deeper investigate and better understand what makes citizens change their mind regarding economic and EU perceptions.

Bibliography

Anderson, C. J./ Reichert, S. M.: Economic Benefits and Support for Membership in the EU: A Cross-National Analysis. Journal of Public Policy, 1995 15(3), pp. 231-249.

Anderson, C. J./ Tverdova, Y. V.: Winners, Losers, and Attitudes about Government in Contemporary Democracies. International Political Science Review, 2001 22(4), pp. 321-338.

Armingeon, K./ Ceka, B.: The Loss of Trust in the European Union during the Great Recession since 2007: The Role of Heuristics from the National Political System. European Union Politics, 2014 15(1), pp. 82-107.

Baten, J./ Mumme, C.: Does Inequality Lead to Civil Wars? A Global Long-Term Study Using Anthropometric Indicators (1816-1999). European Journal of Political Economy, 2013 32, pp. 56-79.

Birdsall, N./ Nellis, J. R.: Winners and Losers: Assessing the Distributional Impact of Privatization. World Development, 2003 31(10), pp. 1617-1633.

Boomgaarden, H. G./ Schuck, A. R.T./ Elenbaas, M./ de Vreese, C. H: Mapping EU Attitudes: Conceptual and Empirical Dimensions of Euroscepticism and EU Support. European Union Politics, 2011 12(2), pp. 241-266.

Burkhauser, R. V.: Winners and Losers over the 1990s Business Cycles in Germany, Great Britain, Japan, and the United States. Schmollers Jahrbuch – Journal of Applied Social Science Studies, 2007 127(1), pp. 75-84.

Caruso, R./ Schneider, F.: The Socio-Economic Determinants of Terrorism and Political Violence in Western Europe (1994-2007). European Journal of Political Economy, 2011 27(Supplement 1), pp. S37-S49.

Ceobanu, A. M./ Escandell, X.: Comparative Analyses of Public Attitudes Toward Immigrants and Immigration Using Multinational Survey Data: A Review of Theories and Research. Annual Review of Sociology, 2010 36, pp. 309-328.

De la Dehesa, G.: Winners and Losers in Globalization. Malden, MA: Blackwell, 2006.

De Vries, C. E./ Edwards, E. E.: Taking Europe to Its Extremes: Extremist Parties and Public Euroskepticism. Party Politics, 2009 15(1), pp. 5-28.

Downs, A.: An Economic Theory of Democracy. New York: Harper & Row, 1957.

Dreher, A./ Gaston, N. G.: Has Globalization Increased Inequality? Review of International Economics, 2008 16(3), pp. 516-536.

Gabel, M.: Interests and Integration: Market Liberalization, Public Opinion, and European Union. Ann Arbor: University of Michigan Press, 1998.

Gabel, M./ Palmer, H. D.: Understanding Variation in Public Support for European Integration. European Journal of Political Research, 1995 27(1), pp. 3-19.

Gabel, M./ Whitten, G. D.: Economic Conditions, Economic Perceptions, and Public Support for European Integration. Political Behavior, 1997 19(1), pp. 81-96.

Geishecker, I./ Görg, H.: Winners and Losers: A Micro-Level Analysis of International Outsourcing and Wages. Canadian Journal of Economics, 2008 41(1), pp. 243-270.

Giddens, A.: Turbulent and Mighty Continent: What Future for Europe? Revised and updated edition, Cambridge: Polity Press, 2014.

Gilley, B.: The Meaning and Measure of State Legitimacy: Results for 72 Countries. European Journal of Political Research, 2006 45(3), pp. 499-525.

Gomez, R.: The Economy Strikes Back: Support for the EU during the Great Recession. Journal of Common Market Studies, 2015 53(3), pp. 577-592.

Heath, A./ Martin, J./ Spreckelsen, T.: Cross-National Comparability of Survey Attitude Measures. International Journal of Public Opinion Research, 2009 21(3), pp. 293-315.

Herzog, A./ Tucker, J. A.: The Dynamics of Support: The Winners-Losers Gap in Attitudes toward EU Membership in Post-Communist Countries. European Political Science Review, 2010 2(2), pp. 235-267.

Hessami, Z.: Globalization's Winners and Losers: Evidence from Life Satisfaction Data, 1975-2001. Economics Letters, 2011 112(3), pp. 250-253.

Hisnanick, J. J.: Who are the Winners and the Losers? Transitions in the US Household Income Distribution. Review of Radical Political Economics, 2011 43(4), pp. 467-487.

Houle, C.: Inequality and Democracy: Why Inequality Harms Consolidation but Does Not Affect Democratization. World Politics, 2009 61(4), pp. 589-622.

Kiewiet, D. R./Lewis-Beck, M. S.: No Man is an Island: Self-Interest, the Public Interest, and Sociotropic Voting. Critical Review – A Journal of Politics and Society, 2011 23(3), pp. 303-319.

Kuhn, T./ Stoeckel, F.: When European Integration Becomes Costly: The Euro Crisis and Public Support for European Economic Governance. Journal of European Public Policy, 2014 21(4), pp. 626-641.

Kuhn, T./ van Elsas, E./ Hakhverdian, A./ van der Brug, W.: An Ever Wider Gap in an Ever Closer Union: Rising Inequalities and Euroscepticism in 12 West European Democracies, 1975-2009. Socio-Economic Review, forthcoming, 2015.

Lewis-Beck, M. S./ Stegmaier, M.: Economic Determinants of Electoral Outcomes. Annual Review of Political Science, 2000 3, pp. 183-219.

Lubbers, M./ Jaspers, E.: A Longitudinal Study of Euro-Scepticism in the Netherlands: 2008 versus 1990. European Union Politics, 2011 12(1), pp. 20-41.

Luttwak, E. N.: Turbo-Capitalism: Winners and Losers in the Global Economy. London: Weidenfeld & Nicolson, 1998.

Mansfield, E. D./ Mutz, D. C.: Support for Free Trade: Self-Interest, Sociotropic Politics, and Out-Group Anxiety. International Organization, 2009 63(3), pp. 425-457.

Marx, K./ Engels, F.: The Communist Manifesto. London: Penguin Books, 2002.

Nissen, S.: The Eurobarometer and the Process of European Integration. Methodological Foundations and Weaknesses of the Largest European Survey. Quality & Quantity, 2014 48(2), pp. 713-727.

OECD: Growing Unequal? Income Distribution and Poverty in OECD Countries. Paris: OECD, 2008.

OECD: Divided We Stand: Why Inequality Keeps Rising. Paris: OECD, 2011.

Offe, Claus: Europe Entrapped. Cambridge: Polity Press, 2015.

Pappas, Takis S./ O'Malley, Eoin: Civil Compliance and "Political Luddism": Explaining Variance in Social Unrest During Crisis in Ireland and Greece. American Behavioral Scientist, 2014 58(12), pp. 1592-1613.

Paus, E. A. ed.: Global Capitalism Unbound: Winners and Losers from Offshore Outsourcing. New York: Palgrave Macmillan, 2007.

Piketty, T.: Capital in the Twenty-First Century. Cambridge: Harvard University Press, 2014.

Ponticelli, J./ Voth, H.-J.: Austerity and Anarchy: Budget Cuts and Social Unrest in Europe, 1919-2008. CEPR Discussion Paper No. 8513, 2011.

Ritzen, J./ Zimmermann, K. F./ Wehner, C.: Euroskepticism in the Crisis: More Mood than Economy. IZA Discussion Paper No. 8001, 2014.

Rüdig, W./ Karyotis, G.: Who Protests in Greece? Mass Opposition to Austerity. British Journal of Political Science, 2014 44(3), pp. 487-513.

Silverman, B./ Yanowitch, M.: New Rich, New Poor, New Russia: Winners and Losers on the Russian Road to Capitalism. Armonk, NY: Sharpe, 1997.

Stiglitz, J. E.: The Price of Inequality: How Today's Divided Society Endangers Our Future. New York: W.W. Norton & Company, 2012.

Teney, C./ Lacewell, O. P./ De Wilde, P.: Winners and Losers of Globalization in Europe: Attitudes and Ideologies. European Political Science Review, 2014 6(4), pp. 575-595.

Tucker, J. A./ Pacek, A. C./ Berinsky, A. J.: Transitional Winners and Losers: Attitudes Toward EU Membership in Post-Communist Countries. American Journal of Political Science, 2002 46(3), pp. 557-571.

Williamson, J. G.: Winners and Losers over two Centuries of Globalization. In: Collier, P./ Gunning, J. W. eds. Globalization and Poverty, Vol. 1: What has Happened? Cheltenham: Edward Elgar, 2008, pp. 19-57.

Seventh chapter
Euro Crisis, German Hegemony and the New Geography of the European Union

Rafal Ulatowski (University of Warsaw)

I. Introduction

After the successful deepening and enlargement of the European Union (EU) in the early 21st century, the process of European integration seemed to be completed. The French–German tandem proved to be effective.

Also, the first years of the currency union suggested its success (Deubner 2001: 5). The economic disparities within the EU have been reduced. But simultaneously, new imbalances have emerged. Since 2010, five Eurozone members (Greece, Ireland, Portugal, Spain, and Cyprus) have received assistance from their European partners and the International Monetary Fund (IMF).[1] The euro crisis and its scale have come as a "surprise" (Cesaratto and Stirati 2010-11: 57). The outbreak of the euro crisis initiated a discussion about the future of the EU (Schild 2013: 24-25). Some of the non-Eurozone EU members also applied for loans to the IMF (European Dialogue 2012). Europe has been the region hit the hardest by the economic crisis, and the euro crisis constitutes an important turning point in the history of European integration.

I will argue that the euro crisis caused three main changes within the EU. First, the inequality in the French–German partnership has deepened so far that the future of this tandem is questionable. German economic dynamism contrasts with the stagnation of the French economy. It presents a challenge to the French–German partnership and to its function as the driving force behind the EU. Second, the division between the wealthy old EU members and the poor new ones has to be questioned. Today, there is a new division between the wealthy core, the economically depressed south and the new members who are catching-up. Third, the euro crisis provided an impetus for deeper economic and political integration.

---

1 Spain is an exception as it was not supported by the IMF.

This chapter has the following structure. First, I will discuss the theory of hegemonic stability. It was brought into discussion by the German finance minister Wolfgang Schäuble during his speech in 2010 at the Paris-Sorbonne University. He argued that the EU and the Eurozone need a benevolent, French-German hegemon. In section III, the political and economic integration in Europe before the outbreak of the Eurozone crisis will be discussed. In section IV, I will analyze the political implications of this crisis. In section V, I will discuss whether the EU is moving toward a hegemonic system. The chapter ends with conclusions in section VI.

II. Hegemony in the European Union – What Hegemony?

The issue of cooperation is broadly discussed in theory of international relations. The hegemonic stability theory offers a hypothesis about the creation and maintenance of institutions contributing to interstate cooperation. It is argued that stability and cooperation are more likely when there is a disproportionally powerful state among the potential co-operators. The hegemonic stability theory arose from the analysis of cooperation before WW I and after WW II, as first Britain and then the USA took the lead in global affairs. Its author, Kindleberger, argued that the failure to establish a sustainable trade and currency system in the interwar period could be explained by the lack of a hegemonic power (Kindleberger 1973).

During his speech at the Paris-Sorbonne University in November 2010, the German finance minister Wolfgang Schäuble referred to France and Germany as playing the role of a "benevolent hegemon" within the European (Currency) Union. He suggested that France and Germany had already taken this role when President Nicolas Sarkozy and Chancellor Angela Merkel agreed on the anti-crisis policy during their bilateral meeting in Deauville in 2010 (Schäuble 2010). But the agreement from Deauville did not enjoy support of the smaller member states of the EU (Mussler et al. 2010). We have to wonder whether the reason behind this was that the other countries were not interested in getting a benevolent hegemon in Europe, or that the hegemon was less benevolent than what was declared.

Kindleberger's approach draws on insights from game theory and the "logic of collective goods". He argues that international stability is a collective good. All members of the system enjoy its fruits, but with the exception of the hegemon, they do not contribute to this stability. The hegemon can and will use its power to secure international stability because it will achieve benefits when stability is established ("benevolent hegemon"). The hegemon's profits will be bigger than the costs, but the biggest winner may be the smaller participants of the system. They do not have to contribute to the creation and sustaining of stability, because their contribution would have little impact on it. They tend to free ride. For Kindleberger, the system with one dominating state is the most conducive to establishing an open and stable economic system (Webb and Krasner 1989: 184).

Stephen D. Krasner and Robert Gilpin have a different opinion on this. They put more emphasis on the consequences of unequal distribution of benefits and free the hegemon from its "benevolent character" (Webb and Krasner 1989: 184). Gilpin argues that the hegemon provides a public good but also 'taxes' the other states, which contribute to the costs of the system. Because they are relatively weak, they do not question this situation. The system is still beneficial for them, what legitimizes the hegemony and secures its acceptance ("coercive hegemony"). The third possibility is hegemony of an "exploitative" character. It imposes on the subordinate states costs that may exceed benefits that these states receive (Snidal 1985: 587-590).

To maintain the system, the hegemon has to perform certain functions. It organizes trade liberalization and keeps its market open during recession. It manages the international monetary system, supplies the international currency, provides liquidity to the system, manages the structure of exchange rates, supplies investment capital, and otherwise encourages development in the peripheral areas of the system (Webb and Krasner 1989: 185). Kindleberger argues that in a world without a hegemon, public goods would be in undersupply. This approach was later relaxed by Krasner and Snidal, who noted that a system with many small countries may also lead to cooperation (Krasner 1976; Snidal 1985).

In the EU, Germany, the United Kingdom and France could be called "Regional Hegemons as Classical Partners and Rivals" (Mayer 2010: 274). Most authors agree on four characteristics of a regional power. First, it is a part of some region; second, it is ready to assume leadership;[2] third, it has material and idealistic capabilities to project regional power; and

---

2   David A. Lake initiated a reinterpretation of the different ways of argumentation (benevolent vs. coercive hegemony) within the hegemonic stability theory toward two distinctive activities: leadership and hegemony (Lake 1993).

fourth, it is highly influential in the region (Flemes and Nolte 2010: 6-7). Despite the fact that regional powers are mostly seen "as states pursuing exclusively benevolent, leading, integrating strategies", such an assumption may be far too optimistic. As Destradi argues, "a much broader range of strategies regional powers can pursue in their relations with neighboring countries" (Destradi 2010: 904-909).

In the EU, the French–German cooperation plays a key role (Pedersen 2002). Lübkemeier suggests that in the EU "leadership" has its "local" specificity and can only be collective. The leaders have to possess not only the will and capability to lead but they have to answer to the needs of all member countries and supply the collective goods (Lübkemeier 2007: 7). This task has been fulfilled for decades by the French–German duo. But did they take the role of a benevolent hegemon during the crisis?

III. European Integration before the Outbreak of the Eurozone Crisis

The development of regionalism in Europe in the late 1940s was fueled by a broad set of circumstances, including the collapse of the colonial empires of the Western European powers, physical destruction and psychological exhaustion of Europeans after the two World Wars, the threat of communism and of the Soviet Union, the emergence of superpowers of a new magnitude, and pressure from the United States to establish close cooperation between its European allies (Hurrell 1995: 47). The "experiment of 1951" proved successful and European leaders followed this path by signing the Rome Treaties in 1957. In the next decades, the European Communities were enlarged and integration was deepened. The decisive move was made in 1992 with the Treaty of Maastricht, which established the EU and paved the way to the introduction of a common currency. The ultimate goal of the founding fathers of European integration was a political union but the means used were economic. Small steps were to lead to an "ever closer union", to replacing the logic of national rivalries by a win–win cooperation (Rachman 2012: 43). Europe was understood as a community of values, which guaranties peace and prosperity (Hüther 2014).

Since the early 1950s, France and the FRG have fulfilled the role of the driving force behind European integration. This partnership, symbolized by the Éllyse Treaty of 1963, proved successful. For decades, the French–German partnership was very true – described by Stanley Hoffman as "symmetry of the asymmetrical". The FRG was economically strong but politically weak, while France had a relatively weak economy but was politically strong (Guérot and Leonard 2011: 4).

Despite the fact that monetary integration was not listed among the primary goals of the Rome Treaty, it was an objective that would periodically win stronger attention (Kondonassis and Malliaris 1994: 292-293). Although France and Germany had different economic expectations toward the common currency, after German unification in 1990 they shared the view about the political necessity to take this step. The euro should bind Germany more tightly into Europe. Because economic wisdom was subordinated to political goals, the roots of the euro crisis go back to the birth of the common currency. As David Marsh argues, the introduction of the euro was a multipurpose operation. "The new money would complete the European program of liberalized cross-border trade, promote the old dream of political unity, rival the dollar as an international reserve currency and — the most complicated objective — prevent an enlarged Germany's domination of Europe by bringing its currency under European control." (Marsh 2010).

France's primary objective was to end the double monetary dependence; first, from the US dollar, and second, toward local hegemony, the Deutsche Mark. Germany was concerned by the steady appreciation of the Deutsche Mark undermining the competitiveness of the German economy (Bibow 2013: 11).

Since 2004, thirteen countries have joined the EU. For the Central European countries, membership in the EU had been a priority of their foreign policy strategies since the early 1990s. Security, political stability and economic progress were the central objects for them (Baldwin 1995). Germany was the driving force behind the enlargement toward the east, and it had successfully convinced the other members of the EU to this project (Tulmets and Cadier 2014: 4).

Before 2009, the success of European integration was explained by its win–win logic. But this way of thinking seems to have disappeared since the outbreak of the euro crisis. The discussion in the first phase of the crisis concentrated around the responsibility for the crisis and the division of costs for rescuing the common currency. The discussion was dominated by zero-sum logic (Rachman 2012: 44-45). The introduction of the euro was a limited project, without a fiscal union or transfer of political sovereignty, with the Stability and Growth Pact (SGP) of 1997 being the only safeguard (Mody 2013: 11). Krugman concludes that the common currency was introduced well before Europe was ready for this step (Krugman 2010), and Eichengreen argues that the Greek crisis shows "that Europe is still only halfway toward creating a viable monetary union" (Eichengreen 2010).

IV. Political Implications of the Euro Crisis

The euro crisis emerged in late 2009 as the dramatic situation of the Greek public finance was made public. After few years of the crisis, its nature is better understood. Today, it is clear that the euro crisis is a consequence of three interlocking crises: the banking crisis, the sovereign debt crisis and the growth crisis (Shambaugh 2012). Thanks to its economic strength, and especially the positive current account balance, Germany has been seen as a key player in resolving the crisis (Cesaratto and Stirati 2010–11: 67).

Since the early days of the FRG, trade balance has been seen as a major indicator of its economic performance. In the Bretton Woods era, positive trade balance was achieved by suppressing consumption demand and wages. Holtfrerich has defined this policy as "monetary mercantilism" (Holtfrerich 2008; Holtfrerich 1998). After the break-up of the Bretton Woods system, Germany was unable to follow this strategy. Only with the introduction of the euro was Germany able to return to this policy. Cesaratto and Stirati call the German economic model "Ordomerkantilismus" (Cesaratto and Stirati 2010-11: 70-73).

As in late 2009 the dramatic situation of the Greek public finance was made public, Europe had no answer for this challenge. France pushed for emergency help, but Germany was strictly against. Only in May 2010 Greece finally got financial support. It was delivered by the Eurozone members and the IMF. After Greece, Ireland, Portugal, Spain, and Cyprus also asked for support. In 2010–2012, the Greek crisis presented the biggest challenge within the Eurozone. The issue of a possible exit of Greece from the Eurozone ("Grexit") was permanently discussed. All supported countries[3] were forced to accept harsh austerity measures and supervision from the so called "Troika" consisting of the European Commission, the ECB and the IMF. Pressure from the financial market spread also toward Belgium, Italy and then even France, putting the future of the

---

3 Spain is an exception.

Eurozone into question (Guillén 2012: 54). The situation has first calmed down in 2012 as ECB President Mario Draghi declared: "the ECB is ready to do whatever it takes to preserve the euro" (Draghi 2012). Despite economic reforms and the expansive monetary policy of the ECB, Greece still represents the biggest challenge for the EU. The future of the Greek membership in the Eurozone is questionable (Hishow 2015).

The euro crisis has been presented as a clash of two worlds. The first one is the world of the "virtuous north" and the second one is the world of fiscal "sinners" of the European south. Also the acronym commonly employed for European countries with the deepest economic troubles, i.e. PIGS or PIIGS (Portugal, Ireland, Greece, and Spain, or Portugal, Ireland, Italy, Greece, and Spain), reflects moral opprobrium and contempt (Rosenthal 2012: 53). German political elites belong to the main supporters of this explanation of the crisis (Joffe 2012).

Germany has been criticized by the European Commission, the United States and the IMF for a reluctant spending policy and keeping a too high current account surplus (Rogoff 2014). It refused all calls for a new "Marshall Plan for Europe" (Crafts 2012). Germany consistently refuses any action in the Keynesian sense. This behavior is backed by the success of the German economic model, based on ordoliberal principles. In the past, German experience with Keynesian policy has been short-lived and negative. In the late 1970s, the FRG participated in the globally coordinated macroeconomic stimulus. Its consequence was a short term economic boom followed by the growth of inflation. In the 1980s, the tight monetary policy together with pro-market reforms proved to be successful and effectively banned Keynesian concepts from the German economy discussion (Bibow 2013: 8-9).

Since the outbreak of the crisis, German politicians have seen Germany as an example of economic stability and are ready to export "stability culture" to other EU members. But Kundnani argues that the German understanding of stability is very narrow. The concentration on inflation does not produce stability in Europe. "In fact, in attempting to export its 'stability culture', Germany has in a broader sense created instability." He also criticizes the German economic policy as unsuitable for a country of its size, saying that "Germany pursues the economic policy of a small country rather than a hegemon" (Kundnani 2012a).

With the end of the Cold War, the role of military power in IR has diminished. Today, the international position of a state depends not on its military strength but on economic power. The French expectations toward the euro have failed. The biggest beneficiary of the common currency is Germany, not France. It is a popular view among French officials, that France loses its economic position and Germany strengthened its position (Nonnenmacher 2013). The current crisis widens the economic gap between both countries, threatening the balance of power between them and deeming France to the role of a "'junior partner". This development threatens the post-WWII relations between them, which were based on the lack of domination (Bibow 2013: 2-3).

According to the McKinsey-Study, Germany is the greatest beneficiary of the common market, the single currency and the "one size fits all" policy of the ECB. As the study shows, Austria, Germany, Finland, and the Netherlands are the countries for which the currency union is the most beneficial (benefits as a percent of the GDP). The biggest beneficiary in absolute numbers is Germany. Only in 2010, the common currency brought it benefits of around 165 billion euro out of the total 330 billion euro for the EMU-17.[4] That made 6.6% of the German GDP. The estimated benefit for the EMU-17 was 3.6% of the GDP. At the same time, the benefits of the introduction of the euro for Italy were 48 billion euro and for France 14 billion euro (McKinsey 2012: 9).

Germany has played a key role in constructing the support programs for the countries of the Eurozone hit by the crisis. They were led by the idea of "structural reforms" and public savings. But they have been criticized and their effectiveness has been questioned. Germany practically imposed an economic model and economic strategy that was labeled the "Berlin consensus" (Cassen 2010: 18-19). There were questions about whether the introduction of the German economic model in other European countries was the right answer to their economic troubles (Dullien and Guérot 2012). The German government was also able to persuade all Eurozone members to participate in rescue packages. Only Slovakia was able to resist in 2010 the pressure and did not participate in the first "Greek Loan Facility" (European Commission 2014).

As Eichengreen wrote, "Germany has benefitted enormously from the creating of euro. It should repay the favor" (Eichengreen 2010). But Germany has refused such proposals. In a budgetary debate of 2014, the Ger-

---

4 "This number is to be interpreted as the additional GDP compared with a growth path in a scenario without the introduction of the euro." (McKinsey 2012: 9).

man finance minister argued that the current austerity policy was right (Schäuble 2014).

V. Toward Hegemony in the EU?

The euro crisis has caused deep changes within the EU. As Leonard, Zielonka and Walton suggest, some countries that used to be seen as the "core" of Europe are moving towards the "periphery" and Germany is growing to the role of "a new decision-making centre". France and Germany celebrate their partnership and try to revive it. However, these efforts are unsuccessful in overcoming the growing differences between them. The deep economic crisis has clear political implications. The euro crisis leads to a new geography of the EU (Leonard et al. 2013: 5-6).

Despite the fact that the terms "core" and "periphery" are broadly used in the discussions about the euro crisis, they were never strictly defined. Their use is based on geographical conditions, changing economic situation or political circumstances. In a chapter published in 2008, Fratzscher and Stracca used the division into "core" and "periphery" based on geographical circumstances. Taking the initial twelve Eurozone members, they called Austria, Belgium, France, Germany, Luxembourg, and the Netherlands the "core". Finland, Greece, Ireland, Italy, Portugal and Spain were called the "periphery" (Fratzscher and Stracca 2008: 6). This division has no emotional dimension. With the outbreak of the crisis, however, the most affected Eurozone members were labeled as the "periphery". With the fast recovery in Ireland, the situation has changed once again. Only South European countries have remained the "periphery", making this term a euphemism for the "South" (Economist 2010). Another aspect of this issue was suggested by Roubini. He indicated that some "core" countries, like France or Belgium, are not economically as strong as Germany, and he called them a "soft core" (Boyle 2012). The same problem is discussed by Cesaratto and Stirati, who describe France and Italy as countries in the middle, between the "core" and the "periphery" (Cesaratto and Stirati 2010-11: 59).

The meaning of the terms "periphery" and "core" has evolved in the last decade. Today, it is used as a shorthand term to distinguish between countries that are economically successful and those that are unsuccessful within the Eurozone. Geographical circumstances play a secondary role.

During the euro crisis, the discussion concentrated on economic issues. But for decades the concepts of "core" and "periphery" were associated with the issue of different levels of political integration in the EU. Such way of thinking has not been abandoned. The term "two-speed Europe" was also proposed by President Sarkozy on November 8th, 2011. He suggested that the integration within the Eurozone should be strengthened and within the EU weakened (Economist 2011). In 2014, Minister Schäuble proposed together with Karl Lamers focusing further development of the European project on the Eurozone, which he labeled the "core". This proposal refers to their proposal from 1994 titled "Reflections on European policy". They propose to "focus on Europe's 'core' – in every sense of the word" and suggest that this can help to keep the UK within the EU (Lamers and Schäuble 2014).

Today, the question of being in the "core" or in the "periphery" of European integration seems for the first time not a question of a sovereign choice of a single country but of power politics based on economic strength. Creditors decisively influence the institutional evolution of the EU, they are able to give narration to the current discussions and dictate the solutions to the debtors (Leonard et al. 2013: 10).

Although in the early 21st century Germany was labeled as "the sick man of the euro" (Economist 1999), later it grew to an "economic superstar" (Dustmann et al. 2014). Germany has won its "unipolar moment" within the currency union (Guérot and Leonard 2011: 1) and achieved the status of the "European Superpower" (El-Erian 2014: 36). Despite this surge of power, Germany stays faithful to the traditionally close relations with France. In 2010-2014, they achieved compromises about the direction of the reform of the EU. The reviving of the French-German partnership took place in Deauville, when the German position as the anchor economy of the EU surged and the French economy's position decreased (Schild 2013: 39). The close coordination between Chancellor Merkel and President Sarkozy led to the emergence of the term "Merkozy" (Schäfers et al. 2011). But it may be misleading. As the former Italian prime minister and President of the European Commission Romano Prodi explained on February 9th, 2011: "It used to be that France was the political driver and Germany the economic one [...]. Now it is the lady that decides and Sarkozy that holds a press conference to explain her decisions" (Guérot and Leonard 2011: 4). This close alignment of France on Germany was criticized by Francois Hollande, at that time a presidential candidate. He called for a rebalancing of the French-German relations. But as president, he has not been able to change the French politics. Three reasons for this could be named. First, the French economy is weak. France lost its AAA rating by Standard and Poor's and Moody's. In consequence, France lost its political role. Second, South European countries do not follow France automatically. Third, Germany has veto power in every issue that is demanded by the French politics. To conclude, the weakness of the French economy is the source of the imbalance in the French-German partnership. That is why Hollande does not intend to build any opposition toward Germany. He tried to strengthen the French position by going beyond the French–German bilateralism and intensifying the relations between Italy and France. But the idea of playing a middle role between the European "North" and the "South" was short-lived (Schild 2013: 41-42). This development has shown French politicians that rebalancing of the French-German relations has to start through a reform of the French economy. Hopes that France could avoid such reforms proved unrealistic (Bibow 2013: 20). Despite this failed attempt, an anti-German alliance with the EU scares German politicians (Brozus 2013).

The German attitude toward the euro crisis has evolved over time. Germany was broadly accused in 2010 and 2011 of being reactive and lacking the necessary vision. But the German approach toward the crisis was accommodated to the worsening financial situation in 2012 (Guérot 2012). During the European summit in June 2012, Chancellor Merkel accepted the right of the ESM to bail out directly troubled Eurozone banks. Many commentators in Germany have seen this as a defeat. The others wanted to see in this step a new phase of the German politics toward the euro crisis (Kundnani 2012b). Chancellor Merkel has argued since 2010 that for Germany, the euro is much more than only a currency and that Germany feels a responsibility to save the euro. She argued "failed Euro, then failed Europe" (Merkel 2010: 4126). She admitted that no other country of the EU profited as much from the euro as Germany (Merkel 2011: 11252).

The German promotion of the austerity policy is supported only by a small group of economically successful countries like the Netherlands, Finland or Austria. But their role is passive and restricted to criticizing Germany for its weakness toward the countries hit by the crisis (Leonard et al. 2013: 13). Germany won also some support from countries that have joined the EU in 2004, e.g. Poland. In his address delivered in 2011 in Berlin, Polish Foreign Minister Sikorski argued: "I fear German power less than German inaction" (Sikorski 2011).

After the outbreak of the crisis, institutional reforms were discussed. One of them was a reform of the Lisbon Treaty. As it proved impossible, however, another way to reform the EU had to be found. Federalists have called for "more Europe"; fiscal and political sovereignty should be transferred to the Community level and "United States of Europe" should be build. But even they have to agree, that the general mood in Europe has to change first, and the goal of a "more perfect union" won superiority over the idea of an "ever closer union" (Mody 2013: 5-6). In line with Chancellor Merkel's speech in Bruges in 2010, an intergovernmental approach was chosen. It reflects the dissatisfaction of many European governments with the European institutions. Most governments prefer intergovernmental cooperation. The second characteristic is the growing integration within the Eurozone. Despite the fact that Germany and many other countries prefer to avoid division within the EU, integration within the Eurozone is deepening (Buras 2013). The French-German position toward the direction of European integration was presented in a joint chapter of May 30th, 2013, which presented the plan to reform the Eurozone. Cooperation within the Euro group should be depended and it should receive a full-time president (France and Germany 2013).

Today, EU members that do not belong to the Eurozone may be divided in two groups: on the one hand, there is the Czech Republic and the United Kingdom, wishing to "bring some powers back" from Brussels, and on the other hand, there are pro-integrationist countries, worrying that deepening economic integration within the Eurozone can strengthen division in the EU into Eurozone members and non-euro countries (Leonard et al. 2013: 12). Despite this danger, they are not willing to join the Eurozone immediately. Poland is a good example of the evolution of their position. Only few years ago, Polish Prime Minister Tusk was an enthusiast of the common currency. Today, the Polish government is much more cautious in its declarations (Orenstein 2014).

The financial crisis hit hard not only the Western European countries but also countries that had joined the EU in 2004 and 2007. Despite differences in the economic performance between the individual countries of the region, most of them have rebuild after the first wave of the crisis and have kept positive growth rates (IMF 2013). In consequence, they were able to continue the catching up process (Table 1). Despite substantial divergence in GDP levels between the old and the new member states, the eastern part of the EU is much more economically dynamic. Putting Cyprus and Malta aside as special cases, in 2004 only the Czech Republic and Slovenia had a higher GDP per capita in PPS than the poorest old member state – Portugal. In 2013, it was also Slovakia. Even more significantly, the three Baltic States (Estonia, Latvia and Lithuania), Poland and Hungary have almost closed the gap and Romania and Bulgaria have achieved significant economic progress as well.

Table 1. GDP per capita in PPS. Index (EU28 = 100). Data from June 1st, 2014.

country/ time	2004	2007	2013	country/ time	2004	2007	2013
Belgium	121	116	119	Bulgaria	35	40	47
Denmark	126	122	125	Czech Republic	78	83	80
Germany	116	115	124	Cyprus	91	94	86
Ireland	143	146	126	Croatia	58	62	61
Greece	94	90	75	Estonia	57	70	72
Spain	101	105	95	Latvia	47	57	67
France	110	108	108	Lithuania	52	62	74
Italy	107	104	98	Hungary	63	61	67
Luxemburg	253	274	264	Malta	80	78	87
Netherlands	129	132	127	Poland	51	54	68
Austria	128	124	129	Romania	35	43	54
Portugal	77	79	75	Slovenia	87	88	83
Finland	116	117	112	Slovakia	57	68	76
Sweden	127	125	127				
United Kingdom	125	118	106				

Source: Eurostat, http://epp.eurostat.ec.europa.eu/tgm/table.do?tab=table&init=1&plug in=1&language=en&pcode=tec00114

Zsolt Darvas predicts that the gap between the GDP per capita of the South European countries (Greece, Italy, Portugal, and Spain) and the Central European countries (the Czech Republic, Hungary, Poland, Slovakia, and Slovenia) may be closed by 2018. Also, the distance to other Western European countries will be reduced (Darvas 2012: 2).

Far reaching changes in the German foreign policy have been observed since German unification in 1990. The transformation process may be divided into three periods. The first one took place from 1990 to 1994 and may be called the "German period". The second period from 1995 till 2004 may be called a "European Period", while the third is the "globalizing period". The last one is characterized not only by intensification of relations with countries outside the Euro-Atlantic world (Mayer 2010: 278) but also by a changing policy toward the EU. As Guerot and Leonhard have indicated, the French–German partnership gained a new nature and is increasingly unbalanced in favor of Germany. The German government reduced its support for the European Commission and for the small countries in the EU. Germany expects that its economic engagement for the EU will be rewarded with much stronger political influence. Chancellor Merkel, like her predecessor, fell free to defend the German national interest without giving it a "European label" (Guerot and Leonhard 2011: 4-5). The euro crisis provoked a discussion about the future of the EU in Germany. Some have called for "more Europe", but they are labeled as "Euro-romanticists". The second camp is called "Euro-pragmatists". Its members do not refuse the EU or the euro, but they are against any steps that could mean additional costs for Germany (Guérot 2012: 6).

Between 2010 and 2012, the German government showed a lack of readiness to compromise. It was focusing instead on exporting the German economic model (Kausch 2011: 46), with the key example of the Treaty on Stability, Coordination and Governance in the Economic and Monetary Union (TSCG). With this treaty, Germany has successfully imposed its economic approach on its European partners (Dullien and Guérot 2012: 1-2). This foreign policy strategy has not only caused worries about the growth of a "German Europe", but also initiated a change in the assessment of the role of the German economy in Europe. It has moved from the previous admiration towards criticism of the German "export obsession" (Kausch 2011: 50). The German pressure caused also government changes in periphery countries such as Greece and Italy, paving the way to accusations that Germany is conducting a colonial-style policy (Guillén 2012: 61).

After the outbreak of the crisis, the self-confident German foreign policy has started raising questions about the future of Germany in Europe. The question of "German Europe" or a "European Germany" came back as a topic of discussion. Based on the belief in the inevitability of the adoption of the German economic model by "peripheral" countries, an additional question was asked: "A German Europe or disintegration?" (Kundnani 2012b).

VI. Conclusions

The euro crisis shows that the process of European integration has not changed the logic of state activity in Europe. The behavior of EU members is still based on national interest and the sense of community reaches only as far as national interests.

During the crisis, Germany grew to the position of the European hegemon. But it does not pretend to fulfill this role as prescribed by Kindleberger. Germany has achieved its current economic position thanks to consistent export-led economic policy. Despite the fact that this model is criticized as inappropriate for an "economic superpower", the German government has no intention to change it. Quite the opposite: with the deep crisis in the demand-orientated economies, it believes even stronger that its economic policy is the right one and should be implemented all over Europe. That is the reason why Germany is a lonely hegemon.

The call for European French–German hegemony in the sense of Kindleberger's theory made by Schäuble in 2010 has to be seen as purely rhetorical. After 2010, Germany has not pretended to fulfill this role. It is ready to invest in the European project, but it demands the same from the other participants. No free riding at German expense should be allowed.

Germany, together with a group of small but economically successful countries, builds a European "core". This development reflects the growing role of economic power in international relations. Other countries are pushed out of the main decision making process. The same concerns the French–German duo. The weakening France has to follow the German strategy to keep its status and the rest of its influence. The economic crisis in the European peripheries separates this region from the European decision-making center. At the same time, the new member states strengthen their position. They are an economically dynamic group that successfully closes the gap to the old member countries and gains access to the European decision-making center.

The euro crisis was an impulse to deepen European integration. It has two characteristics. First, it has an intergovernmental character. Second, there is a clear trend toward stronger integration within the Eurozone.

The Eurozone crisis has deep economic and political consequences for the EU and its political geography. Despite Schäuble's declaration, Germany is not a "benevolent hegemon". The reality of the EU is determined by two factors. The first one is structural, a trend toward strong integration within the Eurozone. The second one is economic development. In consequence, there is a new balance of power with an economically strong "core", a depressed "periphery" and economically dynamic but still much poorer new members. The sustainability of this division will be in the first line the consequence of the outcome of economic reforms within single countries but also of the future politics of the European lonely hegemon.

Bibliography

Baldwin, R.: The Eastern Enlargement of the European Union. European Economic Review, 1995 39, pp. 474-481.

Beck, U.: Germany Has Created An Accidental Empire. Social Europe Journal, 2013, available at: <http://www.socialeurope.eu/2013/03/germany-has-created-an-acciden tal-empire/>.

Bibow, J.: On the Franco-German Euro Contradiction and Ultimate Euro Battleground. Levy Economics Institute of Bard College Working Paper No. 762, New York, 2013.

Boyle, C.: Europe's Core Begins to Look Like the Periphery. CNBC, 2012, available at: <http://www.cnbc.com/id/48646808>.

Brozus, L.: Machtverschiebungen in der EU: wie Deutschland ein »guter Hegemon« bleibt. Stiftung Wissenschaft und Politik, 2013, available at: <http://www.sw p-berlin.org/de/publikationen/kurz-gesagt/machtverschiebungen-in-der-eu-wie-deut schland-ein-guter-hegemon-bleibt.html>.

Buras, P.: The EU's Silent Revolution. ECFR 2013.

Cassen, B.: Un "consensus de Berlin" imposé à l'Europe. Le Monde diplomatique, 2010 57 (681), pp. 18-19.

Cesaratto, S./ Stirati, A.: Germany and the European and Global Crises. International Journal of Political Economy, 2010-11 39(4), pp. 56-86.

Crafts, N.: Saving the Eurozone: Is a 'Real' Marshall Plan the Answer? The CAGE-Chatham House Series, 2012.

Darvas, Z.: The Euro Crisis: Ten Roots, but Fewer Solutions. Bruegel Policy Contribution, 2012.

Destradi, S.: Regional Powers and their Strategies: Empire, Hegemony, and Leadership. Review of International Studies, 2010 36(4), pp. 903-930.

Deubner, C.: Währungsunion ohne Politische Union? SWP-Studie, 2001.

Draghi, M.: Speech by Mario Draghi, President of the European Central Bank at the Global Investment Conference in London, ECB 2012, Available at: <https://www.e cb.europa.eu/press/key/date/2012/html/sp120726.en.html>.

Dullien, S./ Guérot, U.: The Long Shadow of Ordoliberalism: Germany's Approach to the Euro Crisis. ECFR, 2012.

Dustmann C./ Fitzenberger, B./ Schönberg, U./ Spitz-Oener, A.: From Sick Man of Europe to Economic Superstar: Germany's Resurgent Economy. Journal of Economic Perspectives, 2014 28(1), pp. 167-188.

The Economist: The Sick Man of the Euro. June 5, 1999, p. 21.

The Economist: The Myth of the Periphery. Forget Core against Periphery in Europe: The True Divide is North against South. March 27, 2010, p. 42.

The Economist: The Future of the EU. Two-Speed Europe, or Two Europes? November 10, 2011, available at: <http://www.economist.com/blogs/charlemagne/2011/11/future-eu>.

Eichengreen, B.: Europe's Trojan Horse. Project Syndicate 2010, available at: <www.project-syndicate.org/commentary/eichengreen14/English/>.

El-Erian, M.: Deutschland ist die Supermacht. Handelsblatt 26/27/28.9.2014, pp. 36-37.

European Commission: Financial Assistance to Greece. 2014, available at: <http://ec.europa.eu/economy_finance/assistance_eu_ms/greek_loan_facility/index_en.htm>.

European Dialogue: How Central Europe dealt with the global crisis. 2012, available at: <http://www.eurodialogue.eu/How-Central-Europe-dealt-with-the-global-crisis>.

Flemes, D./ Nolte, D.: Introduction. In: Flemes, D. ed. Regional Leadership in the Global System. Ideas, Interests and Strategies of Regional Powers. Farnham, Burlington: Ashgate, 2010, pp. 1-14.

Fratzscher, M./ Stracca, L.: The Political Economy under Monetary Union: Has the Euro Made a Difference? ECB Working Paper Series, 2008.

France and Germany: France and Germany – Together for a Stronger Europe of Stability and Growth. Pressemitteilung Nummer 187/13, 2013.

Guérot, U.: The Euro Debate in Germany: Towards Political Union? ECFR, 2012.

Guérot U./ Klau T.: After Merkozy: How France and Germany can Make Europe Work. ECFR, 2012.

Guérot, U./ Leonard, M.: The New German Question: How Europe can get the Germany It Needs. ECFR, 2011.

Guillén, A.: Europe: The Crisis Within a Crisis. International Journal of Political Economy, 2012 41(3), pp. 41-68.

Hishow, O. N.: Finanzkollaps in Griechenland: Reformen oder Dauer-Bailout? SWP-Aktuell, 2015.

Holtfrerich, C.-L.: Geldpolitik bei festen Wechselkursen (1948-1970). In: Deutsche Bundesbank ed. Fünfzig Jahre Deutsche Mark. Notenbank und Währung in Deutschland seit 1948, München, 1999, pp. 347-438.

Holtfrerich, C.-L.: Monetary Policy in Germany since 1948: National Tradition, International Best Practice or Ideology? In: Touffut, J.-P. eds. Central Banks as Economic Institutions, Cheltenham: Edward Elgar, 2008, pp. 22-51.

Hurrell, A.: Regionalism in Theoretical Perspective. In: Fawcett L./ Hurrell A. eds. Regionalism in World Politics. Regional Organization and International Order. Oxford: Oxford University Press, 1995, pp. 37-73.

Hüther, M.: Hohe Erwartungen geweckt. Handelsblatt, September 2014, 29/30/31, p. 72.

IMF: Central, Eastern, and Southeastern Europe, Regional Economic Issues. 2013.

Joffe J.: I come to praise Angela Merkel, not to bury her, Financial Times, June 19, 2012, available at: <http://www.ft.com/intl/cms/s/0/a438a8a6-b8ab-11e1-a2d6-001 44feabdc0.html#axzz24BvZPu>.

Kausch, K.: A Geo-Economic Germany? In: Martiningui, A./ Youngs, R. eds. Challenges for European Foreign Policy in 2012. What kind of Geo-Economic Europe? Madrid: FRIDE, 2011, pp. 45-52.

Kindleberger, C.: The World in Depression. Harmondsworth: Penguin Press, 1973.

Kondonassis, A. J./ Malliaris A. G.: Toward Monetary Union of the European Community: History and Experiences of the European Monetary System. American Journal of Economics and Sociology, 1994 53(3), pp. 291-301.

Krasner, S. D.: State Power and the Structure of International Trade. World Politics, 1976 28(3), pp. 317-347.

Krugman, P.: The Making of a Euromess. New York Times, February 15, 2010, available at: <www.nytimes.com/2010/02/15/opinion/15krugman.html>.

Kundnani, H.: What Hegemon? Germany's Self-Centeredness and Short-Term Thinking Disqualify it as a Hegemon. DGAP, 2012, available at: <https://ip-journal.dgap.org/en/article/21241/print>.

Kundnani, H.: 'Political Union': A German Europe or Disintegration? ECFR, 2012, available at: <http://www.ecfr.eu/content/entry/commentary_political_union_a_ger man_europe_or_disintegration>.

Mody, A.: A Schuman Compact for the Euro Area. Bruegel Essay and Lecture Series, 2013.

Lake, D. A.: Leadership, Hegemony, and the International Economy: Naked Emperor or Tattered Monarch with Potential? International Studies Quarterly, 1993 37(4), pp. 459-489

Lamers, K./ Schäuble, W.: More Integration is Still the Right Goal for Europe. Financial Times, August 31, 2014, available at: <http://www.ft.com/cms/s/0/5565f134-2d 48-11e4-8105-00144feabdc0.html>.

Leonard, M./ Zielonka, J./ Walton, N.: Introduction. In: Walton, N./ Zielonka, J. eds. The New Political Geography of Europe. London: ECFR, 2013. pp. 5-14.

Lübkemeier, E.: Führung ist wie Liebe. Warum Mit-Führung in Europa notwendig ist und wer sie leisten kann. SWP-Studien, 2007.

Marsh, D.: The Euro's Lost Promise. The New York Times, May 18, 2010, available at: <http://www.nytimes.com/2010/05/18/opinion/18marsh.html?pagewanted=all& _r=0>.

Mayer, H.: France, Germany, UK: Responses of Traditional to Rising Regional Powers. In: Flemes, D. eds. Regional Leadership in the Global System. Ideas, Interests and Strategies of Regional Powers, Farnham, Burlington: Ashgate, 2010, pp. 273-292.

Merkel, A.: Abgabe einer Regierungserklärung durch die Bundeskanzlerin: zu den Maßnahmen zur Stabilisierung des Euro. Deutscher Bundestag, Stenografischer Bericht, Plenarprotokoll 17/42, 2010.

Merkel, A.: Abgabe einer Regierungserklärung durch die Bundeskanzlerin: zum Europäischen Rat am 24./25. März 2011 in Brüssel. Deutscher Bundestag, Stenografischer Bericht, Plenarprotokoll 17/99, 2011.

Mussler, W./ Busse, N./ Sattar, M.: Merkel kann Stimmrechtsentzug nicht durchsetzen. FAZ, 29. Oktober 2010, pp. 1-2.

Nonnenmacher, G.: Das Deutsch-französische Dilemma. FAZ, 4. Juli 2013, p. 1.

Orenstein, M.: Six Markets to Watch: Poland. Foreign Affairs, 2014 93(1), pp. 23-27.

Pedersen, T.: Cooperative Hegemony: Power, Ideas and Institutions in Regional Integration. Review of International Studies, 2002 28(4), pp. 677-696.

Rachman, G.: Europe's Zero-Sum Dilemma. The National Interest, 2012 May/June, pp. 43-48.

Rogoff, K.: Germany's Current Account Surplus is a Wider Issue than it First Appears. The Guardian, April 10, 2014, available at: <http://www.theguardian.com/business/2014/apr/10/germany-current-account-surplus-wider-issue>.

Rosenthal, J.: Germany and the Euro Crisis: Is the Powerhouse Really So Pure? World Politics, 2012 5/6, available at: <http://www.worldaffairsjournal.org/article/german y-and-euro-crisis-powerhouse-really-so-pure>.

Schäuble, W.: Rede des Bundesministers der Finanzen Dr. Wolfgang Schäuble an der Université Paris-Sorbonne, 2010, available at: <http://www.bundesfinanzministeriu m.de/Content/DE/Reden/2010/2010-11-02-sorbonne.html?view=renderPrint>.

Schäuble, W.: Rede des Bundesministers der Finanzen, Dr. Wolfgang Schäuble, zum Haushaltsgesetz 2014 vor dem Deutschen Bundestag am 8. April 2014 in Berlin, available at: <http://www.bundesregierung.de/Content/DE/Bulletin/2014/04/40-1-b mf-bt.html>.

Schäfers, M./ Schubert, C./ Mussler, W.: Berlin und Paris übernehmen die Führung. FAZ, 3. Dezember 2011, p. 13.

Schild, J.: Leadership in Hard Times. Germany, France, and the Management of the Eurozone Crisis. German Politics and Society, 2013 31(1), pp. 24-47.

Shambaugh, J. C.: The Euro's Three Crises, Brookings Papers on Economic Activity. 2012 Spring, pp. 157-211.

Sikorski, R.: Polish Foreign Minister Radosław Sikorski Reminds Berlin of its Special Responsibility in Overcoming the European Debt Crisis. DGAP, 2011, available at: <https://dgap.org/en/node/20055>.

Snidal, D.: The Limits of Hegemonic Stability Theory. International Organization, 1985 39(4), pp. 579-614.

Tulmets, E./ Cadier, D.: French Policies toward Central Eastern Europe: Not a Foreign Policy Priority but a Real Presence. DGAPanalyse, 2014.

Webb, M. C./ Krasner, S. D.: Hegemonic Stability Theory: An Empirical Assessment. Review of International Studies, 1989 15(2), pp. 183-198.

D. Law

Eighth chapter
The Overburdening of European Law through Economic and
Monetary Union

*Christian Joerges (Hertie School of Governance, Berlin, and Centre of
European Law and Politics, University of Bremen)*

I. Introductory Remarks

The times are long gone in which lawyers have dominated the European
agenda in both integration politics and in academic debates. Since the
1980s political science gained a dominating role, accompanied with some
hesitation by sociology and other neighbouring disciplines. By now, in the
decade of crisis, economists are occupying the driver seat. What does all
this mean for the law and its administration? The law remains visible. We
are witnessing intense debates on the transformation of European rule,
Europe's *Verfassungswirklichkeit* and the apparent or real tensions
between its actual operation and European commitments to democracy
and the rule of law. Nothing less is at issue in the proceedings on the OMT
programme of the European Central Bank (ECB) (BVerfGE 2014; the
Advocate General (AG) has delivered his Opinion on 14 January 2015
(Cruz Villalòn 2015) and the Court of Justice of the European Union
(CJEU) handed down its Judgment on 16 June 2015 (CJEU 2015)). The
legacy of law in the integration process has retained its strength – and has
at the same time become more precarious than ever. An understanding of
that legacy is indispensable both for the deciphering of the form in which
monetary union was institutionalized and the understanding of widely
shared views about the proper responses to its failures. There is hence
every reason to take the law seriously, albeit not in the among the legal
community widespread uncritical praise, but instead through a re-configu-
ration of the law-politics relationship in which law can regain a legitimacy
mediating function. This is the objective of the following five sections.
The first will be a very brief critical reconstruction of the so-called 'integration through law' project. An alternative re-conceptualisation of European law is possible, section III will submit and sketch out the idea of conflicts-law constitutionalism which juxtaposes integration through unifor-

mity with the *unitas in pluralitate* vision of the ill-fated Draft Constitutional Treaty.[1] This is the framework within which the Monetary Union as it was established by the Maastricht Treaty of 1993 and complemented by the Stability and Growth Pact (SGP) in 1997[2] will be analysed in section IV. What then follows in section V are comments on Europe's crisis management and crisis 'law'. The epilogue (section VI) is about the need to renew the legitimacy of the integration project through a reconfiguration of the law-politics relationship

II. The Disintegrative Effects of Economic Integration through Law

What else than law was conceivable as the distinctive medium that kept the Community, which the Treaty of Rome had established, together? The story of the early jurisprudence of the European Court of Justice (ECJ), which transformed the articles of the Treaty, in the understanding of its signatories an agreement governed by international law, into a Constitutional Charter (see famously Weiler 1991: 1412), is well known, and not just to lawyers. So is the characterisation of the Community by Walter Hallstein, the first President of the Commission as '*Schöpfung des Rechts, Rechtsquelle, und Rechtsordnung*' (Hallstein 1979: 3). 'Integration through law', was to become the distinctive trademark of the European project and during its most dynamic and promising phase on the road to Maastricht, law was prominently conceptualised as the 'agent and the object of integration' (Dehousse and Weiler 1990: 243).

How can we explain this success story? The assignment of both instrumental functions and legitimating potentials to law was certainly in line with the deliberate design of European integration as an economic project. That affinity was strengthened through the so-called constitutionalisation of the EEC Treaty by the early jurisprudence of the ECJ, now CJEU. In particular the conceptualisation of the economic freedoms as basic rights which Europe's market citizens could invoke against their nation states was in line with that understanding. It seemed after the recognition of

---

1 "The motto of the Union shall be: 'United in diversity', thusly Article 1-8 of the 'Treaty establishing a constitution for Europe'", OJ C 310/16.12.2004, 1.
2 "Council Regulation (EC) 1467/97: On speeding up and clarifying the implementation of the excessive deficit procedure", OJ L 209, 2.8.1997, 1.

these principles now simply logical to assign a constitutional status to the core institutions of the Europeanising market economy.

One aspect and a crucially problematical implication of the integration-through-law agenda was the establishment of a steadily deepening dilemma, namely, the unresolvable tensions between the juridification of European integration according to the 'logic of the market', on the one hand, and the primacy of democratic legitimacy, on the other (see recently Grimm 2015). We are currently witnessing a dramatic intensification of these tensions. But they are not new and not a late by-product of the financial crisis. They originated in the foundational period. Their impact and importance was still marginal. But they already received, in particular in Germany, a highly critical attention (Davies 2007: 68).

The tension between democratic legitimacy as it was institutionalised in the member states of the EC, on the one hand, and the establishment of an order of supranational validity, on the other, is the most problematical legacy of the integration project. But we should substantiate some of its dimensions further. One defect is methodological. The famous formula characterising law as the 'object and the agent of integration' was coined at the height of the American law and society movement which promoted the sociological study of law and all sorts of interdisciplinary 'law-and...' explorations. This revival of legal realism by the American law and society movement has attracted much attention, not least in the 'law-in-context' approach which was very much *en vogue* at the law department of the European University Institute. 'Integration through law', however, was an agenda which disregarded the embeddedness of law in all sorts of social norms thoroughly. The attractiveness of 'integration through law' in European studies is, nonetheless, understandable. Its methodological solipsism, doctrinal rigidity and its formalism enabled transnational interactions and acting; it fostered the emergence of a European community of lawyers and legal scholarship long before social scientists started to take Europe seriously (Schepel and Wesseling 1997).

The primacy of law and its methodological poverty came at a high price, however. 'Progress' in European integration was equated with the accomplishment of ever more legal uniformity, while legal diversity served to provide conclusive reasons for more legal harmonisation. The deficiencies of the integration-through-law fantasy and ideology are precisely the fatal flaws of which Giandomenico Majone (2014) and Fritz Scharpf (2010) keep reminding us: Integration through law rests upon an economically, socially and politically unsustainable 'one-size-fits-all' assumption and proceeds accordingly. In integration-through-law more uniformity figures as a goal itself, as Europe's *finalité*; this could go unnoticed for a good while but was bound to generate disintegrative effects (Joerges 1994: 32) which were to become ever more burdensome with the deepening of Europe's socio-economic diversity.

III. The Alternative of Conflicts-Law Constitutionalism

Legal scholarship is by no means unique with its dedication to harmony and its disregard of conflicts. The economic theory of integration has been eager to underline the beneficial effects of open borders and free trade. Sociology simply eschewed integration studies – with few notable exceptions (Bach 2015; Dahrendorf 2008; on the latter see Everson and Joerges 2012: 650). Neo-functionalism, which dominated political integration theory for so long, sought to identify non-political mechanisms moving integration ahead. Revisions of these orientations have begun prior to the crisis. But the crisis had strong accelerating effects. This is clearly visible in the legal discussion of Europe's responses to the crisis (Dani 2009, 2012; Chalmers 2012; Dawson and De Witte 2013) and in sociological analyses of societal dynamics (Preunkert and Vrobuda 2015). In political science, we are witnessing a turn to the political economy and in economics the emergence of the 'conflict theoretical perspective' on the crisis (Krieger 2015). The move from harmonisation to conflict and contestation seems overdue and is so multifaceted that I have to refrain from any mapping exercise even within my own discipline. What I will do instead in this section is to defend my conflicts-law approach on which I have been working for quite some time (Joerges et al. 2005).

To start with a terminological explanation: 'Conflict of laws' is the Anglo-Saxon *pendant* to the continental 'private international law'. These disciplines are since centuries engaged in the search for the applicable law in cases (legal constellations) with contacts to more than one jurisdiction. The art of selecting the proper law is a fascinating intellectual exercise. It is also one which has become ever more difficult in a world with a multitude of heterogeneous authorities exercising influence and claiming respect as progressive contemporary scholarship realises (see Muir Watt and Fernàndez Arroyo 2014). The European Union provides the most obvious example conceivable. The search for the applicable law in a multi-level system of governance in which the highest lawyer is entrusted with limited powers does not make sense as a comprehensive model of governance. This is why the conflicts-law approach must not be equated with the traditions which its name recalls. The choice of that notion is to signal that legal differences mirror varieties of socio-economic orders, different policy priorities – and governmental interests.

With that message the conflicts-law approach departs quite radically from the integration-through-law agenda which the previous section has reconstructed. What the approach shares with that legacy is the ambition of providing a framework within which European rule can be limited and legitimated. That framework, however, is an alternative to the orthodoxy of European law in essential respects. The conflicts-law approach refrains from conceptualising and portraying European law as an ever growing and more comprehensive body of rules and principles of progressively richer normative qualities. What European law must learn instead after enlargement and in view of its deepening socioeconomic heterogeneity is to live with the varieties of its capitalism. It has to take the fortunate motto presented in Article I-8 of the otherwise unfortunate 2003 Draft Constitutional Treaty seriously. 'United in Diversity' should be understood as Europe's true vocation, and – this is the jurisprudential gist of the approach – its vocation can be realised through a new type of conflicts law understood as Europe's constitutional form. While this proposition has its technical complexities, its core analytical assumptions, sociological premises and normative messages can be simply restated.

To start with the sociological premises: The member states of the EU are no longer autonomous. They are in many ways interdependent, and hence, dependent upon cooperation. This cooperation, however, is unlikely to lead to the establishment of a strong federal entity in the foreseeable future. In view of the histories of European democracies and their uneven potential and willingness to pursue the same objectives of distributional justice, respond consistently to economic and financial instabilities, and cope uniformly with environmental challenges, it is simply unlikely that Europeans will converge in their political perspectives, that the institutional varieties of European forms of capitalism and economic cultures will disappear, or that, considering the enormous complexity of their social systems and the diversity of their entitlements, they will institutionalise a uniform pan-European welfare system (Manow 2015, ch. 7; *contra* Habermas 2014). These challenges are of such dimensions that the sustainability of the whole European project seems to depend upon the construction and institutionalisation of a 'third way' between or beyond the defence of the nation state, on the one hand, and federalist ambitions, on the other. The varieties of capitalism studies as they are by now substantiated in analyses of the European crisis (Iversen and Soskice 2013; Hall 2014), which document a considerable non-convergence and resistance of the social fabric of Europe's economies are of both sociological and normative significance in the present context. They document the resistance of the institutional configuration and the European economies against command-and-control changes; they furthermore militate against the assumption that the destruction of such configuration would generate some superior alternative.

The conflicts-law approach respects diversity not merely on functional grounds. It understands this respect as a democratic commandment. This commandment is derived from a dilemma of democratic will-formation in nation states. Increasingly, nation states which define themselves as constitutional democracies are unable to guarantee the inclusion of all those who are impacted by their policies within their internal decision-making processes. The democratic notion of self-legislation, however, which postulates that the addressees of a law should be able to understand themselves as its authors, demands 'the inclusion of the other'. This is why European law should be re-conceptualised: it should concern itself with a compensation of the democratic shortcomings of national decisional processes. Such re-conceptualisation implies that European law could induce its legitimacy from this compensatory function. It could thereby find a novel response to free the critique of its legitimacy. Instead of asking the Union to correct its democracy deficit, we should understand and develop the potential of European law to compensate for the structural democracy deficits of the European nation states (Joerges and Neyer 1997: 293). This argument has since then often been restated or modified, most prominently by Habermas (2007: 176).[3] But this is just one dimension of conflicts-law constitutionalism. A second one concerns the responses to problem interdependence through form of cooperation which "deserve recognition". An analysis of such modes of cooperation in comitology (the mysterious European committee system) in the foodstuffs sector which revealed a surprisingly deliberative potential of this mode of transnational cooperation has prompted the notion of 'deliberative' supranationalism (Joerges and Neyer 1997). This type of supranationalism, we argued, deserves recogni-

---

3 Similarly most recently Innerarity (2015). For a critique and rejection, see Somek (2010) and Kreuder-Sonnen (2014).

tion where the search for creative problem solving is channelled by procedures which favour deliberative exchanges and impede strategic bargaining. A third dimension of the approach concerns the supervision of transnational governance arrangements which involve non-governmental actors.

There is no space to go into any detail here.[4] I will focus instead on three challenges which are of particular importance for the evaluation of Europe's crisis management. (1) The definition of the undemocratic external impact of national decision-making and the delineation of what it might take to compensate for it through European law. (2) The design of cooperative arrangements and procedures which "deserve recognition". (3) The management of conflict constellations, in which a positive solution cannot be achieved and in which must acquiesce in un-decidability (for the European example of atomic energy, see Joerges 2013).[5] These concerns can be illustrated in an analysis of EMU and the SGP, which will at the same time substantiate the specifics of the approach in exemplary fashion.

IV. EMU as an Irresolvable Diagonal Conflict Constellation

The economy of the Union and its law were so far addressed only in section II. There the affinities between economic integration through market building and the constitutionalisation of the EEC Treaty have been underlined. As has been noted there, 'direct effect', 'supremacy', 'pre-emption' – the doctrinal creed of the integration-through-law project – was very much to the liking of a school of thought which was until very recently hardly known to integration through law scholars and is now often so thoroughly misunderstood: Germany's ordo-liberalism and its vision of a transnational European economic constitution. From early on ordo-liberal scholars have interpreted the freedoms guaranteed in the Treaty of Rome, the opening up of national economies, the anti-discrimination rules, and

---

4 For recent more comprehensive explanations, see Joerges (2014a, 2011); Joerges, Kjaer, and Ralli (2011).

5 Similarly, we have in our defence of 'deliberative supranationalism' (Joerges and Neyer 1997) added that 'deliberation' is unlikely to succeed where controversies over safety standards mirror distributional conflicts; in such cases exit options must be granted.

the commitment to a system of undistorted competition as a principled 'decision' for the establishment of a free market economy and its competitive ordering (crystal clear the account by Mestmäcker 1987: 13). In this reading, the Community acquired a legitimacy of its own. The validity of Europe's economic governance was not dependent upon some foundational political democratic act. To the contrary, the EEC was perceived as a non-majoritarian settlement *par excellence*; its competitive order was based upon law and shielded against political influence (Wigger 2008). Interpreting the pertinent treaty provisions as prescribing a law-based order committed to guaranteeing economic freedoms and protecting competition by supranational institutions resolved the legitimacy *problématique* elegantly. The legitimacy of the economic 'ordo' was independent of the state's democratic constitutional institutions.

Europe is a moving target, however. The ordo-liberal project was confronted with the dynamic growth of regulatory politics since the mid-1980s and a widening of European powers which was not easily reconcilable with assignment of constitutional primacy to the 'system of undistorted competition'. The Maastricht Treaty was perceived by the mainstream of European legal studies as a continuation and a deepening of what had been accomplished, a strong move hence towards 'an ever closer union'. But both the opening of new policy-fields and the crowning of the completion of the internal market by monetary union met with very considerable reserves on the part of leading scholars with strong commitments to the Freiburg School (Streit and Mussler 1995; Hauser 1992; Vaubel 1993).[6]

With the benefit of hindsight the Treaty of Maastricht is very widely characterised as a turning point of utmost, albeit tragic importance. It has in particular become obvious that EMU did by no means lead to a stronger convergence of economic policies. The expectation that the pressure to harmonise, stemming from integration, would become stronger and even irresistible under a common currency (Mestmäcker 1973), which may have had its *fundamentum in re* in the smaller and more homogeneous Community of the 1960s and 1970s, has become implausible. EMU as it was established in Maastricht can no longer be defended as a command of economic reason but is more adequately understood as a political project,

---

6 Instructive also the reserves against entering into the third stage of EMU in Biedenkopf (2012: 78).

assuring Germany's neighbours that the country would be faithful to its European commitments (Dyson 2014: 609ff.; Eichengreen 2015: 90). Conceptually speaking the Maastricht compromise has produced a hybrid, an odd mixture of ordo-liberalism and *planification* with Germany defending its stability philosophy in substantive principles and statutory norms and ceding to French preferences in the procedural norms of the General ECB Council (in the same vein, Fabbrini 2015). Legally speaking the hybrid should – in the parlance of the conflicts-law approach – be characterised as a diagonal conflict constellation.

This notion requires an explanatory remark: Monetary policy has become an exclusive competence of the Union (Article 3(1) c TFEU). With this provision, the Union claims supremacy in the policy area conferred to it, a conferral which did not include economic and fiscal policies. The exercise of these policies can have external effects and lead to 'horizontal' conflicts. As experienced immediately after the establishment of the EMU, monetary policy and the national policies could still come into conflict. This, however, is not a vertical conflict for which supremacy would provide a response. It is a 'diagonal' conflict: both the Union and the member states are certainly interested in the functioning of their economies. But the powers needed to accomplish this objective are attributed to two distinct levels of governance. The type of conflict resolution foreseen in Article 119 TFEU is 'the adoption of an economic policy which is based on the close coordination of member states' economic policies' as substantiated in Article 121 TFEU. As is plainly visible from the legal texts and substantiated by meticulous analyses (Braams 2013), this instrument was a *lex imperfecta*, an order devoid of meaningful sanctions. The 'stability community' of the EMU existed only on paper. Neither did the Treaty of Maastricht provide for mechanisms to enforce its ideational basis nor did the successive SGP of 1997 complement the Treaty accordingly. The functioning of the whole new regime was dependent on good economic luck and constant political bargaining.

If the Maastricht EMU and the SGP are legally speaking too soft why not fix the construct through strong rules? That question which is so often answered in the affirmative, leads to the true gist of the matter both in practical and in constitutional terms. As to the first aspect, it is illuminating to consider the insights of the non-legal disciplines cited in section II. Not only does the diversity of socio-economic conditions even within the Eurozone generate a variety of interests, but the differences in the institutional configurations and economic cultures and in the social norms practiced also explain why European command and control governance cannot accomplish its objectives. The normative and constitutional implications of that conflict constellation are of fundamental importance. There is of course nothing unusual or inherently problematical with compromises, incoherencies, or with hybrids embodied in or generated by legal acts. What is so problematic about the European case and what distinguishes the European order from consolidated constitutional democracies is the lack of a political infrastructure and unavailability of an institutional framework in which democratic political contestation could occur and legitimate a completion or improvement of the imperfect edifice that has been established. We have to conclude, sadly, that the Maastricht arrangement was an ill-defined political compromise, rather than a sustainable accomplishment of constitutional validity and strength.

V. Conflict 'Resolution' through Authoritarian Managerialism

As argued in the preceding section, the fragility of the Maastricht arrangement was a birth defect that remained latent until the economic crisis began to unfold in 2008. Since then, we have witnessed a turbo-speed establishment of new modes of transnational economic governance and unheard of regulatory techniques. Detailed descriptions are readily available[7] but cannot, and need not, be reproduced here. The following observations focus instead on three particularly intriguing features of the regime which affect European law and depart strikingly from both the integration-through-law agenda and the ordo-liberal project of economic constitutionalism.

The first: the supervision and control of macro-economic imbalances, which the two 'six-pack' regulations 1176/2011 and 1174/2011 mandate (see Losado and Menéndez 2014: 443, 449) disregard the principle of enumerated powers, and, by the same token, the democratic legitimacy of national institutions, in particular the budgetary powers of the parliaments of the 'states receiving assistance'. The second: in its departure from the one-size-fits-all philosophy that orients European integration in general and monetary policy in particular, European crisis management nonethe-

---

7 See, comprehensively Losado and Menéndez (2014) and for an analysis Joerges (2014b).

less fails to achieve a variation, which might be founded in democratical-ly-legitimated choices; quite to the contrary, the individualised scrutiny of all member states is geared to the objective of budgetary balances and seeks to impose the functionally seemingly necessary accompanying disci-pline; the 'receiving states' cannot but respond to pertinent requests through austerity measures: reductions of wage levels and of social entitle-ments. The third: the machinery of the new regime with its individualised measures which are oriented only by necessarily indeterminate general clauses is resorting to *Maßnahmen* (regulatory ad hoc interventions); it has established a transnational executive machinery outside both the realm of democratic politics *and* the form of accountability which the rule of law used to guarantee; core concepts used by new economic governance can-not be defined with any precision, either by lawyers or by economists, and are therefore not justiciable; rule-of-law and legal protection requirements are being suspended. This type of de-legalisation is accompanied by assessments of member state performance, which cannot be but highly dis-cretionary.

It seems both remarkable and irritating that similar concerns can be dis-cerned in the Opinion in the OMT Case C-62/14 which the Advocate Gen-eral (AG) of the CJEU has delivered on January 14, 2015 (Cruz Villalòn 2015). The learned AG observes in his discussion of the notions of mone-tary and economic policy:

> "The Treaties are silent ... when it comes to defining the exclusive compe-tence of the Union in relation to monetary policy" (Cruz Villalòn 2015, para. 127).

> "The division that EU law makes between those policies is a requirement imposed by the structure of the Treaties and by the horizontal and vertical dis-tribution of powers within the Union, but in economic terms it may be stated that any monetary policy measure is ultimately encompassed by the broader category of general economic policy" (Cruz Villalòn 2015, para. 129).

It follows that the delineation which the text of the Treaty expects us to make when characterising measures as monetary rather than economic policy has to rely on "the objectives ascribed to that policy" (Cruz Vil-lalòn 2015, para. 127). In contrast to facts, which can be ascertained when a decision is being taken, it is usually uncertain and controversial whether such objectives can be realised at all, and if so, how. What can neverthe-less be ascertained is whether a measure "belongs to the category of instruments which the law provides for carrying out monetary policy" (para. 130). But here the law's conditional programming ends. Independent expertise must step in. The ECB has explained that it *intended* to pursue a monetary policy objective and enjoys broad discretion in its framing and implementation (paras 109-112). "The ECB must ... be afforded a broad discretion for the purpose of framing and implementing the Union's monetary policy. The Courts, when reviewing the ECB's activity, must therefore avoid the risk of supplanting the Bank, by venturing into a highly technical terrain in which it is necessary to have an expertise and experience which, according to the Treaties, devolves solely upon the ECB. Therefore, the intensity of judicial review of the ECB's activity, its mandatory nature aside, must be characterised by a considerable degree of caution" (Cruz Villalòn 2015, para. 111).

The CJEU, in its judgment of 16 June, 2015, endorses this reasoning. Just like the AG, the Court underlines that the "Treaty contains no precise definition of monetary policy but defines both the objectives of monetary policy and the instruments which are available to the ESCB" (para. 41). What the ECB decides to undertake is legal as long as "it does not appear that that analysis of the economic situation of the euro area as at the date of the announcement of the programme in question is vitiated by a manifest error of assessment" (para. 74).

What is left of the powers of the member states in the sphere of economic policy? These powers depend first of all on how the ECB defines its mandate. The implementation of that mandate comprises and even requires the linking of the OMT programme to the conditionality of financial assistance (para. 145). The ECB is also entitled to proceed, selectively in its buying activities, and focus on those states in which the monetary policy transmission channels are blocked (para. 153). The ECJ follows suit. The conditionality of financing which the court had qualified as a matter of *economic policy* in its Pringle judgment in view of their function "to safeguard the stability of the euro area as a whole" (CJEU 2012, para. 56) does not affect the qualification of the OMT programme as monetary policy, because the latter is meant "to support the general economic policies in the Union" as provided for by Article 119(2) TFEU (para. 59).

The unruly conflict between European monetary policy and national economic policy has been settled through a novel regulatory arrangement, in which the ECB is an extremely powerful actor, albeit one, which needs the support of the machinery ensuring the targeted conditionality of financial assistance. "[T]he Union today is governed by a set of principles relating both to its objectives and to its boundaries", the AG assures us and does not hesitate to characterise this arrangement as a "constitutional framework" (Cruz Villalòn 2015, para. 215). It is a framework within which conventional democratic procedures are difficult to discern.

Compliance with the original Maastricht EMU and the SGP, so we have argued, was never an option because Maastricht has generated a truly unruly conflict constellation. This assertion implies that we should be cautious with rejecting the responses to this unruliness as simply wilful and malicious. Ernst-Wolfgang Böckenförde, a renowned constitutionalist and former judge of the German Constitutional Court, was the first to characterise the crisis of EMU as a state of emergency (Böckenförde 2010). Decades earlier, in his Freiburg inaugural lecture which he dedicated to nobody else than Carl Schmitt, the same Böckenförde (1978: 1884) had defined the state of exception as a breakdown of the correlation between the situation implicitly pre-supposed in the law (*'Normallage'*), as the reference point of its regulatory objectives (*'die intendierte Regulierungskraft der Norm'*), as a discrepancy and tension hence between conferred powers and means, on the one hand, and the irrefutable challenges of a state of emergency, on the other. This definition, and even more so, its 'application' to the European crisis is certainly debatable and in need of further substantiation (see Dyson 2013; White 2015; Joerges 2014c). Exegetic exercises on the Schmittian notion are not illuminating here. What is at stake is instead a challenging alternative: Will we have to live with – or rather under – the new modes of economic governance which seem to many by now firmly established after the CJEU has covered these unconventional techniques with a thin veneer of legality (CJEU 2012; 2015)? Is an alternative to such 'normalisation' at all conceivable?

In the wake of the Greek elections, 'normalisers' can hardly be overly confident. Who can exclude that political contestation, however disorganised, will intensify, that the epistemic communities organising Europe's crisis management will be forced to re-consider their recipes, that technocratic rule cannot be shielded against the European public and politicians who are accountable to their constituencies. Such conjectures are far from providing a substantiated alternative *programmatique*. They only assume that Europe's present post-constitutional constellation is far from stable and the type of normalisation which is currently *en vogue* will not go away with the conflict configurations which it seeks to control.

VI. 'Wo aber Gefahr ist, wächst das Rettende auch'[8] or Does It? An Epilogue

If contestation is bound to intensify in Europe, both within national societies and between them, we can at least hope for productive innovations which such conflicts and debates may generate. But we also have to consider and explore socio-economic conditions, chances of deliberate social and legal change. And we should listen to outside observers who take an intense and emphatic interest in the future of Europe. One particularly stimulating commentator is Dani Rodrik, an economist by education and passionate publicist at the Princeton Institute for Advanced Study. In a famous book, Rodrik (2011) has submitted a "trilemma thesis". He asserts the impossibility of the simultaneous pursuit of economic globalisation, democratic politics and national determination (autonomy), highlighting that only two goals can be paired: either economic globalisation and democratic politics, or democracy and national autonomy. He then has underlined that the EU furnishes dramatic illustration of this trilemma (Rodrik 2014). The EU could transnationalise democracy through federalisation and thereby defend the advantages of the common market. Federalisation would imply that it would, at the same time, be forced to establish common European politics to legitimise the necessary assumption of fiscal and social policy, with negative consequences for national sovereignty. In the absence of such a de-nationalising will, he asserts, the EU will have to give up the common currency and accept economic disintegration.

Is federalisation the way out of the crisis? Rodrik's diagnosis is *de facto* deeply pessimistic, because, in his view, the federal vision is an abstract utopia. Political Democratic Union would have to be defined and accomplished in democratic processes. The same holds true for the institutional configurations of the economy. All this would have to happen very soon, but is inconceivable in the foreseeable future. He concludes:

"Instead of deepening integration, policy makers must look for ways of undoing it selectively, opening up policy space for national governments in money, finance, and regulation. Under the scenario, the future of mone-

---

8 "But where danger threatens, that which saves from it also grows", from: Friedrich Hölderlin, *Patmos. Dem Landgrafen von Homburg überreichte Handschrift*, 1802 (quoted from Friedrich Hölderlin, *Werke*, Salzburg-Stuttgart: Bergland, 1954: 379; English translation by Michael Hamburger, in: Friedrich Hölderlin, *Selected Poems and Fragments*, London: Penguin Books, 1994: 243).

tary union looks particularly bleak, as it is hard to see a single currency can be reconciled with multiple (democratic) polities" (Rodrik 2014: 6).

To take outside observers seriously does not mean that we have to subscribe to their argument. In defiance of Dani Rodrik's trilemma thesis, I am by no means persuaded that state- or federation-building is the only conceivable response to the tensions between transnational economic integration and democratic legitimacy. As indicated in the first section, there is a democratic alternative, namely, the 'united in diversity vision" of the 2003 Draft Constitutional Treaty for European Union. Rodrik would agree, but he would also argue that then we would forego the economic benefits of the common market. But would we really? Werner Abelshauser, in a recent *unitas in pluralitate* manifesto (Abelshauser 2014), disagrees on both empirical and normative grounds. His empirical evidence is the resistance of the varieties of capitalism against economic integration. This phenomenon is anything but deplorable if the institutional diversity is economically beneficial, rather than detrimental. The lawyer is not in a position to reject or to subscribe to the findings of economic historians. What he *is* competent to explore is the legal framing of the kind of variety that the historian has in mind. Abelshauser refers, in note 30 of his *Denkschrift*, to the re-conceptualisation of European law as a new type of conflicts law. Conflicts-law constitutionalism is, indeed, a project which conceptualises united in diversity as Europe's constitutional form (Joerges 2014a). What I, sadly, have to add is that the crisis has affected this project strongly (Joerges 2014d). It was designed as an exercise in critical theory with normative perspectives which would not confront the state of the integration project with merely normatively attractive ideas, but which, in the tradition of the Frankfurt School, would identify aspects of the integration process which had a potential for institutional innovations, and might, thanks to the ingenuity of committed actors, be transformed in a constructive way. As it seemed in less troubled times, conflicts-law constitutionalism could eventually be elaborated further and proceed as a *re-constructive* project, *i.e.*, a re-conceptualisation of European law, which would, to a considerable degree, be compatible with European law as it stood, and be able to orient its further development. The re-constructive status was based upon its sociological premises which reflect the conflict-laden European constellation more adequately than the orthodoxy of European law. All that seemed necessary, and, indeed, overdue, was to re-consider the integration project in the light of Europe's ever growing diversity, to take the conflicts which this diversity generated into account, and to re-orient Europe's agenda from harmonisation and unity to the management of complex conflict constellations. The analytics of this approach retain their potential, and the normative commitments have not been invalidated.

Bibliography

Abelshauser, W.: Europa in Vielfalt einigen. Eine Denkschrift, 2014. Retrieved from <http://www.homes.uni-bielefeld.de/wabelsha/Denkschrift.pdf> (accessed on 14 January 2015).

Bach, M.: M. Rainer Lepsius und die Begründung der soziologischen Europaforschung. Berliner Journal für Soziologie, 2015 24, pp. 599-603.

Biedenkopf, K.: Der Weg zum Euro. Stationen einer verpassten Chance. Hertie School of Governance, 2012.

Böckenförde, E.-W.: Kennt die europäische Not kein Gebot? Die Webfehler der EU und die Notwendigkeit einer neuen politischen Entscheidung. Neue Zürcher Zeitung, June 21, 2010.

Böckenförde, E.-W.: Der verdrängte Ausnahmezustand. Zum Handeln der Staatsgewalt in außergewöhnlichen Lagen. Neue Juristische Wochenschrift, 1978 31 (2. Halbbd.), pp. 1881-90.

Braams, B.: Koordinierung als Kompetenzkategorie. Tübingen: Mohr Siebeck, 2013.

BVerfGE (Bundesverfassungsgericht): 2 BvR 1390/12, Judgment of 18 March 2014.

Chalmers, D.: The European Redistributive State and a European Law of Struggle. European Law Journal, 1992 18, pp. 667-693.

CJEU (Court of Justice of the European Union): Pringle v Ireland, Case C-370/12 Judgment (Grand Chamber) of 27 November 2012, nyr (not yet reported).

CJEU: Peter Gauweiler and others and Fraktion DIE LINKE im Deutschen Bundestag v Deutscher Bundestag, Case C-62/14, Judgment (Grand Chamber) of June 16, 2015, nyr.

Cruz Villalòn, P.: Opinion in Case C-62/14 Peter Gauweiler and others and Fraktion DIE LINKE im Deutschen Bundestag v Deutscher Bundestag, delivered on January 14, 2015.

Dahrendorf, R.: Ein Europa für die Zukunft. Der Spiegel, 1994 1, pp. 28-29.

Dahrendorf, R.: The Modern Social Conflict: The Politics of Liberty. New Brunswick: Transaction Publishers, 2nd ed., 2008.

Dani, M.: Economic and Social Conflicts, Integration and Constitutionalism in Contemporary Europe. LEQS Discussion Paper Series 13, 2009.

Dani, M.: Rehabilitating Social Conflicts in European Public Law. European Law Journal, 2012 18, pp. 621-643.

Davies, B.: The Constitutionalisation of the EEC/EC: West Germany between Legal Sovereignty and European Integration 1949-1974. Ph.D thesis, King's College London, *2007*.

Dawson, M./ de Witte, F.: Constitutional Balance in the EU after the Euro-Crisis. The Modern Law Review, 2013 76, pp. 817-844.

Dehousse, R./ Weiler, J.: The Legal Dimension. In: Wallace, W. ed. The Dynamics of European Integration. London: Pinter, 1990, pp. 242-60.

Dyson, K.: States, Debts and Power. Saints and Sinners in European History and Integration. Oxford: Oxford University Press, 2014.

Dyson, K.: Sworn to Grim Necessity? Imperfections of European Economic Governance, Normative Political Theory and Supreme Emergency. Journal of European Integration, 2013 35, pp. 207-222.

Eichengreen, B.: Hall of Mirrors. The Great Depression, the Great Recession, and the Uses – and Misuses – of History. Oxford: Oxford University Press, 2015.

Everson, M./ Joerges, C.: Reconfiguring the Politics-Law Relationship in the Integration Project through Conflicts-Law Constitutionalism. European Law Journal, 2013 18, pp. 644-666.

Fabbrini, S.: The Euro Crisis and its Constitutional Implications. In: Champeau, S./ Closa, C./ Innerarity, D./ Maduro, M. eds. The Future of Europe. Democracy, Legitimacy and Justice after the Euro Crisis. New York: Rowman and Littlefield, 2015, pp. 19-36.

Grimm, D.: Die Stärke der EU liegt in einer klugen Begrenzung. Frankfurter Allgemeine Zeitung, No. 184, August 11, 2014, p. 11.

Grimm, D.: The Democratic Costs of Constitutionalization: The European Case. European Law Journal, 2015 21, forthcoming.

Habermas, J.: Why the Development of the European Union into a Transnational Democracy is Necessary and How it is Possible. ARENA Working Paper 13/2014.

Habermas, J.: Does the Constitutionalization of International Law Still Have a Chance? In: Habermas, J.: The Divided West. Cambridge: Polity Press, 2007, pp. 113–93.

Hall, P. A.: Varieties of Capitalism and the Euro Crisis. West European Politics, 2014 37, pp. 1223–1243.

Hallstein, W.: Die Europäische Gemeinschaft. Düsseldorf: ECON, 5th. ed., 1979.

Hauser, H.: Die Ergebnisse von Maastricht zur Schaffung einer Europäischen Währungsunion. Aussenwirtschaft, 1992 47, pp. 151-171.

Innerarity, D.: Images of Europe around the Crisis. The European Legacy: Toward New Paradigms, 2015 20, pp. 1-11.

Iversen, T./ Soskice, D.: A Structural-Institutional Explanation of the Eurozone Crisis. Harvard University, Department of Government, 2013.

Joerges, C.: Rethinking European Law's Supremacy (with Comments by Chalmers, D./ Nickel, R./ Rödl, F./ Wai, R.). EUI Working Paper Law 2005/12, 2005.

Joerges, C.: Economic Law, the Nation-State and the Maastricht Treaty. In: Dehousse, R. ed. Europe After Maastricht: An Ever Closer Union? München: Law Books in Europe, 1994, pp. 29-62.

Joerges, C.: The Idea of a Three-Dimensional Conflicts Law as Constitutional Form. In: Joerges, C./ Petersmann, E.-U. eds. Constitutionalism, Multilevel Trade Governance and International Economic Law. Oxford: Hart Publishing, 2011, pp. 413-56.

Joerges, C.: The Timeliness of Direct Democracy in the EU—and the Contest over Atomic Energy in Conflicts-Law Perspective. In: Lachmayer, K./ Busch, J./ Kelleher, J./ Turcanu, G. G. eds. International Constitutional Law in Legal Education: Proceedings of the Erasmus Intensive Programme NICLAS 2007-2012. Baden-Baden: Nomos, 2013, pp. 89-100.

Joerges, C.: Unity in Diversity as Europe's Vocation and Conflicts Law as Europe's Constitutional Form. In: Nickel, R./ Greppi, A. eds. The Changing Role of Law in the Age of Supra- and Transnational Governance. Baden-Baden: Nomos, 2014a, pp. 127-76.

Joerges, C.: Europe's Economic Constitution in Crisis and the Emergence of a New Constitutional Constellation. German Law Journal, 2014b 15, pp. 985-1028.

Joerges, C.: Law and Politics in Europe's Crisis: On the History of the Impact of an Unfortunate Configuration. Constellations, 2014c 21, pp. 249-261.

Joerges, C.: Three Transformations of Europe and the Search for a Way Out of its Crisis'. In: Joerges, C./ Glinski, Carola eds. The European Crisis and the Transformation of Transnational Governance. Authoritarian Managerialism versus Democratic Governance. Oxford: Hart Publishing, 2014d, pp. 25-46.

Joerges, C./ Kjaer, P. F./ Ralli, T.: A New Type of Conflicts Law as Constitutional Form in the Postnational Constellation. Transnational Legal Theory, 2011 2, pp. 153-65.

Kreuder-Sonnen, C.: Global Exceptionalism and the Euro Crisis: Schmittian Challenges to Conflicts-Law Constitutionalism. In: Joerges, C./ Glinski, Carola eds. The European Crisis and the Transformation of Transnational Governance. Authoritarian Managerialism versus Democratic Governance. Oxford: Hart Publishing, 2014, pp. 71-82.

Krieger, T.: Any Solution in Sight to Europe's Crisis? Some General Thoughts from a Conflict-Theoretical Perspective. This volume.

Losada, F./ Menéndez, A. J.: The Key Legal Texts of the European Crises. Treaties, Regulations, Directives, Case Law, ARENA Centre for European Studies, 2014.

Majone, G.: Rethinking the Union of Europe Post-Crisis. Cambridge: Cambridge University Press, 2014.

Manow, P.: Social Protection, Capitalist Production – The Bismarckian Welfare State in the German Political Economy 1880-2010. Revised habilitation thesis, Konstanz, 2015.

Mestmäcker, E.-J.: Auf dem Weg zu einer Ordnungspolitik für Europa. In: Mestmäcker, E.-J./ Möller, H./ Schwarz, H.-P. eds. Eine Ordnungspolitik für Europa. Baden-Baden: Nomos, 1987, pp. 9-50.

Mestmäcker, E.-J.: A Legal Theory Without Law. Tübingen: Mohr Siebeck, 2007.

Mestmäcker, E.-J.: Power, Law and Economic Constitution, German Economic Review, 1973 11, pp. 177–92.

Muir Watt, H./ Fernández Arroyo, D. P. eds. Private International Law and Global Governance. Oxford: Oxford University Press, 2014.

Preunkert, J./ Vobruba, G. eds.: Krise und Integration. Gesellschaftsbildung in der Eurokrise. Wiesbaden: Springer VS, 2015 (forthcoming).

Rodrik, D.: The Future of European Democracy. Princeton Institute for Advanced Study, 2014, retrieved from <https://www.sss.ias.edu/files/pdfs/Rodrik/Commentary/Future-of-Democracy-in-Europe.pdf> (last accessed on January 25, 2015).

Rodrik, D.: The Globalization Paradox. New York: W.W. Norton, 2011.

Scharpf, F. W.: The Asymmetry of European Integration, or why the EU cannot be a "Social Market Economy". Socio-Economic Review, 2010 8, pp. 211-250.

Scharpf, F. W.: The European Social Model. Journal of Common Market Studies, 2002 40, pp. 645-70.

Schepel, H./ Wesseling, R.: The Legal Community: Judges, Lawyers, Officials and Clerks in the Writing of Europe. European Law Journal, 1997 3, pp. 165-188.

Somek, A.: The Argument from Transnational Effects I: Representing Outsiders through Freedom of Movement. European Law Journal, 2010 16, pp. 315-344.

Streit, M. E./ Mussler, W.: The Economic Constitution of the European Community. From "Rome" to "Maastricht". European Law Journal, 1995 1, pp. 5-30.

Vaubel, R.: Die zweite Stufe auf dem Weg zur Europäischen Wirtschafts- und Währungsunion: Konsequenzen aus den Maastrichter Währungsbeschlüssen. In: Griller, S. ed. Auf dem Weg zur Europäischen Wirtschafts- und Währungsunion? Wien: Service-Fachverlag, 1993, pp. 65-81.

Weiler, J. H. H.: The Transformation of Europe. Yale Law Journal, 1991 100, pp. 2403-2483.

White, J.: Emergency Europe. Political Studies, 2015 63, pp. 300-318.

Wigger, A.: Competition for Competitiveness: The Politics of the Transformation of the EU Competition Regime. Vrije Universiteit Amsterdam, 2008.

Ninth chapter
Legitimacy, Democracy and the Future of the Monetary Union

Francesco Nicoli (University of Trento)

I. Legitimacy in Good and in Bad Times

The European Union is at a turning point. While its leaders are struggling to find a sustainable settlement of the crisis, the process of integration has somehow accelerated towards the uncharted territories of fiscal integration. In the meantime, the rise of euroscepticism in many countries, the slowing implementation of often-contested austerity measures and the renewed role of intergovernmentalism at the European level have stimulated, once again, the debate over the alleged democratic deficit of the European Union. Against this background, the goal of this chapter is twofold. First, it aims to shed light on the conceptual relation between *democracy* (and *democratic deficit*), *legitimacy* of political systems, and *economic policy-making*. Second, it discusses the fundamental challenge the Eurozone is facing today in light of the previous findings.

Before the crisis: A legitimized European Union

The question whether the European Union is suffering from a democratic deficit has increasingly gained scholarly attention since the decision of the *Bundesverfassungsgericht* (German Federal Constitutional Court, BVerfG) on the Maastricht Treaty in 1993. The Bundesverfassungsgericht stressed that democratic legitimacy "is not to remain a formal principle of accountability" (Bundesverfassungsgericht 1993: 18). Democratic deficit and legitimacy are separate concepts: A political system may suffer from a democratic deficit but still be fully legitimised in front of its citizens, either because of its good policies and/or because legitimacy stems from a different level of representation (other than democratically elected parliaments). Thus, a conclusive investigation on the alleged democratic deficit of the EU requires a two-steps process. First, it must be verified that the EU is precisely in need of the form of legitimacy that is *democratic* legitimacy; second, if this is the case, it must be investigated whether such democratic legitimacy exists or not.

Legitimacy of the EU as a broader concept has been object of intense debating. The idea that the EU relies on indirect legitimacy (or second-order legitimacy) has obtained a wide (although not overwhelming) scholarly consensus, and it is loosely parented with both neo-functionalist and liberal-intergovernmentalist approaches. Although the scholarship on EU legitimacy is extremely rich and creative, indirect-legitimacy theses can be clustered around three main cornerstones: the "regulatory state" argument of Majone (1997); the classical principal-agent framework for international organisations reformulated by Moravcsik (2002); and the output-legitimacy argument made famous by Scharpf (1970, 1998).

Majone (1997) argues that direct democratic legitimacy is required only when the functions transferred to the supranational level entail redistributive policies among the participating countries. While this was clearly not the case before the crisis, it could have substantially changed with crisis-led integration (Majone 2014). Moreover, regulatory bodies work more efficiently when "insulated" from politics, thus strengthening output-legitimacy (Majone 1997: 4). The insulation of decision-making is thus justified, like within nation-states, by the democratic qualification of the principals, so as long as member states preserve their democratic stance, the EU shall be considered equally democratic (Moravcsik 2002). Similarly, Scharpf (1970, 1998, 2009) applies Easton's input- and output-legitimacy to the EU, suggesting that the latter has been thus far legitimated only through output-legitimacy (the effectiveness of its decisions) rather than by input-legitimacy (the democratic election of its leadership). These four elements, considered together, provide a solid framework for understanding indirect legitimacy. As long as the EU does not deal with redistributive policies, does have democratically-elected principals, and does deliver valuable outcomes for the citizens, it will be considered as a fully legitimate undertaking.

The classical indirect legitimacy thesis has been widely criticized. Among others, Follesdal and Hix (2006) claim that regulatory policies often entail distributive and redistributive effects not only between countries, but also within social groups. Raunio (1999) suggests that the fundamental role of governments in the EU institutions has changed the power-balance within nation-states in favour of the executive. MacNamara (2002) and Follesdal and Hix (2006) suggest that the perception of the boundaries between regulative and distributive policies may change, thus creating a democratic deficit. In particular, MacNamara – discussing the democratic oversight of the ECB – collects evidence against (1) the notion that monetary policy has no redistributive effects (MacNamara 2002: 54), and (2) the notion that central banking independence provides better outcomes in fighting inflation than democratic control over monetary policy. Finally, Agné (2007) indicates that the 'chain of delegation' of the EU is both too long and not reversible, constituting a stretching and eventually a violation of the principal-agent framework and creating a deficit of democratic oversight.

The three cited arguments (redistributive effects of regulatory policies; power shifts towards the executive; and an ineffective delegation chain) account for the large majority of claims that the EU suffers from a democratic deficit. Along with Majone (2014), I will argue that while these positions failed to capture the reality of European integration before 2010, the shift of sovereignty occurring since the crisis (embodied both in new institutions and new policies) has changed the nature of the Eurozone, thus producing a democratic deficit *today*. This is not due to the limits of the indirect legitimacy thesis as argued by Hix, Rauino and the other democratic-deficit scholars; rather, it is due to the accrued competences of the Union, which are redistributive in nature and require democratic legitimacy. In particular, Hix's analysis of distributive effects in regulative policies fails to take into account the reality of EU policy-making. As noted, among others, by Scharpf (2009), the decisions undertaken at European level should not be considered individually but rather as parts of larger packages of regulations that aim at making every participating country better off with respect to the entire regulative package. Therefore, while individual regulations may make certain countries worse off, this effect is counter-balanced by the negotiation of additional measures that are more favourable to the given country. If the whole country is better off in each round of negotiations, this implies that it disposes of resources to compensate – if it wishes so – the social groups that individually find themselves worse off. Whether it does happen or not is purely a matter of domestic preferences within the Parliament and not a defining feature of the EU construction.

Similarly, Rauinio's claim (the EU decisional procedures shift power from the parliaments to the governments) overlooks reality on the ground. In fact, countries wishing to provide a stronger level of scrutiny of executives' decisions by domestic parliaments are not prevented to do so in any way: As Rauinio himself acknowledges, certain countries have gone so far to empower national parliaments' committees to adopt binding positions for their ministries in the Council. In other words, the EU as such does not strengthen the executives *vis-à-vis* domestic parliaments, which can exert any control they wish; rather, executives (and not the Parliaments) are hold accountable, at EU level, for their actions. In addition, national constitutional courts can intervene to protect parliamentary rights, as done by the German Bundesverfassungsgericht in 2012. It follows that, again, it is a matter of national preferences to adopt such supervision procedures, not an institutional feature of the EU.

The impact of the crisis: Rise of the democratic deficit

As shown, if we narrow our analysis to the EU as it looked *before* the crisis, the claim that its institutions were not legitimated is weak. Not only theoretical arguments in favour of democratic deficit *before the crisis* can be, to some extent, easily dismissed; but also trust in institutions remained relatively stable until 2007, while eurosceptic parties maintained a low profile in many countries until 2009. However, as a response to the European crisis, several institutions and procedures were introduced, which slowly moved the Eurozone in the minefield of fiscal integration. While a precise measure of EU legitimacy can be hardly provided, information concerning legitimacy of EU institutions and adherence to the project of European integration can be extrapolated from existing data.[1] In particular, two approaches can be followed. On the one hand, one can look to *hard euroscepticism* (in accordance with the definition of hard euroscepticism by Taggart and Szczerbiak 2002) by pursuing an analysis of electoral cycles in an attempt to identify leading factors behind the rise of eurosceptic and anti-European forces. On the other hand, one can look at Eurobarometer time series to extrapolate information about *attitudinal euroscepticism* and the general stance towards the EU. Analysis of Eurobarometer data shows that, until 2009/2010, only a small minority of European citizens was against EU membership.

---

1 Serricchio et al. (2013) claim that they find no evidence of a correlation between euroscepticism and the crisis. However, their analysis not only focuses on attitudinal rather than electoral data, but also ends in 2010, before the Europeanisation of the crisis.

Two Eurobarometer indicators matter: opposition to EU membership and mistrust in the EU. *Opposition to membership* has been, overall, rather low. It achieved the highest value in 2010, at 18% of the EU population, both in the Eurozone and in the EU. In the Eurozone, the trend is particularly striking: two clear episodes identify growing opposition to membership, the eastern enlargement and the euro crisis. As data for membership-opposition have not been coherently collected after 2011, I look at the second indicator, *mistrust in the EU*. The trend shows a strong increase in the Eurozone after 2010, where the mistrust towards the EU is today even higher than outside the monetary union. It must be noted that, being the elasticity of opposition to mistrust close to one for the available years, it can be assumed that increases in mistrust entail a comparable rise in opposition. Such conclusions seem to corroborate the classical understanding of democracy (Bundesverfassungsgericht 1993). What really matters when determining the need for democratic legitimacy is the *range* of policies enacted at European level: the redistributive policies introduced since 2011 have generated a need for legitimacy that was not there before. The next sections show that while no need of direct democratic legitimacy existed before the European economic crisis, the policies enacted so far – and the policies that the Monetary Union will need to introduce in the future – imply a substantial leap forward in integration. This will generate a rise in social conflict: as rebellion against democratic deficit if no additional democratic legitimacy is provided, or as national-conflict if the institutional setting plays nations against each other, or finally as a democratic class struggle at EU level if appropriate democratic institutions are provided.

Fiscal integration during the crisis

Since 2010, a series of policies has been introduced under the pressure of the economic crisis, aiming to increase the effectiveness of supervision over national finances, to achieve a better economic policy coordination, as well as to ensure financial stability of the Eurozone. The finality of these initiatives is to heal the shortcomings of the European Monetary Union as they have appeared since the beginning of the crisis. From a theoretical perspective, it has become increasingly clear, over the last few years, that the Eurozone's institutional framework was missing the institutions, procedures and economic flexibility needed to deal with such a crisis. According to the *Optimal Currency Area* framework, as shown by Merler and Pisani-Ferry (2012), without perfect labour and capital mobility, the solution to the crisis must include either a proper fiscal union, or a full-fledged banking union, or a central bank with a widened mandate.

However, despite their functional differences, all the aforementioned options require some degree of fiscal integration; no credible solution excludes it. Fiscal transfers between countries, by definition, require fiscal integration. A full-fledged banking union is in need of a common fiscal backstop for the joint deposit guarantee (Pisani-Ferry and Wolff 2012); and – as shown by Sinn and Wollmershäuser (2011) and by De Grauwe and Ji (2013)[2] – a wider mandate for the European Central Bank (ECB) would have fiscal implications.

In other words, a leap towards fiscal and economic policy integration – although this may acquire different forms – is needed to ensure the stability of the Eurozone: failure in proceeding with some degree of fiscal integration may trigger the collapse of the single currency. Since 2010, substantial progress has been made: Fiscal policy coordination has been strengthened with the Treaty on Stability, Coordination and Governance (TSCG) and with the reform of the Stability and Growth Pact; three pillars (regulation, supervision, resolution) of the Banking Union have been initiated; economic policy coordination has been redesigned into the European Semester; and the ECB has widened the interpretation of its mandate. While the institutional effort is far from exhaustive, the path towards full-fledged economic integration is now hardly reversible without disruptive actions. Such fiscal and economic integration constitutes a major change in the scope and the reach of the Union itself, with important implications concerning its legitimacy and democratic qualification.

Fiscal integration and legitimacy

Fiscal integration touches the very core of democratic systems, whose Europeanisation – either in the form of a strengthened cooperation or with a full transfer of competences – does not simply represent a marginal incremental change in the EU competences. Rather, it constitutes a

---

2 With symmetrically different results concerning the direction of fiscal transfers in comparison to Sinn (2011).

paradigm shift in the nature of the EU and in the way the EU itself shall be legitimised.

The theories of indirect legitimacy presented above describe a European Union dealing mainly with regulative policies, insulated institutions, and limited distributional effects. In other words, indirect democracy may well apply when the range of competences that are object of coordination/ integration do not include essential features of contemporary democracies. The idea that a 'ranking' of competences exists within democracies has also been affirmed by the jurisprudence of the Bundesverfassungsgericht. In the 2009 Lisbon Judgement, the court proposes, in fact, a list of fields of competence that determines the content of democracy:

> "Particularly sensitive for the ability of a constitutional state to democratically shape itself are (...) *fundamental fiscal decisions on public revenue and public expenditure*, the latter being particularly motivated, inter alia, by social policy considerations (...)." (Bundesverfassungsgericht 2009, para. 252, emphasis mine).

A loss of parliaments' decision-making rights in these fields would not represent a marginal transfer of competences towards an institution legitimated through a classical principal-agent relation, but would instead constitute a true deprivation of substantial democracy for the concerned constituencies. As Fabbrini (2002: 24) notes, fiscal and economic policy decisions are substantially adopted today by intergovernmental decision making, while "the legitimacy of decisions taken on behalf of the EU cannot be a derivative of the legitimacy enjoyed by the governments of its member-states". Consequently (and in absence of a body truly representative of the European people), the transfer of these competences would spoil the effectiveness of the citizens' political rights to vote. Friedrich and Kroger (2013: 4) suggest that "(p)olitical procedures and practices are democratic if they are firmly based on political equality as the 'foundational idea' of democracy". This implies that decisions shall be collectively binding and achieved by majority voting: the EU needs a shift from input to output legitimization (Habermas 2011) as witnessed by the famous *adagio* "no taxation without representation".

This is not an easy undertaking. Being parliamentary control on fiscal matters essential for democracy, the Bundesverfassungsgericht notes that – when there is no parliamentary control of fiscal policy whatsoever – we are outside the democratic framework: The famous adagio may then become "*no true representation* (i.e., no true democracy) *without taxation* (i.e., without control on fiscal issues)".[3] If *no* parliament controls fiscal policy, there is no democracy. In principle, then, fiscal integration may endanger the democratic qualification of the EU: transferring fiscal powers to the EU without strengthening its democratic legitimacy would deprive European citizens of the decision-making power over an issue absolutely essential for democracy, as noted by the Bundesverfassungsgericht.

Of course, different forms of fiscal integration might require different forms of democratic legitimacy – but regarding fiscal matters, they all require *input* legitimacy, as defined by Scharpf (1998). Any form of indirect legitimacy on fiscal issues violates the democratic conditions of political equality; however, the introduction of input legitimacy can hardly be handled without raising problematic issues. At the same time, as noted by the Bundesverfassungsgericht in 2009, the simple transfer of fiscal power to the European Parliament would not preserve the political equality criterion, as the European Parliament is elected based on geographical constituencies with a regressive proportionality principle, and there is no second federal chamber where the equality of states is represented (Bundesverfassungsgericht 2009, para. 274 and following).

The no demos thesis and its implications

More importantly, the transfers of economic and fiscal powers to a supranational assembly[4] would be insufficient if we maintain that identity is a precondition for democracy when democracy has redistributive implications. The relationship between redistribution and collective identity has noble fathers in political philosophy: it can be perceived already in David Hume's theory of morality as described in the *Treatise*, which assumes that one's feelings intensity for another human being increases as one's proximity to the individual strengthens (Cohon 2010, para. 7), thus justifying stronger redistributive policies within nations than between. Ferdinand Tönnies' *Gemeinschaft* concept also reflects the idea of societies built

---

3 Menéndez (2000) originally proposed the reversion of this famous principle albeit with a different meaning.
4 This holds even when respecting the criteria laid down by the Bundesverfassungsgericht, for example, by creating a federal parliament where people are represented both as citizens of a state and as individuals.

upon shared community beliefs rather than upon rational contractualism. In the second half of the twentieth century, the debate over the societal boundaries of democracy and redistribution has revamped on both sides of the Atlantic. In North-America, the renewed discussion addressed the issue of the origins and limits of redistributional justice, being marked by contributions like Rawls' *A Theory of Justice* (1971), MacIntyre's *After Virtue* (1981) and Walzer's *Spheres of Justice* (1983). In Europe, the debate – ignited by the controversial Maastricht decision of the Bundesverfassungsgericht – focused on the limits of a democratic transformation of the European Union alongside the emergence of a collective European identity. In this context, the so-called *no demos thesis* was developed, among others, by Bryde (1994), Kielmansegg (1994; 1996), and, to a lesser extent, by Grimm (1995), Weiler (1996; 2000) and Zürn (2000). As Zürn writes, the foundation of the no demos thesis is that "majoritarian decision-making is hardly achievable beyond the national level since it requires some form of collective identity that includes trust and solidarity" (2000: 195). Some proponents of the thesis, like Bryde (1994), ground the *demos* into ethnical, linguistic and cultural features, which create links of solidarity among the demos members, thus justifying redistribution through majority voting. Outside the demos, these boundaries disappear, making the deployment of a working democracy impossible.

Weiler's[5] depiction of the no demos thesis is likely the most articulated: "democracy does not exist in a vacuum (...) if there is no demos, there can be no operating democracy" (1996: 523). The nature and the ultimate goal of the European constitutional construct (its *telos*) is indeed not to proceed towards the creation of a single European demos, but rather to preserve peacefully the distinct demoi.[6] Consequently, a true majority-voting democracy at EU level is not possible, and the departure from unanimity vote that occurred with the Single European Act coincides with the beginning of the crisis of the European construction: "no matter how close the union, it is to remain a union among distinct peoples" (Weiler 2000: 14).

---

5 Weiler's position on the argument has evolved over time from an initial sceptical position (1995) into a moderate agreement (1996) and finally towards his "constitutional tolerance" approach (2001).

6 "Europe is not yet a Demos in the organic national-cultural sense and should never become one" (Weiler 1996: 528).

The no-*demos* argument, as reconstructed by Weiler, is composed of a positive statement ("Europeans are not a *demos*") and a normative claim ("Europeans shall not become a *demos*"). While the normative claim is controversial, many citizens (including committed Europeans) and political leaders would likely agree with the positive claim. For instance, the Bundesverfassungsgericht (2009, para. 279) writes: "The democratic fundamental rule of the equality of opportunities of success ("one man, one vote") only applies within a people, not in a supranational body of representation, which remains a representation of the peoples linked to each other by the Treaties."

In a way, the 2009 ruling on the Lisbon Treaty constituted an extraordinary compendium of the defining principles of classical democracy, providing a (legally binding) interpretation of the relations between the fundamental political competences sovereignty, parliaments, *demos,* and representativeness. The Bundesverfassungsgericht appears to share the positive part of the no demos thesis concerning democracy, including the basic arguments for which democracy (majority-voting) is possible only within one demos. Although the Court does not rule out the emergence of a European demos, especially through institutional reforms, it recognises that such a demos is still yet to emerge; and thus only inter-governmental politics are possible provided the existing institutional balance. However, the Bundesverfassungsgericht reverses the classical argument of the no demos proponents: it is democracy, defined by political equality and its essential functions (like fiscal and economic policy) that defines the demos. Where individuals enjoy political equality and their decisional power concerns essential democratic functions, we have democracy and thus the demos is established.

A legitimacy trilemma?

The no demos thesis generates a major issue: either we decide to proceed with securing the EMU with fiscal integration giving up any claim of democratic control over it, thus creating a purely inter-governmental (output-legitimized) fiscal union; or we decide to maintain democracy at the national level, avoiding fiscal integration, and therefore receding from monetary integration. In other words, the EU is facing a true *governance trilemma,* which may be resumed by Figure 1. We can preserve democratic decision-making, the monetary union, and the no demos assumption, but only two of these features at a time. Pursuing all three features simultaneously would prevent any resolution to the crisis. In fact, democratic decision making and fiscal integration are consistent, but this would require the creation of a European Parliament that is enabled to deal with fiscal and economic policy. This would be in contrast to the demos thesis which assumes that fiscal policy cannot be the object of democratic decision making outside the demos because of its redistributive implications. Similarly, we could maintain the demos thesis and proceed towards fiscal integration at the condition that any decision on fiscal and economic policy that is undertaken in the newly established fiscal union is taken by consensus of governments, thus removing democratic decision making from controlling these policies. Finally, we could maintain the demos thesis and a majority-voting control over fiscal and economic policies, only if these are not integrated at the EU level. The next sections will discuss each of the alternatives in more detail.

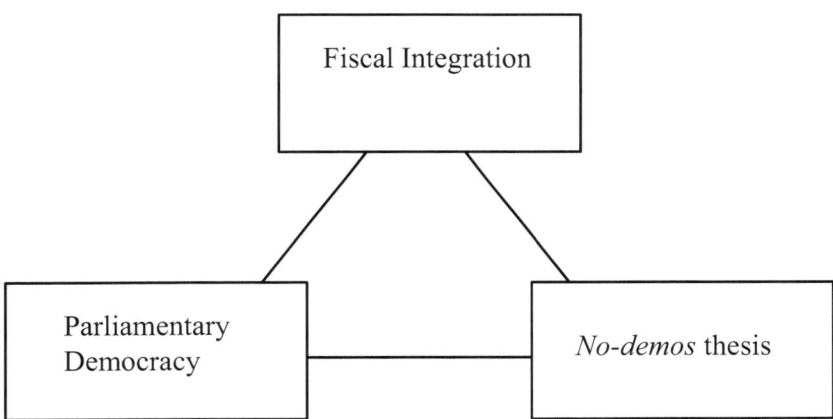

Figure 1: The legitimacy trilemma of EU governance

II. Democratic Legitimacy after the Crisis: A Legitimacy Trilemma

I previously showed that the EU was not in need of direct democratic legitimacy *before the crisis,* so the question whether the EU suffered a democratic deficit was, at the time, redundant. However, I also showed that the post-crisis integration, concerning fiscal and economic policies, could not be insulated any longer. Today, the range of policies undertaken at the EU level does need democratic legitimacy. If the EU is not able to provide it, it would suffer a democratic deficit. However, if confronted with the no demos understanding of democracy, we end up being trapped in a trilemma with no apparent way out.

The implications for the European Union and its quest of legitimacy differ under each of the different options. From this point onwards, we enter a rather uncharted territory. Rodrik (2011) has proposed an apparently similar trilemma. In his trilemma, he relates, on a global level, *nation state, democracy* and *globalisation.* In Rodrik's view, globalization constitutes a threat to either democracy or the existing political order based upon sovereign nation states. In this volume, Joerges (2015) has presented a substantial criticism of Rodrik's approach. However, even if we accept the general structure of the trilemma, it cannot be simply transposed as it stands into the European situation for several reasons. First, as argued above, not every level of globalization/integration threatens democracy, only integration phases requiring the sharing of essential democratic functions with clear redistributive implications, such as fiscal and economic policy.[7] Second, the concept of nation state in Rodrik's trilemma is misleading and, I believe, ultimately wrong. Nation states, in fact, constitute the solution (in a specific geographical area) to the more substantial problem posed by the demos, as much as a European Federation would constitute a solution to the same trilemma on a larger geographical area. If the EU were to be forged into a federal state, Rodrik's trilemma would not hold anymore. Statehood represents a solution to the problem of the demos. Nation-states are under threat only in the measure they represent the *milieu* of the democratic process as it stands today: in this particular function, they enter in the trilemma. Because of this reasoning, even if Rodrik's work may provide some insights concerning the long-term outcomes of the trilemma's pairs, it is insufficient to provide a correct understanding of the crisis of the European Union. A discussion of the trilemma's solutions follows in the next subsections.

---

7 This may change across time and societies. As noted by Moravcsik (2002: 614), although monetary policy might have redistributive implications, it was possible to create the ECB because the redistributive function of monetary policy was widely rejected at the time of its creation.

Democratic principle, no demos thesis

The first option for resolving the trilemma implies the choice of democracy and no demos thesis, while rejecting fiscal and monetary integration. Is the dissolution of the Eurozone a viable option? Theory and historical experience seem to suggest that the dissolution of monetary unions would not move the institutional-economic system into a stable equilibrium. Further institutional adjustments would be needed, endangering the European Union and the Single Market.

Moving monetary integration to its end is a risky decision. Besides the short term effects of a similar decision (which according to several studies – UBS [Deo et al. 2011] and Bertelsmann Stiftung [Belke 2012] – might acquire a global magnitude several times higher than the collapse of Lehman Brothers), it endangers especially long-term stability. The Monetary Union, in fact, was introduced for specific reasons. On the one hand, there was a sincere political willingness to push forward European integration; on the other hand, there was also a clear macroeconomic concern behind the inception of the EMU. It constitutes, in fact, a solution to Mundell's (1961) famous "Impossibility Trilemma". A group of countries cannot simultaneously pursue unrestricted flows of capital, independent monetary policy and fixed exchange rates. The EMU is an institutional solution to this trilemma, in favour of free movement of capital and fixed exchange rates (thus repelling independent monetary policy). The collapse of the EMU would raise the same question again, namely how to create monetary stability in Europe. If the EMU collapses, it would be because a fixed exchange rate system is not sustainable. Therefore, the choice will be to have free movement of capital, independent monetary policy and flexible exchange rates.

This combination of factors, however, may well constitute the first step towards further disintegration, endangering the Single Market for goods and capital. As suggested by Meade (1957: 385) and more recently by Eichengreen (2008) and Kawai and Akivama (2003), if short term preferences over the inflation-unemployment trade-off are different (and indeed, they are different among European countries) and if monetary policy is independent, it is unrealistic to think that free-trade agreements (and as a consequence, the Single Market) would survive in the long term.

The Single Currency surely was a political project, but it was also justified as a rational solution to Mundell's trilemma. The European solution to Mundell's trilemma has been to permanently remove the possibility of diverging monetary policies in order to preserve the free movement of capital and fixed exchange rates. However, why are fixed exchange rates so important? The rationale for fixed exchange rates is to ensure a level playing field in the single market for goods. Meade (1957) suggests that an effective level-playing field single market for goods cannot endure in a floating exchange rate system if countries hold different inflation preferences. If there are no trade barriers, countries with higher inflation preferences have an incentive to expand continuously their monetary base, thus depreciating their currencies, in order to boost short-term price competitiveness, adopting a beggar-thy-neighbour policy. Partner countries with lower inflation preferences have little options against this behaviour: they can either (a) do nothing and accept a higher level of unemployment, or (b) change their own inflation preference and accept a higher level of inflation, or (c) change their preference concerning free trade and recede from the single market.

In other words, Meade's economic reasoning – requiring the choice of pairs between differentials in inflation preferences, flexible exchange rates, and a level-playing field single market – implies a third trilemma. From this perspective, it is straightforward to understand the pressure that the European single market for goods would suffer in case of a dismantling of the Eurozone: a disintegrative decision on the third trilemma (legitimacy) would prevent a forward-looking solution on the second trilemma (monetary) thus generating pressure on the first (trade). The logic of this chain of disintegration is proposed in Figure 2. Of course, being the entire European construction somehow dismantled in the process, the issue of democratic legitimisation disappears: not only fiscal integration, but also monetary policy and potentially trade policy (at a later stage in the disintegration chain) are kept at the domestic level. The need for a democratically legitimised EU fades away alongside the deconstruction of the EU itself.

Monetary union, no demos thesis

The second option with respect to the legitimacy trilemma concerns monetary union and no demos thesis, leading to an inter-governmental type of fiscal integration (or executive-federal in the words of Habermas). Clearly, it would produce a shift from input (democratic) legitimisation to an output legitimisation of fiscal policies. Indirect legitimacy for insulated insti-

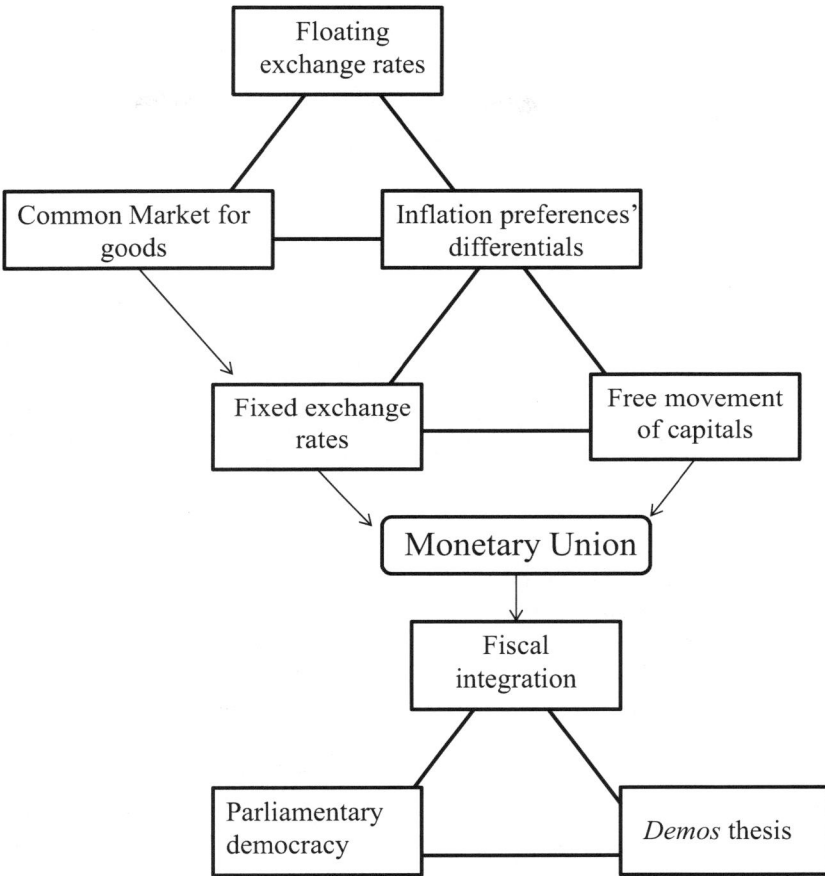

Figure 2: Sequence of integration trilemmas

tutions worked as long as the EU could be qualified as a regulatory, non-redistributive polity, but adding the redistributive functions would constitute a fundamental change of the Union and, if pursued without democracy-enhancing reforms, would constitute a net loss of democratic stance (Majone 2014).

Nevertheless, such arrangement may work in practice: its logic is straightforward. The formal equality of states, including their veto powers on fiscal matters, shall be preserved in order to fulfil the no demos assumption. However, the credibility of commitments is still essential: credibility must cover not only the willingness of peripheral countries to adopt reforms, but also the willingness of core countries to pay. If each fiscal transfer were to need 28 majorities in 28 national parliaments, the whole system would end-up being completely non-credible in face of the financial markets and the voters. Moreover, the whole 'grand-bargaining' still needs to be protected by electoral politics. Fiscal and economic integration (with legal responsibilities for both net recipient and net contributor countries) is thus again insulated and protected by unilateral changes through constitutionalisation in a fiscal treaty with redistributive features. Indeed, the "insulation logic" observed by Majone constitutes not only a requirement to achieve effectiveness avoiding decisional traps, but also a strategy to ensure compliance (Wolf 1999: 341). The goal is precisely the *de-democratization* of a given competence. The respect of national sovereignty turns a purely fictional stratagem into an insulation setting. Clearly, the respect of the no demos thesis is apparent: in order to grant to each national demos equal and non-majoritarian rights on fiscal and economic policies, these policies must be excluded from the fields of action of democratic policy-making. Such an arrangement, albeit eventually effective, would violate both *input* and *output congruence* as defined by Zürn (2000), thus further weakening the democratic stance of the system.

Furthermore, output-legitimated fiscal policies have two main hurdles to overcome: (1) *variations* of constituencies' interests and preferences after the constitutional agreement, and (2) *time inconsistency* problems. In fact, output legitimacy requires *horizontal* effectiveness of the implemented policies. In other words, if a policy ends up producing welfare losses in a given constituency, output legitimacy is not achieved. Therefore, output legitimisation is not an agreement about the rules of the game, but about the winners of the game. Of course, no constituency would (in theory) agree to a 'quasi-constitutional' agreement that is structurally against its interests. During the negotiations, the delegates would use their veto powers to block any agreement that does not respect (overall) their own preferences, so the loss of democracy experienced by the constituency that is bound by the agreement is matched with the material gains that provide output legitimacy. For a single fiscal decision to be output-legitimised, therefore, a relevant level of ex-ante economic convergence is required. If we assume that adjustment and convergence processes are effective, long-term convergence could happen; but in order to have effective convergence, we need (for economic reasons, see above) fiscal integration.

Can we legitimise fiscal integration with a legitimisation vector requiring, to be effective, actual convergence, thus fiscal integration? Temporal expectations play here an essential role. Agents may support a loss in actu-al democratic stance only if concrete advantages show up timely. The higher the loss, the faster results shall be delivered.[8] Naturally, the 'time-ly' definition may vary across regions and individuals: some may accord high values to short terms gains, while others prefer long-term advantages. However, as explained above, these arrangements are credible only if we focus on the long term, that is, if their content does not depend on the national political cycle. Thus, as long as multiple constituencies exist, and as long as these constituencies hold different interests, it seems hardly possible to find an agreement that satisfies the long-term commitment condition and the short-term effectiveness condition for any constituency.

Monetary union, democratic principle.

There is a third possible outcome of the trilemma, a *federal* integration pattern combining supranational democracy and monetary union. Several concerns can be raised, however, despite the clear political appeal of such an option. These concerns rely on a simple observation: Getting out of the no demos thesis might not be as easy as it could appear. There is little doubt concerning the fact that Europeans are not (yet) a 'people': the no demos thesis – for which redistribution and thus democracy cannot sur-vive outside the demos – is therefore relevant, if it is proven true.

As stated above, the no demos thesis is actually composed of two dif-ferent parts, a normative and a positive one. Under the federal integration perspective, we can easily dismiss (as a political choice) the normative claim. However, it is not so easy to dismiss the positive part (that democ-racy cannot be deployed outside a single people defined in ethnic and cul-tural terms). On the one hand – regardless of our theoretical opinions on the possibility of redistribution outside the demos –, we will still have to deal with Mme Le Pen, Geert Wilders and Prof. Lucke. On the other hand, the experience of many democratic fiscal federations like the UK, Spain and Belgium, demonstrates that even consolidated systems may not be in a final functional equilibrium. Even functionalists with rather federal feel-

---

8 Empirical studies on the European identity and the legitimacy of the institutions demonstrate that there is an extremely sensitive component in the individual atti-tude towards EU institutions in relation to short-term achievements (see Bruter 2003: 116).

ings, like Haas (1964) and Schmitter (2002), consider a quick federalisation of the EU unlikely to happen without traumas. The former, in his analysis of international integration patterns, considers that federal integration would succeed only after the instauration of a "liberal nationalism". In other words, after a conflicting phase between original national identities, the supranational authorities may succeed to build up a true federation overcoming the nationalist oppositions with the creation of a strong and shared body of beliefs and values. In addition, Schmitter considers that governments would resist with some forms of "power protectionism" boosting national identities.

This is an essential question: the viability of a truly input-legitimised EU depends on the extent to which the no demos assumption might effectively be ignored. Hypothetically, democratic fiscal integration might be self-legitimising. This hypothesis can be presented as follows: if the power of an elected assembly over fiscal issues is increased, then political parties will increase their efforts to take control of the assembly, investing more in collecting votes, mobilizing consensus and building up organizational structures. Because of the organizational efforts and the search for consensus, two effects are likely to arise: (1) increased political polarization, and (2) increased participation rates in the elections.

This hypothesis has been criticized by Hix (1998) with respect to the overall powers of the European Parliament, but remains to be tested with particular reference to fiscal powers, which represent the core of the democratic process. In this regard, Hix et al. (2007) recognise that a relevant increase of the parliaments' powers to shape the outcomes of the political process can indeed increase their legitimacy. If this correlation is true, a democratic fiscal integration might indeed be self-legitimising, opening the doors for a fast-track federalisation of the Eurozone. If it were wrong, however, creating a fiscal union without an underlying demos would have disruptive consequences, eventually leading to the triumph of eurosceptics and the dismissal of the European integration project for good.

III. Conclusions

The analysis of the European disease presented in this chapter has implications for both theory and policy-making. The chapter has shown that while talking of a democratic deficit before the crisis may have been redundant according to both theoretical reasoning and empirical evidence, the wave of crisis-led integration that occurred since 2010 has changed the picture. The EU is not simply facing the need for further democratization: Instead, we show that the Union is trapped in a policy and legitimacy deadlock from which there are no easy ways out. Fiscal integration (or monetary disintegration) is unavoidable; and it will substantially transform the Euro-zone into a redistributive polity. Depending on the institutional setting, the ensuing conflict could either be qualified as a national struggle or as a societal struggle. Similarly, inaction will equally fuel social conflict, as indicated by the rising populism in many EU member states.

None of the possible choices is costless: Dismantling the Monetary Union could not only push the continent towards a new financial disaster, but also release disintegrative dynamics which ultimately would end only with the collapse of the Single Market for goods and capital. Proceeding with output-legitimated fiscal integration (thus avoiding federalism and the political costs it entails) will have huge costs in terms of democratic legitimacy, may fuel national conflict and may constitute a solution not lasting sufficiently long to achieve true economic convergence. The out-put-legitimacy provided would thus be dramatically asymmetric, creating the conditions for renewed national hate. The risk that short- and medium-term losers of such a process would rebel before accessing long-term gains is high. Finally, a federal integration pattern is equally risky, as it will require a democratically legitimised sharing of resources among communities that do not have a truly unified public sphere, identity, or sense of common belonging. Experience shows that this is hard to achieve without political conflict and potential break-ups even within long-standing established communities.

The analysis suggests that the EU is caught in a 'functional trap': Policy makers should be aware of the risks entailed with each of the possible choices over the trilemma, and must identify a clear integration pattern shaped not only by immediate economic needs and political fears, but also by the economic and democratic challenges over the medium term. Failure of doing so may substantially increase the perceived democratic deficit of the EU, effectively expropriating citizens of their democratic decision power. Alternatively, it may create a dysfunctional system hostage of minority blockages in national parliaments and characterised by recurrent instability on the financial markets. Ultimately, such sub-optimal solutions may not be sustainable and may end up provoking the collapse of the EMU. Even a true federation, however, may not be self-sufficient without a demos: whether a common polity could ensue common (fiscal) policies, and thus a common public sphere, that would result from need and not from a pre-existing shared identity, is the deeper question behind any programme for democratically-legitimised fiscal integration, a question so far without a convincing answer.

Bibliography

Agné, H.: The Myth of International Delegation: Limits and Suggestions for Democratic Theory in the Context of the European Union. Government and Opposition, 2007 42(1), pp. 18-45.

Belke, A.: Doomsday for the Euro Area: Causes, Variants and Consequences of Breakup. Working Paper, Bertelsmann Stiftung, Gütersloh, 2012.

Bryde, B. O.: Die bundesrepublikanische Volksdemokratie als Irrweg der Demokratietheorie. Staatswissenschaften und Staatspraxis: rechts-, wirtschafts- und sozialwissenschaftliche Beiträge zum staatlichen Handeln, 1994 5(3), pp. 305-330.

Bruter, M.: Winning Hearts and Minds for Europe: The Impact of News and Symbols on Civic and Cultural European Identity. Comparative Political Studies, 2003 36(10), pp. 1148-1179.

Bundesverfassungsgericht: "Maastricht case", Cases 2134/92 & 2159/92, Decision of October 12, 1993.

Bundesverfassungsgericht: "Lisbon case", Case 02/08, Decision of June 30, 2009.

Bundesverfassungsgericht: "ESM case", Case 1390/12, Decision of September 12, 2012.

Cohon, R.: Hume's Moral Philosophy. In: Zalta, E. ed. The Stanford Encyclopaedia of Philosophy. Center for the Study of Language and Information, Stanford University, 2010.

De Grauwe, P./ Ji, Y.: Fiscal Implications of ECB's Bond Buying Programme. Vox Policy Portal, June 14, 2013.

Deo, S./ Donovan, P./ Hathaway, L.: Euro Break-Up – The Consequences. Global Economic Perspectives. UBS Investment Research Department, London, 2011.

Eichengreen, B.: The Breakup of the Euro Area. NBER Working Paper No. 11393, 2008.

Fabbrini, S.: Intergovernmentalism and its Outcomes: The Implications of the Euro Crisis on the European Union. Draft Working Paper, University of California, 2012.

Friedrich, D./ Kroger, S.: Democratic Representation in the EU: Two Kinds of Subjectivity. Journal of European Public Policy, 2013 20(2), pp. 171-189.

Follesdal, A./ Hix, S.: Why there is a Democratic Deficit in the EU: A Response to Majone and Moravcsik. Journal of Common Market Studies, 2006 44(3), pp. 533-562.

Grimm, D.: Does Europe Need a Constitution? European Law Journal, 1995 1(3), pp. 282-302.

Habermas, J.: Europe's Post-Democratic Era. The Guardian, November 10, 2011.

Haas, E. B.: Beyond the Nation State. Functionalism and International Organization. European Consortium for Political Research, 1964.

Hix, S.: Elections, Parties and Institutional Design: A Comparative Perspective on European Democracy. Western European Politics, 1998 3(21), pp. 19-52.

Hix, S./ Noury, A./ Roland, G.: Democratic Politics in the European Parliament. Cambridge: Cambridge University Press, 2007.

Joerges, C.: The Overburdening of European Law through Economic and Monetary Union. This volume, 2015.

Kawai, M./ Akiyama, S.: Implications of the Currency Crisis for Exchange Rates Arrangements in Emerging East Asia. Policy Research Working Paper, No. wps2502, World Bank, 2003.

Kielmansegg, P. G.: Läßt sich die Europäische Gemeinschaft demokratisch verfassen? Europäische Rundschau, 1994 22(2), pp. 23-33.

Kielmansegg, P. G. : Integration und Demokratie. In: Jachtenfuchs, M./ Kohler-Koch, B. eds. Europäische Integration, Opladen: Leske+Budrich, 1996, pp. 47-71.

MacIntyre, A.: After Virtue: A Study in Moral Theory. Notre Dame/IN: University of Notre Dame Press, 1981.

MacNamara, K.: Rational Fictions: Central Bank Independence and the Social Logic of Delegation. West European Politics, 2002 25(1), pp. 47-76.

Majone, G.: The Regulatory State and its Legitimacy Problems. Western European Politics, 1997 22(1), pp. 1-24

Majone, G.: From a Regulatory State to a Democratic Default. Journal of Common Market Studies, 2014 52(6), pp. 1216-1223.

Meade, J.: The Balance-of-Payments Problems of a European Free-Trade Area. Economic Journal, 1957 67(267), pp. 379-396.

Menéndez, A. J.: Another View of Democratic Deficit: No Taxation without Representation. In: Joerges, C./ Meny, Y./ Weiler, J. H. H. eds. What Kind of Constitution for What Kind of Polity? Responses to Joschka Fisher. Robert Schuman Centre for Advanced Studies, European University Institute, Florence, 2000, pp. 126-138.

Merler, S./ Pisani-Ferry, J.: The Euro Crisis and the New Impossible Trinity. Bruegel Policy Contribution, 2012, Issue No. 1.

Moravcsik, A.: In Defense of the "Democratic Deficit": Reassessing Legitimacy in the European Union. Journal of Common Market Studies, 2002 40(4), pp. 603-624.

Mundell, R.: The Monetary Dynamics of International Adjustment under Fixed and Flexible Exchange Rates. Quarterly Journal of Economics, 1960 74(2), pp. 227-257.

Mundell, R.: A Theory of Optimal Currency Areas. American Economic Review, 1961 51(4), pp. 657-665.

Pisani-Ferry, J./ Wolff, G.: Fiscal Implications of a Banking Union. Bruegel Policy Brief, 2012, Issue No. 2.

Rawls, J.: A Theory of Justice. Cambridge/MA: The Belknap Press of Harvard University Press, 1971.

Raunio, T.: Always a Step Behind? National Legislatures in the European Union. Government and Opposition, 1999 34(2), pp. 180-202.

Rodrik, D.: The Globalization Paradox: Democracy and the Future of World Economy. New York: Norton, 2011.

Scharpf, F.: Demokratietheorie zwischen Utopie und Anpassung. Konstanz: Universitätsverlag, 1970.

Scharpf, F.: Interdependence and Democratic Legitimation. MPIfG Working Paper No. 98/2, 1998.

Scharpf, F.: Legitimacy in the Multilevel European Polity. MPIG Working Paper No. 2009/01.

Schmitter, P.: Neo-Neo-Functionalism. Working Paper, European University Institute, 2002.

Serricchio, F./ Tsakatika, M./ Quaglia, L.: Euroscepticism and the Global Financial Crisis. Journal of Common Market Studies, 2013 51(1), pp. 51-54.

Sinn, H.-W.: The ECB's Stealth Bailout. VoxEu, June 1, 2011.

Sinn, H.-W./ Wollmershäuser, T.: Target Loans, Current Account Balances and Capital Flows: The ECB's Rescue Facility. International Tax and Public Finance, 2011 19(4), pp. 458-508.

Szczerbiak, A./ Taggart, P.: The Party Politics of Euroscepticism in EU Member and Candidate states. Sussex European Institute, Working Paper No. 51, 2002.

Walzer, M.: Spheres of Justice: A Defense of Pluralism and Equality. Basic Books Inc., New York, 1983.

Weiler, J. H. H.: Does Europe Need a Constitution? Reflections on Demos, Telos and the German Maastricht Decision. European Law Journal, 1995 1(3), pp. 219-258.

Weiler, J. H. H.: European Neo-Constitutionalism: In Search of Foundations for the European Constitutional Order. Political Studies, 1996 XLIV, pp. 517-533.

Weiler, J. H. H.: Federalism without Constitutionalism: Europe's Sonderweg. In: Nicolaidis, K./ Howse, R. eds. The Federal Vision: Legitimacy and Levels of Governance in the United States and the European Union. Oxford: Oxford University Press, 2001, pp. 54-72.

Wolf, K. D.: The New Raison d'Etat as a Problem for Democracy in World Society. European Journal of International Relations, 1999 5(3), pp. 333-363.

Zürn, M.: Democratic Governance beyond the Nation State: The EU and other International Institutions. European Journal of International Relations, 2000 6(2), pp. 183-221.

Tenth chapter
Conflict at the Interface of Economic Policy and Law –
Cognitive Dissonance in the German Constitutional Court's
OMT Case Reasoning

Stefan Oeter (University of Hamburg)

I. Starting Point

Europe has gone through a sequence of dramatic events of financial crisis
(Schuppan 2014: 95-124; Illing 2013: 47-96; Hellwig 2011: 3-11). All
started with the real estate bubble in the United States, the breakdown of
the market for structured bonds based on real estate loans and the subse-
quent insolvency of Lehman Brothers (Scharpf 2011: 25-27). The crisis in
Ireland followed suit, the real estate market in Spain also breaking down,
with a severe crisis in the asset structure of Spanish banks. Finally, the
markets lost confidence and started to look closer to sovereign debt, with
Greece as an obvious candidate for debt failure. The risk of Greece being
cut off from the financial markets and finally forced to leave the Eurozone
was too much a danger for the European financial system (Illing 2013:
31-34). Ireland, Portugal, Spain and Greece had to be rescued by a combined emergency effort of the other Eurozone states and the European
Central Bank (ECB). All this triggered an overhaul of the institutional set-
up of the EU in financial matters as well as a series of far-reaching fiscal,
economic, social and political reforms in a number of EU states – reforms
that are highly unpopular in most member states concerned.

Accordingly, we can observe strong societal resistance against these
reforms, supported by parts of the legal academia and courts. The Por-
tuguese Constitutional Court several times declared austerity measures of
government and parliament unconstitutional, forcing them to shift the burden of austerity to other parts of society (see the references in Wendel
2014: 266 Fn. 18; as to the background see Rato 2013: 411-447). Judicial
courts in other states of the Mediterranean South of the EU attempted to
follow the same way, with less success in most cases. Rebalancing the
budget and pursuing radical austerity programs has been a policy path far

from a broad societal consensus in the states concerned (Scharpf 2013: 22-27; Goulard 2013: 237-247).

Resistance, however, is not limited to directly affected states, but occurs also in states that seem more or less spared from the direct effects of the crisis, like Germany. The extensive rescue packages that had to be adopted in parliament led to anger and resentment, with parts of the governing parties only grudgingly accepting to vote in favor. One of the major results of the enormous amount of financial exposure to be taken by all member states is the ensuing conflict between European and national elites in politics, but also in economic and legal academia, visible in particular with the concerns voiced by national constitutional courts. These concerns are not only explainable in terms of political resistance against intrusive reforms drastically changing the internal social and political fabric, but also expose some fundamental unease with the course of European integration (Piris 2013: 317-327).

Some of the resistance thus is also the product of conflicting visions of the fabric of European integration and differing constructions of EU law. The most striking example for such a line of conflict is the recent conflict between the European Central Bank and the German Constitutional Court. The German Constitutional Court follows a very traditionalist idea of economic sovereignty with national parliaments as the guardians of national sovereignty, perceiving delegated competences as narrowly limited, with the parliaments policing the limits of delegation of competences (Huber 2014: 53-76).

An outside observer of the political system might be tempted to put such trust in national parliaments in the (somewhat heretical) question whether this does not entrust a drug-addict with the task of controlling the supply of drugs. Parliaments – a perspective of political economy tells us quite clearly – are addicts to deficit spending, since only this allows political actors to distribute financial advantages to their clientele of voters. However, debt financing with government loans depends on incentives for banks to buy state-bonds, since the whole machinery of debt-financed welfarism works only if potent financial institutions are willing to buy large amounts of state bonds.

II. The OMT Decision of the Bundesverfassungsgericht

A symbolic point of reference for the principled resistance of constitutional courts against the rescue measures of European ministers of finance (and the ECB) is the notorious OMT decision of the German Bundesverfassungsgericht of 14 Jan. 2014 (see Siekmann and Wieland 2015: 6-10; Simon 2015: 107-130; Mayer 2014: 111-146; Bast 2014: 167-181; Thiele 2014: 241-264; Heun 2014: 331-337; Wendel 2014: 263-307). This decision is noteworthy for its line of reasoning, but also – for the first time ever – initiated a referral of the Bundesverfassungsgericht to the European Court of Justice, or ECJ.

The decision concerns decisive questions of the future development of European monetary policy. In light of the importance of the questions involved, one might expect particular diligence in the constitutional court's reconstruction of ECB policies and of the economic background of the case. This assumption, however, proves false when one starts to analyze in detail the decision – one cannot but phrase the sad results of such analysis in the finding of a certain carelessness of the court (see in detail Heun 2014: 331-337).

Procedural issues

Already the object of the constitutional complaint procedure is strange. Usually the object of constitutional complaints is an act of public authority issued by a German state organ (v. Münch et al. 2012: Art. 94, para. 54; Degenhart 2015: 31). The jurisdiction of the (German) Federal Constitutional Court encompasses only such acts of public authority as are attributable to German state organs – be it organs of the Federation, of the Länder or of local authorities. Acts of EU organs as such are not acts of (German) public authority that fall in the remit of the constitutional court's jurisdiction (v. Mangoldt et al. 2010: Art. 94, para. 175). The OMT procedure before the Bundesverfassungsgericht thus had an initial problem – there is no act taken by a German state authority to fall under the jurisdiction of the court. In order to find a constitutional complaint procedure admissible, the complainants and the Court thus had to develop some degree of legal phantasy (Heun 2014, 331). Without a positive act attributable to anybody of German state authority, one had to construe an omission of German state organs where these organs were under a constitutional obligation to act (c.f. BVerfG 2014, OMT dec., Diss. Op. Lübbe-Wolff, para. 18). Basis of the proceedings thus was the idea that the federal parliament (the Bundestag) was culpable of omitting an action that it was obliged to take against a measure of EU policy, in order to fend off an intrusion of EU authorities in the realm of public authority exclusively attributed to German authorities (Heun 2014: 331). Such an omission was not easy to construe – the ECB acted in a domain where the treaties accord the bank exclusive competence, namely in the field of monetary policy. In order to argue a relevant omission, the complaint (and the interim measures of the court) had to start from the assumption that the object of attack – the announcement of outright monetary transactions by ECB President Draghi – was an intrusion in a field constituting the sole prerogative of German statehood, with the German authorities being obliged to prevent such intrusion by an ultra vires act (Gärditz 2014: 193-195). It is even not clear whether the OMT statement of ECB President Draghi had the character of a decision at all (see Wendel 2014: 288-289, now affirmatively answered by Advocate General Cruz Villalón in its opinion on the OMT case of 14 Jan. 2015 – ECJ 2015, Op. AG Cruz Villalón, paras. 82-90).

In a perspective critical to the decision one might say that the real object of the complaint was the decision by the European Central Bank on future OMT measures – and such a decision (or perhaps only public announcement of future OMT measures) is by definition not open to judicial control by the Bundesverfassungsgericht, but only can be challenged (if procedurally possible) before the European Court of Justice. The complainants and the judges constituting the majority knew this – and thus had to take the detour of making an omission of the federal organs the primary object of complaint. As a result, the Federal Constitutional Court had not to decide on the OMT announcement of President Draghi as such, but instead the complaint is formally directed against the inactivity of German constitutional organs in controlling the activities of ECB (Heun 2014: 331).

It is difficult to imagine, however, what might be the actions of German authorities in limiting the scope of action of the ECB (Gärditz 2014: 194). If the federal government or the Bundestag would try to curtail the scope of action of the Bundesbank, a public outcry would run through the Federal Republic, as being directed against the (sacred) independence of the German Bundesbank. It seems that such sacralisation has not been extended to the ECB. What should German state authorities do if they think that the ECB is acting contrary to the law? Any direct action of national control of the ECB would be contrary to the guarantees of independence of the ECB, with the only way left to the German authorities being a judicial procedure against the ECB before the ECJ. The Karlsruhe court here was obviously in a dilemma, out of which the court attempted to escape by some kind of a trick. The omission that the court has found is the lack of any (critical) debate on the limits of ECB action in dealing with the financial crisis. According to the court, there existed a duty to have a debate on ECB policies in German parliament (BVerfG, 2014 OMT dec., para. 53). Such an assumption seems quite hazardous (see Wendel 2014: 281-282). Is there a constitutional obligation of the Bundestag in any case where one might think an EU organ acts beyond its competence and thus encroaches upon the realm of (German) democracy? Is the Bundestag under an obligation to take up and debate any issue that might be argued to fall in its own remit, and not the one of European organs? Such a duty rests on a very fundamentalist conception of (national) democracy, a concept that forces German parliamentary institutions to defend any centimeter of democratic decision-making attributed to German representative democracy.

Judge Lübbe-Wolff has fiercely objected to such a conceptualisation of (national) democracy: "I doubt that any of the motions can be interpreted as being directed against the omission of an open-ended governmental or parliamentary debate. In relation to the specified objects of challenge, this is not a *minus* but an *aliud*. Apart from that, where the Federal Constitutional Court finds itself unable to identify specific decisions as mandatory under the Constitution, it is in my view not entitled to order, as an alternative or as a preliminary to further obligations not yet specified, that parliament or other supreme organs conduct a debate." (BVerfG 2014, OMT dec., Diss. Op. Lübbe-Wolff, para. 22).

The fundamental quarrel behind such dissent is the discontent of a number of judges (and of an important current in constitutional doctrine) with the rules on standing in constitutional complaint procedures that the Constitutional Court has developed as a particular device in EU cases (see Gärditz 2014: 190-198). The court – thus goes the critique – has completely inflated the filter of standing. Usually a complainant has to demonstrate that a subjective right of a personal nature might have been violated by the act of public authority against which the complaint is directed. In the series of EU-related decisions starting with the Maastricht decision and now culminating in the OMT decision, the court has developed an extremely generous perspective of the subjective rights content of Art. 38 para. 1 BL, the article guaranteeing free and fair elections and the corresponding electoral rights (Gärditz 2014: 186-190). In a way, these electoral rights have degenerated – so the critics are complaining – into some kind of an „actio popularis", an unlimited right of action against political acts that the constitutional court ardently tries to avoid in all the other domains of constitutional law (see Heun 2014: 332; Gärditz 2014: 190).

Again looking at the dissenting opinion of Judge Lübbe-Wolff elucidates the point: "An even more blatant innovation for which the Court cannot rely on determinative standards from previous case-law lies in the assumption that under specified conditions not only acts of German federal organs which positively transfer or restrict sovereign rights, but also mere inaction in the face of qualified transgressions on the part of the European Union can be challenged on the basis of Art. 38 sec. 1 GG (…). With this assumption, the Senate departs from earlier case-law, just recently corroborated." (BVerfG 2014, OMT dec., Diss. op. Lübbe-Wolff, para. 17).

Referral to the European Court of Justice

The path taken by the court created a problem that was difficult to solve with ordinary means. According to the procedural construction explained above, the constitutional court could decide that the Bundestag has violated rights of voters on democratic participation by omitting to discuss in the plenary some qualified transgressions on the part of the European Union (resp. its organs). What Karlsruhe cannot do, however, is declaring these (assumed) transgressions by EU organs illegal and thus null and void. That would clearly encroach upon the competence attributed to the ECJ. There was only one way out of the dead end in which the court had manoeuvred itself – a referral procedure to the ECJ. The German Bundesverfassungsgericht until now never had referred any question of legality of acts of German (or EU) organs under EU law to the ECJ (see Di Fabio 2014: 107-110; Mayer 2014: 118; Thiele 2014: 246-250). The referral in the OMT case is the first case of such a referral by the BVerfG. One might say that the referral is the product of a logical trap created by the Constitutional Court in its previous jurisprudence (c.f. Mayer 2014: 118). The court might have decided that a certain act of the EU (like the OMT declaration of ECB President Draghi) constitutes a blatant violation of the distribution of competences, an evident case of an ultra vires act that should be dealt with as null and void by German state authorities since such act is not based on any delegation of competences according to Art. 23 BL. In its recent jurisprudence, however, the court required a „sufficiently qualified violation of the integration program" (Bundesverfassungsgericht 2010, Honeywell dec., BVerfG 126, 286, 303-307) if such transgression of the limits of EU competences shall be of any relevance. The rationale behind such limitation is obvious: If such qualification would not have been incorporated, any German state organ could have declared an act of EU law null and void (as being ultra vires) and thus could have brushed aside wantonly the normative superiority of EU law (Mayer 2014: 118). This was not the intention of the constitutional court, thus the need for a severe limitation of German state organs (and courts) in raising the issue of an ultra vires character (see Wendel 2014: 274).

As the court formulated it in its resumé of the previous jurisprudence in para. 37 of the OMT decision: "A sufficiently qualified violation of the integration programme requires that the violation is manifest and that the challenged act entails a structurally significant shift in the allocation of powers to the detriment of the member states (cf. BVerfGE 126, 286 <304 and 305 with further references>). Transgressions of the mandate are structurally significant especially (but not only) if they cover areas that are part of the constitutional identity of the Federal Republic of Germany, which is protected by Art. 79 sec. 3 GG, or if they particularly affect the democratic discourse in the member states" (BVerfG 2014, OMT dec., para. 37). As a result of such a line of argumentation, a referral to the ECJ is necessary (according to the reasoning in Honeywell) if an ultra vires act is at stake (Bast 2014: 168-171) – but the assumption of an *ultra vires act* requires a „manifest" violation (Degenhart 2015: 31), a condition difficult to argue in the OMT case (Heun 2014: 332; Wendel 2014: 275-277).

If one follows the previously set precedents of the Honeywell jurisprudence, the better arguments speak for the assumption that there is only a "simple" violation of EU law, if at all, in the OMT case (Heun 2014: 332). It is far from evident, as will be demonstrated below, that the announced OMT program, as an unconventional monetary policy measure, falls completely outside the scope of the ECB's competence of 'monetary policy' according to Art. 127 TFEU. One might debate about this: Since the measure is "unconventional" if compared to classical measures of monetary policy, a very restrictive interpretation of the realm of monetary policy might see it outside the ECB's ambit; at the same time, there are good arguments in favour of the competence of the ECB to take such "unconventional" measures under the heading of Art. 127 TFEU (see Heun 2014: 333-334). Economists as well as lawyers might be found that argue both positions – but a heavily disputed question of interpretation of a competence norm, with arguments pro and contra raised in the debate, cannot seriously be qualified as a 'manifest' violation of the competence provision (Heun 2014: 332). The same may be argued for the Honeywell requirement of a structurally significant shift in the allocation of powers to the detriment of the member states: An 'unconventional' measure that might still be argued to fall in the ECB's competence under Art. 127 TFEU can only under serious difficulties be argued to shift – in a structurally significant way – the allocation of powers to the detriment of the member states. The member states could not really take such a measure, and the fact that the ECB takes it (or better announces it) does not shift the allocation of powers since the power to buy state bonds on the secondary markets, in order to influence the interest spread of such papers on the financial markets, is a power attributed to the ECB under Art. 127 TFEU (Heun 2014: 332).

The assumption underlying the referral thus can only be judged as hazardous: "It would have to be considered a manifest and structurally significant transgression of its mandate if the European Central Bank acted beyond its monetary policy mandate (aa), or if the prohibition of monetary financing of the budget was violated by the OMT programme (bb)." (BVerfG 2014, OMT dec., para. 38). The court here sets up a claim that is difficult to substantiate in detail, as will be shown subsequently.

Interpretation of Art. 119 (3) and 127 (1) TFEU

The remarks on the procedural issues have already made clear that the Bundesverfassungsgericht interprets the TFEU in a very particular way, narrowing considerably the range of possible options how to construe the provisions of Arts. 119 (3) and 127 (1) TFEU in its reciprocal relationship: "According to Title VIII of the Treaty on the Functioning of the European Union and notwithstanding the special powers expressly assigned to the Union (e.g. Art. 121, 122, 126 TFEU), the responsibility for economic policy lies clearly with the member states. In this field of economic policy, the European Union is – apart from individual exceptions that are in particular regulated in Part Three of the Treaty on the

Functioning of the European Union – essentially limited to a coordination of member states' economic policies (Art. 119 sec. 1 TFEU). The European Central Bank may only support the general economic policies of the member states (Art. 119 sec. 2, Art. 127 sec. 1 sentence 2 TFEU; Art. 2 sentence 2 ESCB Statute). It is not authorised to pursue its own economic policy. If one assumes – subject to the interpretation by the Court of Justice – that the OMT Decision is to be qualified as an independent act of economic policy, it manifestly violates this distribution of powers." (BVerfG 2014, OMT dec., para. 38).

The first part of this formulation constitutes more or less a truism. Art. 119 (1) as well as 121 (1) TFEU clearly reserve the domain of economic policy to the member states and provide only for a 'coordination' of economic policies by the member states (Simon 2015: 114). The ECB has no genuine competence in the core field of 'economic policy', but may 'support' the economic policy of member states by measures falling in its competence under Chapter 2 of Title VIII of the TFEU (Thiele 2013: 33-36). The last sentence of the citation from para. 38 of the German Constitutional Court's OMT decision, however, sets out an assumption that is far from trivial – namely the assumption "that the OMT Decision is to be qualified as an independent act of economic policy". Such an assumption requires a narrow reading of Art. 127 TFEU that remains to be illustrated as a plausible interpretation of the treaty (Heun 2014: 333-334; Wendel 2014: 292-298).

The OMT measures of the ECB as an act of general economic policy?

The assumption put forward by the Karlsruhe court relies on an astonishing reconstruction of the objectives of OMT. The constitutional court did not limit itself to reconstruct the objective given by the ECB for its unconventional measure, but gives it a much broader meaning than was expressed in the statements of the ECB, by claiming: "The OMT Decision aims to neutralise spreads on government bonds of selected member states of the euro currency area which have emerged in the markets and which adversely affect the refinancing of these member states (thus ECB, Monthly Bulletin September 2012, p. 7; ECB, Monthly Bulletin October 2012, pp. 7 and 8)." (BVerfG 2014, OMT dec., para. 65).

This clearly misinterprets the statements of the ECB. The message attributed to the ECB by this passage is not contained in the sources referred to. The cited statements in the ECB's monthly bulletin only state that there is a disturbance of the transmission mechanism that needs a correction (Heun 2014: 333-334; Gerner-Beuerle et al. 2014: 298-304; Wendel 2014: 296; as to the economic logic of 'transmission' see Riso 2015: 20-22). The German constitutional court even radicalizes its (mis-)construction of the ECB's objectives in stating: "In any case, according to explanations given by the *Bundesbank*, one cannot in practice divide interest rate spreads into a rational and an irrational part." (BVerfG 2014, OMT dec., para. 71). Has the ECB really claimed that it wants to divide interest rate spreads in rational and irrational parts? The ECB's statements do not speak for such an interpretation. One might question what the sense is of such a manipulative reconstruction of the ECB's policy objectives. Is the interest of the ECB in the issue of spreads indeed irrelevant for monetary policy, purely motivated by reasons of economic policy, namely facilitating the access of member states to further credit on international financial markets at a low interest rate? That might be one of the results of an OMT program – the concern of the ECB with interest rate spreads and the disturbed transmission mechanism on financial markets, however, does not become completely irrelevant due to these budgetary side-effects (Goldmann 2014: 276) Is any action of the ECB that lowers spreads outside its competence, because it also has repercussions on economic policy?

It seems the Constitutional Court thinks exactly in these terms: "As for the European Central Bank claiming to safeguard the current composition of the euro currency area with the OMT Decision (cf. ECB Press Release of 26 July 2012), this is obviously not a task of monetary policy but one of economic policy, which remains a responsibility of the member states." (BVerfG 2014, OMT dec., para. 72). But this is again a misinterpretation of the ECB statement – ECB President Draghi only spoke of a duty "to preserve the Euro" as a motivation of the Central Bank's activities in coping with the crisis (Heun 2014: 334). His statement did definitely not imply that "preserving the euro" was the only and primary reason for announcing the OMT program – and, the other way round, that it is the duty of the ECB to do the utmost to preserve the Euro is more or less a triviality (c.f. Goldmann 2014: 277).

The Constitutional Court, however, uses such statements to construct a 'transgression' of the ECB's mandate (Heun 2014: 334): "In the view of the Federal Constitutional Court, the objective mentioned by the European Central Bank invoked to justify the OMT Decision, namely to correct a disruption to the monetary policy transmission mechanism, can neither change the above-mentioned transgression of the European Central Bank's mandate, nor the violation of the prohibition of monetary financing of the budget." (BVerfG 2014, OMT dec., para. 95). And a paragraph later: "The fact that the purchase of government bonds can, under certain conditions, help to support the monetary policy objectives of the European System of Central Banks does not turn the OMT Decision itself into an act of monetary policy (…) The (economic) accuracy or plausibility of the reasons for the OMT Decision are irrelevant in this respect." (BVerfG 2014, OMT dec., para. 96). This is hard stuff: Even if the ECB uses a set of measures that "help to support the monetary policy objectives of the European System of Central Banks", this does not count as a measure of monetary policy as long as it creates serious effects which – as a primary objective – could only be pursued under the heading of 'economic policy'. But does that make sense? Are monetary policy and economic policy so neatly separated that the effects of measures taken in the area of monetary policy can be limited strictly to that area? Experience in monetary as well as economic policy speaks decidedly against such a separation doctrine (Hellwig 2014: 2-5, 13-21; Simon 2015: 114; Goldmann 2014: 269-272; Gerner-Beuerle et al. 2014: 295-304; see also ECJ 2015, Op. AG Cruz Villalón, para. 129). The sole orientation of monetary policy on price stability cannot work, because financial stability concerns unavoidably have an important place in the mandates of central banks (Hellwig 2014: 13-19). Moreover, the last remark in the cited passage makes the reasoning of the constitutional court even worse: "The (economic) accuracy or plausibility of the reasons for the OMT Decision are irrelevant in this respect." Does that mean that – even if the measures are economically plausible as measures of monetary policy – this is irrelevant as long as they produce significant effects in economic policy, a field that is thought by the German Constitutional Court to belong exclusively to the domain of member states (Wendel 2014: 293), with a potential coordination at European level only by intergovernmental means? The issue of intended effects and side effects becomes completely mixed up here (Riso 2015: 23-25; Goldmann 2014: 274-276). The reasoning of the court also completely neglects that measures of monetary as well as economic policy are based on prognostic models – prognoses and models highly disputed between economists (Goldmann 2014: 269-272). As Martin Hellwig formulated it, "there are ample grounds for such 'professional' disputes because the pursuit of price stability in an area with multiple non-integrated market systems presents a difficult new challenge" (Hellwig 2011: 2). Judges regularly do not possess the qualification (nor any legitimacy) to decide disputes in academic debates on economics (Herrmann 2012: 810-811; Goldmann 2014: 271). Measures of monetary and economic policy thus are paradigmatic cases where a wide margin of appreciation should be accorded, going along with a very limited standard of judicial review, restricting legal review more or less to a plausibility test (Goldmann 2014: 266-268, 272-274; Simon 2015: 114-116; see also ECJ 2015, Op. AG Cruz Villalón, para. 111).

The OMT measures of the ECB and political conditionality

The German Constitutional Court uses an additional argument to denounce the OMT measures as a 'transgression' of the ECB's mandate. The phenomenon taken up in this line of reasoning is the overlap (and linkage) between the OMT program and the assistance programs under EFSF and ESM. The member states of the Eurozone have given fresh money to the program countries in order to support them in their restructuring efforts, mainly via the mechanisms of the EFSF and the ESM (Hilpold 2014: 62-67). This fresh money, however, is tied to a strict conditionality (Scharpf 2011: 27-32). Such conditionality puts the ECB in a certain dilemma: Should it risk eroding the conditionality of EFSF and ESM support by pumping money in the financial markets that becomes available to program states without conditionality? The ECB decided that it should build a systematic interface in its program that secures the working of conditionality (Riso 2015: 25-26). The German Constitutional Court now turns this deference to the measures taken by the member states in an intergovernmental mechanism completely around: "By tying the purchase of government bonds of selected member states to full compliance with the requirements of the assistance programmes of the European Financial Stability Facility and the European Stability Mechanism and thus retaining its own conscientious examination, the European Central Bank makes the purchase of government bonds on the basis of the OMT Decision an instrument of economic policy. This is also confirmed by the fact that it plans to refrain from buying government bonds if the member state concerned does not meet the economic policy" (BVerfG 2014, OMT dec., para. 77). What if the ECB would have decided to omit such tying of OMT purchases to the conditionality of EFSF and ESM programs? Would that have made the Constitutional Court more positive in its judgment on the OMT program? One might doubt that, because such a construction would have eroded the conditionality of EFSF and ESM and would have created a serious problem of moral hazard (Goldmann 2014: 277-278; see also ECJ 2015, Op. AG Cruz Villalón, para.141).

The OMT measures of the ECB as a monetary financing of state budgets?

The Constitutional Court goes even further by implying that the OMT program creates a path enabling the ECB to intervene at any time when the credit rating of a Eurozone member state deteriorates and interest rates go up: "If purchases of government bonds were admissible every time the monetary policy transmission mechanism is disrupted, it would amount to granting the European Central Bank the power to remedy any deterioration of the credit rating of a euro area member state through the purchase of that state's government bonds. This would suspend the prohibition of monetary financing of the budget." (BVerfG 2014, OMT dec., para. 97). The statement is doubtful because it assumes that "any deterioration of the credit rating of a euro area member state" automatically expresses itself in the disruption of the monetary policy transmission mechanism (Heun 2014: 336). It is hazardous to construe such a linkage because most changes in the credit rating – and interest spreads – do not per se lead to a disruption of the monetary policy transmission mechanism. This might in some cases be the result, but only in some. The Court thus implies an expansion of ECB's mandate that is in fact implausible, because the ECB does not care about interest spreads as such (Gerner-Beuerle et al. 2014: 314-315). Simply because the ECB concludes that in a specific case a dramatic deterioration of credit ratings of members states (with the according rise of interest rate spreads) leads to a disruption of the monetary policy transmission mechanism, this does not say that it claims to be authorized to intervene in any case of deterioration of credit ratings. But only with such an assumption the Court can come to the conclusion that the OMT program collides with the prohibition of monetary financing of the budget.

The Court here shifts the borderlines of the European treaties. It is true that the ECB may not directly finance the budget of member states. But the Court assumes that any market operation undertaken by the ECB in the field of monetary policy, as soon as it affects the monetary financing of the budget of member states, needs a specific justification in order not to be qualified as a (prohibited) monetary financing of the budget (Wendel 2014: 298-300). However, where does such an expansive version of the prohibition of monetary financing of state budgets come from? Any facilitation of refinancing of banks at the national level, e.g. via ELA credits, affects their capability to buy state bonds, and thus has repercussions on monetary financing of the budget (see Mensching 2014: 333-346; Hellwig 2014: 11). But does that exclude such measures? If that were true, the ECB could forget about most of its measures of monetary policy, in particular all its market operations, since they always will have (indirect) effects on monetary financing of state budgets (see Riso 2015: 19, 27; Uhlig 2015: 46).

Already the sweeping formula of a general "prohibition of monetary financing of the budget" used by the Bundesverfassungsgericht is a peculiar construct: "Art. 123 TFEU and Art. 21.1. ESCB Statute forbid the purchase of government bonds "directly" from the emitting member states, i.e. the purchase on the primary market. This prohibition is, however, not limited to this interdiction, but is an expression of a broader prohibition of monetary financing of the budget (...). Union law recognises the legal concept of bypassing as do the national legal systems. It is ultimately based on the principle of effectiveness ("effet utile") and has repeatedly been alluded to in the Court of Justice's jurisprudence (...)." (BVerfG 2014, OMT dec., para. 85). The Constitutional Court itself admits here that the explicit prohibition in Art. 123 TFEU and Art. 21.1. ESCB Statute covers only the purchase of government bonds 'directly' from the emitting member states (Simon 2015: 119). However, this does not hinder the Court to formulate a much broader prohibition of monetary financing of the budget that the judges claim to form the basis of European monetary law (Heun 2014: 335; Wendel 2014: 298). However, can one postulate a broad and sweeping general prohibition of also 'indirect' financing when the authors of the treaty expressly limited the prohibition formulated in the treaty to 'direct' purchases on the primary market? The Court bases such conclusion on some (relatively peripheral) voices in European legal literature that even – if one reconstructs the references in detail – do not support the position (Heun 2014: 335; Wendel 2014: 298), ignoring the mainstream not supportive of its underlying thesis – and does so because in essence it seems to share the anxieties of the ECB's critics painting the dangers of 'fiscal redistribution' and a 'Joint Liability Union' to the walls (see in this regard Degenhart 2015: 34; Kahl 2013: 203-204). But isn't this (mis-)construction of the meaning of Art. 123 TFEU a transgression of a national constitutional court's competence (Kumm 2014: 209-214; Wendel 2014: 300-302), an attempt to correct the authors of the treaty with a much broader rule that the judges like more than the narrow prohibition laid down in the treaty? Exactly such a correction of the treaty wording is needed, however, if the accusation of "bypassing" of the treaty rules on the prohibition of monetary financing of the budget shall make sense – and thus the claim of an 'ultra vires' act (Simon 2015: 119-120; Heun 2014: 335).

If one construes Art. 123 TFEU in a meaning loyal to the subjective intention of the drafters as well as to a grammatical and systematic interpretation, one must come to the conclusion that it merely prohibits 'direct' financing, and perhaps also the circumvention of the prohibition of direct financing of state budgets (Riso 2015: 26-28). It is difficult, however, to see how this could also comprise market operations with government bonds on secondary markets, if not used exceptionally as a means to openly finance state budgets via the back door (Simon 2015: 119-122).

The argumentation of the Court is sloppy: "It can be an (…) indication for a circumvention of the prohibition of monetary financing of the budget if government bonds are purchased on the secondary market to a considerable extent and shortly after their emission by the Eurosystem (market pricing)." (BVerfG 2014, OMT dec., para. 92). If only 'direct' financing by purchases on the primary markets is prohibited, why are purchases to a considerable extent an "indication for a circumvention of the prohibition of monetary financing of the budget"? Moreover, why is the timing of the purchase – shortly after emission or much later – an indication? The Court leaves us alone with such questions.

It must be admitted: The boundary line between monetary policy and economic policy is not that easy to draw (Simon 2015: 114; Thiele 2013: 27-32). However, does that not speak in favour of a large margin of appreciation (see Simon 2015: 114-116; Thiele 2013: 27-32) which the ECB as the organ entrusted by the treaties with the task of monetary policy should enjoy? If such margin of appreciation is not recognized, we unavoidably end up in what is called in Hayekian terminology a "pretense of knowledge". Can law – or better: a constitutional court – really determine what is the right type of monetary policy entrusted to the competent central bank? Where does the qualification of national constitutional court judges to replace the ECB's economic judgment by their own economic judgment come from? Is there not a deeper sense in entrusting monetary policy to a

body of experienced economists with a longstanding trajectory in monetary policy at national level?

Proposed restrictive reading of OMT measure of the ECB

The resulting sceptical perspective on the Constitutional Courts' transgression into the epistemic domain of economic policy affects also the proposed narrow reading of the OMT measure taken by the ECB (see Heun
2014: 336). The Court postulates: "The Federal Constitutional Court
believes that these concerns regarding the validity of the OMT Decision,
based on the interpretation used here, could be met by an interpretation in
conformity with Union law. This would require that the content of the
OMT Decision, when comprehensively assessed and evaluated, essentially
complies with the above-mentioned conditions. In the view of the Federal
Constitutional Court, the OMT Decision might not be objectionable if it
could, in the light of Art. 119 and Art. 127 et seq. TFEU, and Art. 17 et
seq. of the ESCB Statute, be interpreted or limited in its validity in such a
way that it would not undermine the conditionality of the assistance programmes of the European Financial Stability Facility and the European
Stability Mechanism (…), and would only be of a supportive nature with
regard to the economic policies in the Union (...). This requires, in light of
Art. 123 TFEU, that the possibility of a debt cut must be excluded (…),
that government bonds of selected member states are not purchased up to
unlimited amounts (…), and that interferences with price formation on the
market are to be avoided where possible." (BVerfG 2014, OMT dec.,
paras. 99-100). A nice catalogue – but is it task of a constitutional court to
determine in detail what type of monetary policy makes sense in a given
situation?

Implications of the path taken by the Bundesverfassungsgericht

The implications of the path taken by the Bundesverfassungsgericht are
potentially dramatic. It does not require prophetic gifts to predict that the
European Court of Justice will not follow the line proposed by the German
Constitutional Court. The reasoning given in the opinion of Advocate
General Cruz Villalón points very much in that direction. In substance, the
ECJ will affirm the competence of the ECB to take a set of measures like

those outlined in the OMT program. There might be some symbolic gesture to the Constitutional Court, a gesture of peace giving the judges at Karlsruhe some sense of victory, but the core reasoning of the BVerfG will not prevail in the ECJ (Mayer 2014: 122-123; Kumm 2014: 206-207).

If the ECJ declares the OMT program of the ECB to be (in essence) compatible with the provisions of the TFEU that might provoke a harsh reaction from Karlsruhe (see Mayer 2014: 124). The German Constitutional Court has taken a tough stance and has taken a relatively extreme position. If it feels to be disregarded by Luxemburg, what will be its reactions? This is difficult to forecast. It might be that the Bundesverfassungsgericht again ends up as – how Joseph Weiler phrased it – the „dog that barks but does not bite" (Weiler 2009: 505). However, this is not sure. It might also be that the Constitutional Court takes a decision of the ECJ confirming the ECB's competence as an invitation to fight through the struggle on jurisdictional supremacy.

But what would it mean if the Bundesverfassungsgericht would confirm that the OMT measure of the ECB was an ultra vires act? The Court then would have to declare the constitutional complaint to be founded. The consequences of such a decision in practical terms, however, would again be rather limited (see Mayer 2014: 126-128). Such a decision would not bind the ECJ or any other EU organ. It could accordingly not change the policy of the ECB. The decision would only bind German state organs. What could be the resulting obligations for German state organs? If one follows the reasoning of the Constitutional Court decision of January 14, 2014, the Bundestag, the first chamber of the German parliament, would be obliged to hold a debate? Wow! However, does that change anything?

III. Cognitive Dissonance as a Driver of Crisis?

So far a critical reading and narrative of the story of the OMT decision of the German Constitutional Court. What does that narrative tell us in a larger perspective? In my reading, the decision shows a strong cognitive bias that attempts to construe any – conventional or unconventional – market operation of the ECB as measures of economic policy outside the mandate of the ECB. While reading the Constitutional Court decision, this cognitive bias is obvious (as to the concept of 'cognitive bias' e.g. Harker 2015; Dutta et al. 2012; Haselton et al. 2005). The Court wants to find a 'transgression' of the ECB's mandate – and in wanting to find it, it finds it. But there is a price to be paid for that. For doing so, the court systematically misinterprets the statements and policies of the ECB (as demonstrated above).

Probably it is going too far if one assumes a wantonly manipulation of the ECB's position. To me it seems better – in the sense of being more plausible than a conspiracy theory – to assume a conflicting epistemology of German constitutional judges. The epistemology of the judges is based on a reasoning of constitutional law – and constitutional law works with assumptions of neat separations of competences. If monetary policy and economic policy are separate categories attributed to different actors, it must be possible to separate clearly both types of competences. And if the economists are so stupid and ignorant that they do not present a neat separation of both fields, the Court has to do it. There will always be some economists that argue exactly the line the court must take in order to separate the two competences. Economics is a pluralist discipline with a huge variety of different schools of thought and a vast discrepancy of opinions. If the economists on whose wisdom the Court relies are not the mainstream, but more or less sectarian – who cares? They argue the right position, the position that fits into the category the constitutionalists want to uphold.

In essence, this is the description of an epistemic bias – the court is seeing what it wants to see. The basic problem with this bias, however, is its misfit to reality. Economics is not as precise a science as it often pretends to be; in essence, it is part of humanities, which means that different authors have very different ideas and models in constructing reality. The German constitutional court seems to think that its construction of the basics of European monetary and economic policy are without alternative – although there exist plenty of intellectual alternatives, and most of them more plausible than the construct the court (with its limited expertise) has tried to put together. The court's perception shows a strong mismatch with the facts on the ground. Social psychology has become used of calling this a cognitive dissonance (see Nail and Boniecki 2011: 44-71; Cooper 2007). Different types of actors with different epistemologies perceive the same phenomenon in completely different intellectual constructions – and some of these constructions simply do not fit (in this case unfortunately the constructs of the constitutional court's second senate).

For the long-term sustainability of a sound monetary policy in reaction to the crisis, such cognitive dissonance might be fatal. If one draws the precedent to its logical end, one might imagine a constellation where one of the major payers of all rescue packages, and a decisive actor in the European Union and the Eurozone, namely the Federal Republic of Germany, might be forced to drop out from the joint exercises in stabilizing the euro. Radicalizing the logic of the German Constitutional Court, the end result of the Court's endeavour would be to force a decisive member state like Germany in a futile political conflict over basic issues of monetary policy. Fortunately, the whole issue will not end up as radically as intended. As already mentioned above, the Court cannot oblige the ECB to any action or omission – it can only oblige German state organs. The OMT program – or better: its announcement – has never put into practice, however. What could accordingly happen? There is nothing the Federal Republic could deny to participate in – as said, the OMT announcement was never put in practice, and probably also never will be put in practice, because in substantive terms the program has been overtaken by the measures of 'quantitative easing' that the ECB started in spring 2015 (Bernoth et al. 2015: 189-198).

However, the question remains: What may be the reasons for such a radical version of cognitive dissonance? A constructivist perspective on institutionalism teaches us that institutions have a strong power of cognitive framing. Its members – and the longer they are members the more deeply – are epistemically socialized in the cognitive patterns that are coded into the institution. The BVerfG – one might excuse me such a blunt statement – is epistemically caught in a world of sovereigntism, is coded in a world view where it is the guardian of national sovereignty and of the autonomy of the national constitution (see Mayer 2014: 143-144). The sovereigntist bias described above is the result of such an epistemic framing, with an assumption that democratic legitimacy is possible only at national level – and thus a normative 'ought' that the importance of national parliaments must be preserved. The jurisprudence of the Karlsruhe court is coded deeply in these terms – from the Maastricht decision via Lisbon to the ESM and the OMT decision (Mayer 2014: 137-142; Bast 2014: 168-171). This epistemology construes the integration programme – and its delegation of competences to the EU – in rather narrow terms that allow national parliaments to 'police' any EU measure against potential *ultra vires* acts.

The concept of *ultra vires* acts in itself demonstrates such a narrow perspective on delegation of competence, since it implies (and requires) a strict limitation of competences transferred to the European level (Bast 2014: 174-178). Such a framing forces the Court implicitly to impose a very narrow and rigid reading of European treaties, otherwise *ultra vires* control would be impossible. The OMT decision is full of examples of such epistemic framing – think only of the Court's reading of Art. 123 TFEU with its broad construction of the prohibition of monetary financing of state budgets, extending the prohibition – contrary to the wording and the spirit of Art. 123 – also to 'indirect' forms of financing of purchases on secondary markets, in order to create a strict protection against anything which might look (in the eyes of the court) as an abusive circumvention of the prohibition.

Result of such a narrow reading is a denial of any margin of appreciation in core issues of economic policy judgment. It is the Constitutional Court that endeavours to determine which types of activities constitute monetary policy and which economic policy. Under the system of the treaty, one might assume that such judgment is primarily in the realm of the ECB, as the organ primarily mandated with operating the provisions of monetary policy. However, in a perspective of policing the limits of delegation, such margin of appreciation seems dangerous – and thus cannot be conceded.

The described bias might be explained in terms of the sociology of knowledge. The epistemic framing of national constitutional court judges relies on cognitive patterns that have been acquired in distinguished national careers – and these patterns are often characterized by a strong distrust against the ample powers delegated to the European institutions. Preserving the prerogatives of the nation state means construing narrowly the delegated competences of the European Union, and this again requires a strict interpretation of the powers and competences of European organs and speaks against any margin of appreciation in filling out the mandate entrusted to the organ under the treaties. The resulting problem: Judges enter epistemic areas where they tend to act beyond their intellectual competence. Some epistemic modesty would have been needed in this regard – and the procedural expression of such modesty should have been the recognition of a wide margin of appreciation in favour of the ECB.

IV. Conclusions

This chapter tried to demonstrate that not only colliding interests are a strong source of crisis. In issues of European monetary and economic policy, it is not that easy to pinpoint down who exactly might have what interests. Collective interests here depend very much on the social construction of reality, on the intellectual frames in which economy and politics are understood. Gross forms of a cognitive bias, however, plague such intellectual frames. Institutional socialization and organizational culture frame the worldviews of their members – and constitutional court judges do not escape such fundamental problem. The desperate search for a narrow reading of the treaty provisions according competences to European institutions such as the ECB drives national constitutional court judges in dubious intellectual constructs that – under a perspective of social psychology – might be termed as a phenomenon of 'cognitive dissonance'.

This is the basic lesson that the text wanted to convey: Also phenomena of cognitive bias and cognitive dissonance may create or exacerbate a severe crisis, as a detailed analysis of the OMT decision of the BVerfG has demonstrated. Behind such cognitive dissonance, we find a concept of the rule of law that is impossible to match with the realities of European economic policy. Law as a detailed work plan for future political action where all the later decisions are already stored in the legal norms is an outdated concept under a perspective of legal theory – constitutional courts desperately cling to such a concept because judges seem to think that their role depends on upholding such an (illusionary) image of law. However, in dealing with complex fields of social action such as monetary and economic policy, where decisions are taken under high degrees of uncertainty, relying on disputed theoretical models and with no clear prognosis of what the decisions taken might mean for future developments, courts should develop an outright policy of intellectual modesty. In such fields it is definitely impossible to know exactly what is right or wrong; as a result, judges should accord the competent organs equipped with the necessary expertise and experience a strong dose of trust – and expression of such institutional trust needs to be an extended margin of appreciation where it is clear that judges (already for epistemic reasons) cannot know better what is the right course of action. In other words: the opposite understanding of law as a loose institutional framework that leaves decisive issues to be decided in the political process seems to be the adequate concept in dealing with all the known and unknown 'unknowns' of economic policy. The Hayekian question of knowledge and its limitations should not get lost.

Bibliography

Bast, J.: Don't Act beyond your Powers: The Perils and Pitfalls of the German Constitutional Court's Ultra Vires Review. German Law Journal, 2014 15(2), pp. 168-181.

Bernoth, K./ König, P./ Raab, C./ Fratzscher, M.: Unchartered Territory: Large-Scale Asset Purchases by the European Central Bank. DIW Economic Bulletin, 2015 3, pp. 189-198.

Bundesverfassungsgericht, Case No. 2 BvR 2728/13 (Jan. 14, 2014), OMT Case (cited as BVerfG 2014, OMT dec.)

Bundesverfassungsgericht, Case No. 2661/06 (July 6, 2010), BVerfGE 126, 286, Honeywell Case (cited as BVerfG 2010, Honeywell dec.).

Cooper, J.: Cognitive Dissonance – Fifty Years of a Classic Theory. Los Angeles: Sage, 2007.

Degenhart, C.: Legal Limits of Central Banking. In: Siekmann, H./ Vig, V./ Wieland V. eds. The ECB Outright Monetary Transaction in the Courts. IMFS Interdisciplinary Studies in Monetary and Financial Stability, 1/2015, pp. 30-36.

Di Fabio, U.: Karlsruhe Makes a Referral. German Law Journal 15 (2), pp. 107-110.

Dutta, T./ Mandal, M. K./ Kumar, S. eds.: Bias in Human Behaviour. New York: Nova Publ., 2012.

ECJ, Opinion of Advocate General Cruz Villalón, delivered on 14 Jan. 2015, Case C-62/14, Request for a preliminary ruling from the Bundesverfassungsgericht, Gauweiler et al./Deutscher Bundestag (cited as ECJ 2015, Op. AG Cruz Villalón).

Gärditz, K. F.: Beyond Symbolism: Towards a Constitutional Action Popularis in EU Affairs? A Commentary on the OMT Decision of the Federal Constitutional Court. German Law Journal, 2014 15(2), pp. 183-201.

Gerner-Beuerle, C./ Küçük, E./ Schuster, E.: Law Meets Economics in the German Federal Constitutional Court: Outright Monetary Transactions on Trial. German Law Journal, 2014 15(2), pp. 281-320.

Goldmann, M.: Adjudicating Economics? Central Bank Independence and the Appropriate Standard of Review. German Law Journal, 2014 15(2), pp. 265-280.

Goulard, S.: Mehr als eine Finanzkrise. Eine Perspektive aus dem Europäischen Parlament. In: Ingolf Pernice ed. Europa in der Welt – von der Finanzkrise zur Reform der Union. Baden-Baden: Nomos, 2013, pp. 237-248.

Harker, D. W.: Creating Scientific Controversies – Uncertainty and Bias in Science and Society. Cambridge: Cambridge University Press, 2015.

Haselton, M. G./ Nettle, D./ Andrews, P. W.: The Evolution of Cognitive Bias. In: Buss, D. M. ed. Handbook of Evolutionary Psychology. Hoboken: Wiley, 2005, pp. 724-746.

Hellwig, M.: Quo Vadis, Euroland? European Monetary Union between Crisis and Reform. Preprints of the Max Planck Institute for Research on Collective Goods, 2011/12.

Hellwig, M.: Financial Stability, Monetary Policy, Banking Supervision, and Central Banking. Preprints of the Max Planck Institute for Research on Collective Goods, 2014/9.

Herrmann, C.: Die Bewältigung der Euro-Staatsschulden-Krise an den Grenzen des deutschen und europäischen Währungsverfassungsrechts. Europäische Zeitschrift für Wirtschaftsrecht, 2012 23(21), pp. 805-812.

Heun, W.: Eine verfassungswidrige Verfassungsgerichtsentscheidung – der Vorlagebeschluss des BVerfG vom 14.1.2014. Juristenzeitung, 2014 69, pp. 331-337.

Hilpold, P.: Eine neue europäische Finanzarchitektur – Der Umbau der Wirtschafts- und Währungsunion als Reaktion auf die Finanzkrise. In: Hilpold, P./ Steinmair, W. eds. Neue europäische Finanzarchitektur. Heidelberg: Springer, 2014, pp. 3-82.

Huber, P. M.: Verfassungsstaat und Finanzkrise. Baden-Baden: Nomos, 2014.

Illing, F.: Die Euro-Krise – Analyse der europäischen Strukturkrise. Wiesbaden: Springer VS, 2014.

Kahl, W.: Bewältigung der Staatsschuldenkrise unter Kontrolle des Bundesverfassungsgerichts – ein Lehrstück zur horizontalen und vertikalen Gewaltenteilung. Deutsches Verwaltungsblatt (DVBl.), 2013 128(4), pp. 197-207.

Kumm, M.: Rebel without a Good Cause: Karlsruhe's Misguided Attempt to Draw the CJEU into a Game of "Chicken" and What the CJEU Might Do About It. German Law Journal, 2014 15(2), pp. 203-215.

v. Mangoldt, H./ Klein, F./ Starck, C.: Kommentar zum Grundgesetz. Vol. 3, 6th ed., München: Vahlen, 2010 (cited as: v. Mangoldt/Klein/Starck/author).

Mensching, C.: Das Verbot der monetären Haushaltsfinanzierung in Art. 123 Abs. 1 AEUV – eine kritische Bestandsaufnahme. Europarecht, 2014 49(3), pp. 333-345.

v. Münch, I./ Kunig, P.: Grundgesetz Kommentar. 6th ed., München: C.H. Beck, 2012 (cited as v. Münch/Kunig/author).

Nail, P. R./ Boniecki, K. A.: Inconsistency in Cognition: Cognitive Dissonance. In: Chadee, D. ed. Theories in Social Psychology. Malden, Mass.: Wiley Blackwell, 2011, pp. 44-71.

Piris, J: The Euro Crisis, Democratic Legitimacy and the Future Two-Speed Europe. In: Pernice, I. ed. Europa in der Welt – von der Finanzkrise zur Reform der Union. Baden-Baden: Nomos, 2013, pp. 317-328.

Rato, H.: Portugal – Structural Reform Interrupted by Austerity. In: Vaughan-Whitehead, D. ed., Public Sector Shock – The Impact of Policy Retrenchment in Europe. Cheltenham: Edward Elgar, 2013, pp. 411-448.

Riso, A.: An Analysis of the OMT Case from an EU Law Perspective. In: Siekmann, H./ Vig, V./ Wieland, V. eds. The ECB Outright Monetary Transaction in the Courts. IMFS Interdisciplinary Studies in Monetary and Financial Stability, 1/2015, pp. 19-29.

Scharpf, F. W.: Monetary Union, Fiscal Crisis and the Preemption of Democracy. Max-Planck-Institut für Gesellschaftsforschung MPIfG Discussion Paper No. 11-11, 2011.

Scharpf, F. W.: Political Legitimacy in a Non-Optimal Currency Area. Max-Planck-Institut für Gesellschaftsforschung MPIfG Discussion Paper No. 13-15, 2013

Schuppan, N.: Die Euro-Krise – Ursachen, Verlauf, makroökonomische und europarechtliche Aspekte und Lösungen. München: Oldenbourg, 2014.

Siekmann, H./ Wieland, V.: The German Constitutional Court's Decision on OMT: Have Markets Misunderstood?. In: Siekmann, H./ Vig, V./ Wieland, V. eds. The ECB Outright Monetary Transaction in the Courts. IMFS Interdisciplinary Studies in Monetary and Financial Stability, 1/2015, pp. 6-13.

Simon, S.: "Whatever it takes": Selbsterfüllende Prophezeiung am Rande des Unionsrechts? Eine unionsrechtliche Bewertung der OMT-Entscheidung der EZB. Europarecht, 2015 50(1), pp. 107-130.

Thiele, A.: Das Mandat der EZB und die Krise des Euro – eine Untersuchung der von der EZB im Zusammenhang mit der Eurokrise ergriffenen Maßnahmen auf ihre Vereinbarkeit mit den rechtlichen Vorgaben des europäischen Primärrechts. Tübingen: Mohr Siebeck, 2013.

Thiele, A.: Friendly or Unfriendly Act? The 'Historic' Referral of the Constitutional Court to the ECJ regarding the ECB's OMT Program. German Law Journal, 2014 15(2), pp. 241-264.

Uhlig, H.: Remarks on the OMT Program of the ECB. In: Siekmann, H./ Vig, V./ Wieland, V. eds. The ECB Outright Monetary Transaction in the Courts. IMFS Interdisciplinary Studies in Monetary and Financial Stability, 1/2015, pp. 6-13.

Weiler, J. H. H.: The "Lisbon Urteil" and the Fast Food Culture. European Journal of International Law, 2009 20(3), pp. 505-509.

Wendel, M.: Exceeding Judicial Competence in the Name of Democracy: The German Federal Constitutional Court's OMT reference. European Constitutional Law Review, 2014 10(2), pp. 263-307.

About the authors

CHRISTIAN JOERGES is since 2013 Senior Professor for Law and Society (part-time) at the Hertie School of Governance in Berlin, Germany, and since 2007, a Co-director of the Centre of Law and Politics at the University of Bremen, Germany. Until 2007, he has been a Professor of Economic Law at the European University Institute in Florence, Italy. His most noted book is *Darker Legacies of Law in Europe: The Shadow of National Socialism and Fascism over Europe and its Legal Traditions*, edited with Navraj S. Galeigh (Oxford: Hart Publishing 2003). His current research focuses on the transformation of the European economic constitution through the financial crisis and on the politicisation of transnational trade governance. A pertinent recent publication is *The European Crisis and the Transformation of Transnational Governance. Authoritarian Managerialism versus Democratic Governance*, edited with Carola Glinski (Oxford: Hart Publishing, 2014).

ROBERT KAPPIUS is working at Deutsche Bundesbank in banking regulation. He earned his doctorate at University of Freiburg. His dissertation addresses equal opportunity policies' inherent conflict structures as well as scope for consensus (German title: Chancengleichheit als Leitkonzept der Bildungs- und Gesellschaftspolitik: Eine ordnungsökonomische Untersuchung zu Konflikt- und Konsenspotenzial). His research focuses interactions between economics and politics, justice and conflict issues, and the evolution of norms.

MARTHA KONTODAIMON is a Research Associate and Ph.D. Candidate at the Chair of Economic Policy and Constitutional Theory at Albert-Ludwigs-University Freiburg. Currently she is working as a Research Associate and Project Manager for the Konrad-Adenauer-Stiftung Greece. She has received her Master's degree in Economics from University of Freiburg and her Bachelor in Political Science and History from Panteion University of Athens. As responsible for the design of experiments in the SoCoLab at the University of Freiburg, she has covered topics on the constitutional approach of old age provision and basic income, the constitutional regulation of public private partnerships and general topics on social contract formation. Her main research areas are social market economy, constitutional reform, interstate contractual formations, justice and fairness of income distributions and reforming tax schemes.

TIM KRIEGER is since 2012 Wilfried Guth Professor of Constitutional Political Economy and Competition Policy at Albert-Ludwigs-University Freiburg. He holds a master degree from the University of Kiel, Germany, and received his Ph.D. from the University of Munich, Germany. He was an assistant or visiting professor at the Universities of Mainz, Marburg and Paderborn, Germany. He works mainly on economic, social and education policies in aging and globalizing societies with a special focus on the conflict-economic dimension of these developments. In addition, he is specialized in the economics of terrorism and crime. In these fields, he has published in several scholarly journals in both economics and political science (including Journal of Public Economics, Journal of Conflict Resolution and Journal of Peace Research).

KARSTEN MAUSE is Assistant Professor of Political Economy in the Department of Political Science at the University of Muenster, Germany. His current research interests include the Political Economy of fiscal policy and the New Political Economy/Public Choice of politicians, bureaucrats, and interest groups.

BERNHARD NEUMÄRKER is since 2003 Professor of Economic Policy at Albert-Ludwigs-University Freiburg. He is the director of the Division of Economic Policy and Constitutional Theory and of the Social Contract Laboratory (SoCoLab). He received his Ph.D., Habilitation and venia legendi from Ruhr-University Bochum and was assistant professor of economics/public finance at the Ruhr-University Bochum as well as acting professor at the University of Saarland, Saarbrücken. He held visiting research and teaching appointments at the University of Sofia, at the Public Sector Economics Research Centre (PSERC), University of Leicester and at UNAM and ITAM universities, Mexico City. His main research areas are constitutional economics and sustainable collective rules, the economic analysis of social justice, the political economy of reforms, soft paternalism and long-term paradigm shifts, conflict economics, and the economics of land grabbing.

FRANCESCO NICOLI is a Ph.D. researcher at the University of Trento, Italy, where he is working on the political implications of the euro crisis. He is also a Visiting Fellow at the Centre for European Policy Studies (CEPS) in Brussels. Prior to joining the Trento School of International Studies, Francesco served as a research assistant at the Brussels based think tanks Bruegel and European Policy Centre (EPC). His publications concern the euro crisis, EU economic governance, and labour mobility in the Eurozone. He holds a bachelor degree in European and International Studies and a master degree in economics.

STEFAN OETER is since 1999 Professor for German and Comparative Public Law and Public International Law at the University of Hamburg Law School in Germany. He is a member (and vice-chairman) of the Independent Committee of Experts of the European Charter for Regional or Minority Languages at the Council of Europe; the president of the Historical Commission of the International Society for Military Law; a member of the Permanent Court of Arbitration, of the German Committee for the Red Cross Conventions and of the Academy of Science in Hamburg. His current research interests include comparative federalism, minority protection and human rights law, humanitarian law, European and international economic law, the theory of international law and international relations, as well as global constitutionalism.

DIMITRIS PAPANIKOLOPOULOS (Dr.) is an assistant researcher at the University of Crete. His work focuses on social movements and collective action, especially in Greece. He is currently working in the Greek-German research project GGCRISI (The Greeks, the Germans and the Crisis).

DIANA PANKE holds the Chair for 'Multi-Level Governance' at Albert-Ludwigs-University Freiburg. Her research interests include international negotiations, multilateral diplomacy, comparative regionalism, small states in international affairs, European Union politics as well as compliance and legalization. In these fields, she has published five monographs (the latest one with ECPR Press) and more than 30 journal articles (including EJIR, CPS, Cooperation and Conflict, Millennium, JCMS, JEPP, WEP, JEP and International Politics).

JOCHEN ROOSE (Prof. Dr. for Sociology, Freie Universität Berlin) holds the chair for Social Sciences at the Willy Brandt Center for German and European Studies, University of Wrocław. His research interests are Europeanization (esp. European discourses, identification, cross border links, attitudes), participation (esp. social movements, volunteering, participation beyond politics), and methods of social research. Currently, he is leading the Greek-German research project GGCRISI (The Greeks, the Germans and the Crisis).

BERND SCHLIPPHAK is a (Junior) Professor for Quantitative Methods at the University of Muenster, Department of Political Science. His research interests focus on the social legitimacy of international organizations as well as on the backlash effects of international events on domestic politics. Recent publications include 'Measuring Attitudes Toward Regional Organizations Outside Europe' (Review of International Organizations 2014) and 'Actions and Attitudes Matter: International Public Opinion Towards the European Union' (European Union Politics 2013).

FRANZISKA SCHOLL (M.A. in Sociology, Freie Universität Berlin) is a doctoral candidate and researcher in the Greek-German research project GGCRISI (The Greeks, the Germans and the Crisis) at Freie Universität Berlin. Her research interests are social movements, protest and volunteering.

MORITZ SOMMER (M.Sc. in Political Sociology, London School of Economics and Political Science) is a doctoral candidate and researcher in the Greek-German research project GGCRISI (The Greeks, the Germans and the Crisis) at Freie Universität Berlin. His research interests are (European) Political Sociology, Social Movement Studies and politicization research.

MAXIMILIAN STEPHAN is since 2013 a Ph.D. student and research assistant at Albert-Ludwigs-University of Freiburg, Germany. His research focuses on strategic behavior during debt restructurings. He studied economics at the University of Freiburg and the University of Copenhagen, Denmark.

RAFAL ULATOWSKI is Assistant Professor at the Institute of International Relations at the University of Warsaw in Poland. He earned his Ph.D. from the University of Bonn, Germany, in 2011 with a dissertation on „Die deutsch-polnischen Wirtschaftsbeziehungen in der europäischen Perspektive: 1990-2007". He was awarded scholarships of the Konrad Adenauer Fundation (2007-2010), the DAAD (2013 and 2014/2015) and the University of Warsaw (2013). He was a visiting Scholar at the Kyungpook National University in the Republic of Korea (2014 and 2015). His research focuses on German foreign policy, the global economy, international financial and trade issues, global energy market, as well as issues of European economic integration.